Ageing, Ageism and the Law

ELGAR STUDIES IN LAW AND SOCIETY

Elgar Studies in Law and Society brings together critical and thought-provoking works by scholars from around the globe, on the most pressing topics and issues within the field of Law and Society. The books in this series reflect original, cutting-edge scholarship on aspects of the Law's role in modern society and its intersection with social structures and institutions, such as politics, gender, race, religion and ethics.

Titles in this series include:

Ageing, Ageism and the Law

European Perspectives on the Rights of Older Persons

Edited by

Israel (Issi) Doron

Head of the Center for Research and Study of Aging, Department of Gerontology, University of Haifa, Israel

Nena Georgantzi

Human Rights Officer, AGE Platform Europe, Belgium and PhD Fellow, National University of Ireland Galway, Ireland

ELGAR STUDIES IN LAW AND SOCIETY

Cheltenham, UK • Northampton, MA, USA

Cover photo by eberhard grossgasteiger on Unsplash

Published by
Edward Elgar Publishing Limited
The Lypiatts
15 Lansdown Road
Cheltenham
Glos GL50 2JA
UK

Edward Elgar Publishing, Inc.
William Pratt House
9 Dewey Court
Northampton
Massachusetts 01060
USA

A catalogue record for this book
is available from the British Library

Library of Congress Control Number: 2018946009

This book is available electronically in the **Elgar**online
Law subject collection
DOI 10.4337/9781788972116

ISBN 978 1 78897 210 9 (cased)
ISBN 978 1 78897 211 6 (eBook)

Typeset by Columns Design XML Ltd, Reading
Printed and bound in Great Britain by TJ International Ltd, Padstow

Contents

About the authors

Marijke De Pauw is a legal and policy officer at UNIA, the Belgian Interfederal Centre for Equal Opportunities. Her work focuses on the implementation of the CRPD at the national level. Dr De Pauw holds a Master's degree in law from Vrije Universiteit Brussel (VUB) and a doctoral degree in international human rights law from the VUB and Université Saint-Louis – Bruxelles. Her doctoral thesis researched the fundamental rights of older persons from a comparative perspective at the international and regional level. She is currently also an associate postdoctoral researcher at VUB, a member of the editorial board of the Flemish human rights journal *Tijdschrift voor Mensenrechten* and an active member of the EU COST Action on Ageism.

Israel (Issi) Doron is an Associate Professor and the Head of the Center for Research and Study of Aging at the University of Haifa, and the Past President of the Israeli Gerontological Society. He specializes in the fields of law and ageing, social policy and ageing, ethics and ageism. Professor Doron has written extensively on topics such as law and ageing, and human rights of older persons and is the editor of key books in the field such as *Theories on Law and Ageing: The Jurisprudence of Elder Law* (Springer, 2009). Finally, Professor Doron is also the founder of an Israeli NGO, "The Law in the Service of the Elderly", which was involved in key strategic-litigation regarding rights of older persons in Israel.

Nena Georgantzi is a trained lawyer specializing in human rights (MA, Université de Strasbourg, France) and social protection (MA, KU Leuven, Belgium). Since 2010 Nena has been working for AGE Platform Europe (AGE), an EU network, which aims to voice and promote the rights of the 190 million citizens aged 50+ in the European Union and to raise awareness on the issues that concern them most. Nena is currently finalizing her PhD on the human rights of older persons at the National University of Ireland in Galway (NUIG). Nena has participated in the drafting of the Council of Europe recommendation on the rights of older persons and has consulted the UN Office of the High Commissioner for

Human Rights. She is also involved in the political process around a new UN convention on the rights of older persons.

Ayelet Gur is a lecturer at the School of Social Work at Bar Ilan University. Her interest lies at the intersection of social policy and disability, with emphasis on issues related to the social inclusion and human rights of people with disabilities in light of the Convention on the Rights of Persons with Disabilities. She is currently involved in two major national studies in Israel: an evaluation study on the transition of persons with intellectual and/or developmental disabilities from institutional care facilities to community-based settings, and a households study on the families of children with intellectual disabilities.

Rosie Harding is Chair in Law and Society at the Birmingham Law School, University of Birmingham, UK and Chair of the Socio-Legal Studies Association. She won a Philip Leverhulme Prize for Law in 2017, and was a 2016/17 British Academy Mid-Career Fellow. Her research focuses on the place of law in everyday life, with a particular focus on the regulation and legal recognition of intimate and caring relationships. She is author of *Duties to Care: Dementia, Relationality and Law* (2017, Cambridge University Press) and *Regulating Sexuality* (2011, Routledge Social Justice, winner of the 2011 SLSA-Hart Book Prize and the 2011 SLSA-Hart Early Career Prize), and editor of *Revaluing Care in Theory, Law and Politics: Cycles and Connections* (2017, Routledge Social Justice), *Ageing and Sexualities: Interdisciplinary Perspectives* (2016, Ashgate), and *Law and Sexuality* (2016, Routledge Critical Concepts).

Paul de Hert is co-director of the multidisciplinary Research Group on Law, Science, Technology & Society (LSTS) at the Vrije Universiteit Brussel (VUB). Professor Paul de Hert's work addresses problems in the area of privacy and technology, human rights and criminal law. Currently he is expanding his scope of interest including research on issues with regard to the human rights status of the elderly and the principle of neutrality in a democratic state. To satisfy his multiple curiosities de Hert teams up regularly with other authors. A human rights approach combined with a concern for theory is the common denominator of all his work.

Eugenio Mantovani works at the multidisciplinary Research Group on Law, Science, Technology & Society (LSTS) at the Vrije Universiteit Brussel (VUB). His research interests include the human rights status of older persons and health law.

Titti Mattsson is a Professor of Public Law at the Faculty of Law, Lund University, Sweden and coordinator for the Norma Elder Law Research

Environment as well as the Law and Vulnerabilities Project at the University. She is a board member of the Swedish Agency for Health and Care Services Analysis and is involved in several national and international research networks, including the COST Action on Ageism. Her current research lies primarily in the intersection between jurisprudence, ethics and social work, with focuses on social welfare policy and the regulation of healthcare services and housing for older people.

Barbara Mikołajczyk is a Professor at the Faculty of Law and Administration of the University of Silesia in Katowice, Poland and the head of the Department of International Public Law and European Law. She has been involved in the COST Action on Ageism (IS1402) and in works of the Polish Commissioner for Human Rights' Group of Experts on Older Persons. She is a member of the Odysseus Academic Network for Studies on Immigration Asylum in Europe. She was also appointed as the ad hoc judge in the European Court of Human Rights (2012–14). She has authored books and articles dedicated to human rights of various categories of vulnerable persons, as migrant workers, asylum seekers, children, ethnic minorities, sexual minorities and older persons.

Ann Numhauser-Henning is Professor of Private Law at the Faculty of Law, Lund University, Sweden and the former Pro-Vice-Chancellor of the same university. She has been the head of the Norma Research Programme since its start in 1996 and initiated the Norma Elder Law Research Environment in 2012. She has written widely on labour law, especially employment law and non-discrimination law, but also on law in the social dimension more generally.

Gerard Quinn holds a Wallenberg chair at the Wallenberg Institute (University of Lund, Sweden) and a research chair at Leeds University (UK). A graduate of Harvard Law School, he was the founding director of the Centre for Disability Law at the National University of Ireland. He has three lifetime achievement awards in the field of disability and was named a "champion of EU research" by the government of Ireland. He has worked for and led major research projects for the UN, the EU and the Council of Europe. He led the delegation of Rehabilitation International during the drafting of the UN Convention on the Rights of Persons with Disabilities and has served on the boards of many international philanthropies. One of his main interests is intersectionality and particularly between old age and disability. He is currently spearheading the development of a Leeds/Lund Open Personhood Project that brings many research institutes around the world together to reflect on personhood and old age as well as disability. He currently sits on the Council of State in Ireland that advises its President on constitutional law issues.

Paul Quinn works at the multidisciplinary Research Group on Law, Science, Technology & Society (LSTS) at the Vrije Universiteit Brussel (VUB) and has also been active in research into issues associated with stigmatization and anti-discrimination approaches. He has been particularly active in developing a normative argument concerning the threats posed by stigmatizing expressions and language when used by the state. His PhD thesis was entitled "Stigmatizing Expressions of the State and the Problems they Pose for the Law". It was concerned with the harm that such expressions can cause and the difficulties that legal systems may have in regulating such harms.

Bridget Sleap is the Senior Rights Policy Adviser at HelpAge International. After working at Universidade Eduardo Mondlane in Mozambique for three years, Bridget completed a Master's degree in International Human Rights at the Institute of Commonwealth Studies, University of London. Since then she has worked on human rights and development at the Panos Institute, International Family Health and now HelpAge International, where she focuses on strengthening the rights of older people through the use of human rights mechanisms.

Benny Spanier earned his PhD from the University of Haifa Law School, Haifa, Israel. He is a research associate in the Center for Research and Study of Aging at the University of Haifa. His research focuses on ageism, soft law and the rights of older persons on the International arena and he has published numerous studies and articles in this field. He was a Visiting Scholar at Syracuse University College of Law. Currently he is working with colleagues on establishing a new International Older Persons Human Rights Index (IOPHRI), which will monitor the legal rights of older persons around the world.

Joanne Watson is a Speech Pathologist employed as a lecturer and researcher in Disability and Inclusion at Deakin University in Victoria, Australia. Joanne's current research interests are centred around the impact of the United Nations Convention on the Rights of Persons with Disabilities on signatory nations' capacity to maximize the self-determination for all citizens. She is particularly focused on the realization of self-determination for people with intellectual disability with complex communication support needs through supported decision-making mechanisms. Joanne's publications include book chapters and peer and non-peer reviewed academic journals and publications. Joanne presents widely in the area of disability and communication disorders within Australia and internationally.

Foreword: ageism affects all of us negatively – and the law can help

Ageing has become an almost universal experience. A century ago, only a small minority of the population was fortunate enough to live up to old and very old age. Since then, life expectancy has increased considerably, in many countries coming close to (or exceeding) the age of 80 years. This is good news: we are able to live a full life span, from childhood and adolescence over young and middle adulthood to old age. Compared to the living situation of older people a century ago, in many countries the material living conditions of older people with respect to income and wealth as well as health and long-term care have improved, although there are still large inequalities between and within countries.

Despite the undeniable progress in life expectancy and the standard of living, we are struggling with stereotypes, prejudice and discrimination concerning older people. These stereotypes, prejudice and discrimination are the basis for ageism, the complex and usually negative social construction of old age. Ageism is based on social constructions. It is manifested in the ways we think, feel and act towards age and ageing – and these social constructions influence the way people grow old. This concerns not only "them", but all of us, as we move towards old age. Ageism restricts the realm of opportunity for older people: societal norms control the way older people are allowed to behave. Just think about indignant responses when older people violate these expectations. For instance, an old woman who spends all her money on luxury cars and travels all over the world, "wasting" her children's future inheritance, violates the expectations of old mothers. Or imagine an old man, dressing in fashionable and provocative outfits – "not appropriate for his age". Sharp reactions, from malicious remarks to open outrage, demonstrate the power of ageism.

More severely, ageism can lead to discrimination. This is the case when older people are denied access to jobs or to healthcare services, simply because of their age. And, let's not fool ourselves: ageism does not start when people turn 65; ageism often starts much earlier. In certain business sectors, turning 40 can make you "too old" for a job. Ageism reinforces social inequality as it is more pronounced towards older women, poor people, people with disability or those with dementia. Moreover, ageism hurts society as a whole as it hinders older people from realizing their full potential.

Ageism is not a rare phenomenon, just the opposite is true: a recent study based on the European Social Survey (The Everyday Ageism Project, www.eurage.com) found that ageism is the most prevalent type of discrimination reported by almost 35 per cent of all participants over the age of 18. Hence, ageism can (and eventually will) affect most of us as we move along the life course.

The basis of ageism is mechanisms of social categorization and stereotyping. As humans, we deal every day with huge amounts of information, and categorization is a useful mechanism to assist individuals with processing the large amounts of information we are confronted with. Categorization allows us to handle diversity and enables us to make quick decisions, especially in social contexts. There are negative effects of overgeneralization, however. If a person is classified as a member of a social group, all properties of the group are ascribed to the individual person. Hence, if a person is seen as "old", the features of the category "old" are attributed to this individual person. Properties of the social category "old" are features like "chronically ill", "functionally impaired", and "cognitively slowed down" – even if an individual older person is neither ill nor functionally and cognitively impaired. Social categorizations come with positive or negative attitudes towards members of a group solely because of their group membership. Social psychological theories suggest that in the case of a negative group identity people try actively to dissociate from this group (for example social identity theory or terror management theory). This leads to social and spatial segregation between younger and older age groups, and reinforces societal beliefs about age groups.

What can we do against ageism? At the present time, research with regard to effective anti-ageist interventions is limited. We know, however, from other fields about potentially effective interventions. These may include raising public awareness and sensitizing civil society about ageism (for example, pointing out the ways in which the media contribute to ageist beliefs and stereotypes) and correcting false beliefs (for example, educating healthcare professionals that certain processes are due to illness and not to ageing per se). Finally, enacting, enforcing and changing laws is one important avenue to change ageism in contemporary societies. The current book is about ageing, ageism, and law in Europe. Israel "Issi" Doron from the University of Haifa (Israel) and Nena Georgantzi from the AGE Platform Europe (Brussels, Belgium) have brought together experts from Europe to comprehensively address this topic. The book has two parts. In the first part, Theories and Concepts, topics such as equality, inclusion/exclusion and autonomy are discussed. The second part, Realities and Legal Experiences, addresses the way laws interact with ageism, either as amplifiers or as attenuators of ageism. Taken as a whole, the book informs as to how to use the law as a tool against ageism.

This book grew out of a European research network, the COST Action "Ageism – A Multi-National, Interdisciplinary Perspective" (IS1402). COST is an EU-funded programme that enables researchers to set up interdisciplinary research networks in Europe and beyond. The researchers in this network come from 35 countries and represent a highly diverse group of established and early stage researchers as well as policy makers. As leaders of this COST Action we are grateful to our colleagues Issi Doron and Nena Georgantzi that they have used the network to produce a timely book on the role of the law in the field of ageism.

Liat Ayalon and Clemens Tesch-Romer

Introduction: between law, ageing and ageism

Israel (Issi) Doron and Nena Georgantzi

PROLOGUE

This book is about law, ageing and ageism in Europe. Generally speaking, European countries, as well as the European public media and interest are well aware of the ageing of Europe, the demographic shift it is facing, and the future challenges which are related. Nevertheless, much less attention was given in Europe to the social construction of old age, the prejudices, biases, stigmas and discrimination the older Europeans experience in their daily lives. Moreover, the different European legal systems, for example legislators, judges and lawyers, were mostly unaware of or blind to the fact that older persons have unique legal challenges, and that these challenges are the outcome of the way society treats and constructs old age.

LAW AND AGEING

Historically, law – meaning lawyers, judges, legislators or the scientific or philosophical (jurisprudential) aspects of the legal body of knowledge – was not interested in "ageing" or "older persons" as such (Doron, 2008). Typically, the interface between law and the older population was within the broader context of treating the poor, those who were unable to care for themselves (for example "lunatics" or "idiots"), or in the context of filial responsibility (for example the duty to care for older parents who were not able to care for themselves) (Doron, 1998). Even in more modern times, when law and society started to recognize the significance of "social groups" as the societal way of systematically discriminating (for example based on religion, nationality, gender, sexual orientation or disability), "age", a unique legal category, was usually missing or invisible (Rodriguez-Pinzon and Martin, 2002).

This reality has changed dramatically since the 1970s. Beginning in the USA (Frolik, 1993), and then spreading to Canada (Herring, 2016; Soden, 2005), the UK (Foster et al., 2014), and other common-law jurisdiction, and finally reaching continental Europe in recent years, the field of "law and ageing" (or "elder law") had gained visibility and recognition within the legal discipline, the legal profession and beyond. New books, publications, research centres, private-bar associations, high-profile legal cases, and media appearances have all been seen in recent years in the field of law and ageing in Europe (Mikołajczyk, 2013; Numhauser-Henning, 2013b).

This change or shift of reality is commonly attributed to three key developments: First, the demographic shift and its socio-legal impli-cations. At this stage of history, it is quite clear that one of the most important global challenges for the 21st century is global ageing. All over the globe societies are experiencing the combination of a dramatic increase of life expectancy, along with a sharp decline in fertility rates (and, for some countries, this combines with either internal migration of young people to big cities, or international immigration of young people to richer countries). The overall outcome of these trends is no less than dramatic: a significant growth both in total numbers, as well as with relative percentage rates, of the older population (Kalache et al., 2005). This historical development could not have been ignored by law, and the various "actors" within this field have started to either be exposed to it (for example older persons' issues coming to courts or raising public legal debates), or are becoming interested in it (as part of looking for new clientele or a unique field of expertise). Older persons themselves have also started not only to organize, but to voice their claim for the legal recognition of their human rights.

Second, the recognition of the private bar, law firms and lawyers to the potential needs of older clientele: the demographic rise of older persons and their role and place in societies have naturally given rise to the interest of private lawyers in this population. In an ever growing competitive legal world, with growing numbers of lawyers, there is a constant search for new legal fields, with potential economic gain. More and more private lawyers have come to recognize the potential legal interest that older persons bring with them to the field of law. Specific-ally, within the American context, ageing comes with very specialized knowledge in fields such as the right to healthcare in old age (for example, programmes like Medicaid, which is the unique healthcare insurance for poor, older Americans, which is legally very complicated), or in the field of estate planning (focused more on the rich who look for means to evade inheritance tax or to transfer assets while evading the tax system) (Frolik, 1993).

Academia and the world of science have also realized that there are unique theoretical, methodological and empirical issues in the inter- and multi-disciplinary study of law and ageing. Both lawyers and gerontologists have realized that one cannot fully understand the interaction between legal systems and the lives of older persons without combining both social and legal bases of knowledge (Doron, 2006).

Finally, these developments did not remain at national level, but appeared at international level as well. More specifically, and as argued by Sciubba (2014), norm diffusion from Latin America to the international level and from the debate and passage of the Convention on the Rights of Persons with Disabilities (CRPD) steered some awareness of rights in older age and drove the campaigning around a convention.

The outcome of all these developments has been expressed in a growing interest in improving the knowledge, the data, the theories and the methodologies within the field of law and ageing in recent years.

AGEISM

But what is it in old age that makes it interesting for law? Why do older people "deserve" to be recognized as a distinct societal group which receives "special" legal treatment? These are actually very important questions for the field of elder law. The answers are not simple and some would argue that indeed there is no such justification. However, as we will try to argue below, there is some justification to realize that older persons experience a unique social phenomenon which raises a legitimate concern for a proper rights-based response.

At least one justification would be found in the social concept of "ageism". In recent years there has been a significant growth in interest and research in this field. This book is based upon work from COST Action IS1402, supported by COST (European Cooperation in Science and Technology), which was fully dedicated to looking into the various aspects of ageism (www.cost.eu). Hence it is beyond the scope of this chapter to fully cover the rich knowledge and understanding of this phenomenon. However, in order to provide the basic foundations which will provide the theoretical context for the rest of this book, we will try to provide some key aspects of this term.

From a definitional perspective, the first to coin the term "ageism" and to attempt to define it was Dr Robert Butler. One of his best known early definitions for the term was as follows:

> Just as racism and sexism are based on ethnicity and gender, ageism is a form
> of systematic stereotyping and discrimination against people simply because
> they are old. As a group, older people are categorized as rigid in thought and
> manner, old fashioned in morality and skills. They are boring, stingy, cranky,
> demanding, avaricious, bossy, ugly, dirty and useless. An ageist younger
> generation sees older people as different from itself; it subtly ceases to
> identify with its elders as human beings. (Butler, 1969)

Since Dr Butler's original definition many other attempts were made to
define ageism, mirroring the growing understanding of the phenomenon.
One of the more recent definitions in the field reflects these newer
definitional developments well:

> Ageism is defined as negative or positive stereotypes, prejudice and/or
> discrimination against (or to the advantage of) elderly people on the basis of
> their chronological age or on the basis of a perception of them as being 'old'
> or 'elderly'. Ageism can be implicit or explicit and can be expressed on a
> micro-, meso-, or macro-level. (Iversen et al., 2009)

While the definitional task is ongoing, another important journey began
with trying to explain the reasons and foundations of ageism. Various
theoretical approaches have been proposed in recent years. Some have
focused on the psychology of the individual, for example the Social
Identity Theory (SIT) with its understanding of the importance of group
identity for the individual, while allowing the creation of the "young"
group identity as opposed to the "old" group (Bodner, 2009). Others have
focused on the more macro or institutional and societal levels, such as the
capitalistic organization of the modern society, and its division and
segregation of functional age groups (for example, young – trained for
production; mature – actively productive and breeding the future workers;
old – non-productive and inactive) (Hagestad and Uhlenberg, 2005).

One of the more well-known individual-level based theories which
tries to explain the phenomenon of ageism is the TMT – Terror
Management Theory. This theory stresses the psychological human
nature and its fear of death. From that perspective, in many ways ageing
and older persons are the real face and reminder of death, which most of
us either deny or try to avoid (Burke et al., 2010).

Finally, while the challenges of both defining and explaining ageism
continue, yet another growing body of research has been conducted into
the ways in which ageism manifests itself in everyday life. Indeed
numerous studies in the field of healthcare have shown how physicians,
nurses, physiotherapists and more, not only hold ageist attitudes towards

older patients, but also operate in discriminatory ways, providing older patients with inappropriate care (Inbar et al., 2012; Topaz and Doron, 2013).

Overall, then, it seems that current theoretical and empirical knowledge points to the fact that one cannot ignore both the existence of ageism and its real life consequences on the lived experience of older Europeans. One cannot understand the full meaning of "being old" without taking into account how society views and values older persons.

LAW AND AGEISM

If we realize that for various reasons the field of "law and ageing" has emerged in recent years, and that we have a much better awareness and understanding of the social phenomenon of ageism, this raises the obvious question: how do they both interact or interrelate? As a matter of fact, one can conceive of various points of potential interactions, which we will try to describe below.

Statutory Law and Other Binding Legal Instruments

One of the key means by which law operates is statutory law (or legislation). From a sociology of law perspective, one can learn a great deal about the values and cultures of societies simply by looking into the language of their black-letter laws. More specifically, within the context of ageism and legal rights of older persons, one could argue that "show me your laws, and I'll know how ageist you are".

Various specific examples exist on the books of national legislation which reflect ageist attitudes towards older persons. Such examples can be found in the absence of "age" within human rights and equality legislation (Rodriguez-Pinzon and Martin, 2002); in legislation which allows or even mandates workforce retirement solely based on chronological age (Numhauser-Henning, 2013a); in statutory frameworks which use chronological age limits (for example for transplantation) (Katvan et al., 2017); or in social protection legislation which allows for the nomination of a guardian over older persons as part of the notion that they cannot take care of themselves because of their age (Doron, 2004).

Interestingly, the ways in which ageism shapes legislation can be found not only at the local or national levels, but also at the international, regional and global level. The simplest examples can be found in the fundamental human rights texts. For example, at the UN level, key legal instruments such as the Universal Declaration of Human Rights, or the International Covenant on Economic, Social and Cultural Rights either do not mention "age" as a unique category (within the context of right to equality) or mention "age" in a very limited and narrow context. For example, according to General Comment No. 6 of the International Covenant on Economic, Social and Cultural Rights, age discrimination is prohibited only in several contexts and not in all, which is completely different language from that used for the General Comment on disability, for instance, which includes a clear prohibition of discrimination based on disability.

More specifically, at the European level, the European Convention of Human Rights also does not include a specific article regarding the rights of older persons, and its "equality" article does not mention "age" as a specific category (Spanier et al., 2013). Moreover, prior to 2009 and the coming into force of the Lisbon Treaty, the European Charter of Fundamental Rights also did not include a specific article regarding older persons as such, and their rights were specifically referred to in a very limited way (Doron, 2013).

A very recent example of the interplay of ageism and binding legal instruments has been displayed on the international level within the context of the UN Open-Ended Working Group on Ageing, and the debates around the need for a new and specific international convention for the human rights of older persons (Doron and Apter, 2010). On the one hand, the formation of the Open-Ended Working Group on Ageing in 2010, which was followed by the nomination of an Independent Expert on the enjoyment of all human rights by older persons by the Human Rights Council in 2014, reflected a growing awareness on the global level for the need to legally address the human rights challenges facing older persons. On the other hand, both these bodies have failed so far to be successful in actually promoting the advancement of a new international convention in the field. One potential reason for this failure can be found in an ageist attitude towards human rights of older persons.

Lawyers

Most people encounter law through the mediation of the legal professional, that is, the lawyers. However, potentially, lawyers (like other professionals) can hold biases, stereotypes and stigma regarding old age and older persons. These personal attitudes can potentially be manifested through discriminatory practices: refusing to accept older clients, treating older clients in a less professional way, adopting more paternalistic approaches in their legal strategies, or even settling cases for lower amounts of money in the view that the "value" of compensation for older clients should be lower than for younger ones.

Not many empirical studies have been conducted on lawyers with regard to ageism. One study measured both the knowledge and the attitudes of lawyers toward ageing and older persons (Ontzik-Heilburn, and Or-Chen, 2014). The finding showed that lawyers expressed low levels of knowledge in the field of ageing, but at the same time expressed mostly neutral and non-ageist attitudes towards their older clients. One of the key recommendations of this study was the need to study further the ways in which lawyers construct their relationships with older clients.

Judges and Courts

Eventually, legal disputes surrounding older persons reach the courts. These legal disputes are eventually settled by judges. These judges are potentially also exposed to ageism, and may be influenced both by their own as well as by the broader cultural values and traditions with regard to the meaning and place of ageing in society.

In recent years various new studies have been published that analyzed – both quantitatively and qualitatively – to what extent court rulings represent "ageist" approaches towards older persons. For example, on the European level, quantitative studies of the rulings of the European Court of Human Rights (ECHR) have shown that the ECHR is mostly unaware of or reflects "blindness" to the phenomenon of ageism (Spanier et al., 2013). Qualitative studies have shown more mixed realities. For example, a study into the ways courts in Israel construct dementia found that judges express both stigmatic and anti-stigmatic approaches towards older persons with dementia (Doron et al., 2018).

The "Clients" – the Older Adults

Like many other gerontological fields, which try to explore the phenomenon of human ageing, the authentic voice of the older population itself is lost. Similarly, for many years, within the field of law and ageing the experience of the older persons themselves within the legal system was not explored or captured. To what extent do older persons themselves experience ageism in their interactions with the legal system?

There are not too many studies which explore this point of view. One such qualitative study was conducted with older women about their legal experience during their divorce proceedings in later life (Ohayon-Glicksman, 2018). Many of these women reported in the interviews how they experienced a mix of both negative and positive ageism in the way their lawyers and the judges treated them.

Witnesses and Jury Members

Finally, it should be reminded that older persons appear before the courts not only as plaintiffs of defendants, but they also appear as witnesses and participate in the judicial process as jurors. These unique legal contexts can raise interesting questions. For example, they may raise questions about how courts "evaluate" (e.g. credibility or truthfulness) the testimony of older persons in the context of an ageist culture. Once again, some studies have been conducted in this field. For example, a study conducted on 1267 undergraduate students who read a case summary and witness statement, while the sex and age of the witness (49, 69, 79 or 89 years) varied, found an age effect for honesty, particularly for comparisons of the 79/89-year-olds versus the 49-year-olds (Mueller–Johnson et al., 2007). However, the study by Kwong See et al. (2001) found that while their study's participants perceived a witness described as young to be more competent than a witness described as old, the opposite was found regarding the description of the witness as honest.

A different question can be raised regarding the attitudes, stereotypes and behaviour regarding older persons within their role as jurors and their actual cognitive performance. Some empirical studies have tried to compare the performance of younger and older jurors. For example, the research by Fitzgerald (2000) has found that age (along with vocabulary and education) influenced performance (for example in the field of recognition memory). However, it also found that simple interventions to improve cognitive performance (for example pre-trial instructions) can improve the performance of older jurors.

CONCLUSION: ABOUT THIS BOOK

Realizing how complex and diverse are the interconnections between ageing, law and ageism has brought about the creation of this book. From the review provided above one can realize how limited is the existing knowledge, both in general, and – within the European context – in specific. In many ways, the European interest in the specific and focused interactions between law, ageing and ageism is in its infancy. It is against this scientific background that this book attempts to try and start to fill in the existing gaps in this important field.

Therefore, the structure of this book tries to mirror our realization of the different ways one can approach our topic, and was constructed in the following manner.

The first part of the book is focused more on conceptual or theoretical aspects of how ageism can be related to law.

The book opens with the chapter by Rosie Harding, which explores the concepts of equality and social justice for older people in the context of arguments for and against the need for a new Convention on the Rights of Older Persons. Professor Harding interrogates the effectiveness of different theoretical approaches to equality (equality of resources, equality of recognition, equality of power and equality of condition) that could underpin arguments about the need for new international human rights protection for older people. In evaluating each of these "equality"-based approaches, the chapter demonstrates why each falls short as a justification for a new Convention. In response to the limitations of an equality approach, Professor Harding argues that we need to turn towards an understanding of social justice for older people, and suggests that a capabilities approach, building on the work of Amartya Sen and Martha Nussbaum, offers the most persuasive conceptual basis for a new Convention. Moreover, she argues that the capabilities approach, which requires not only the discursive and rhetorical enunciation of rights but also their substantive realization, is the most effective way to understand equality and social justice for older people.

The book continues with the chapter by Titti Mattsson, with a discussion that focuses on the relationship between vulnerability and ageism in the light of age limits in social welfare legislation. Professor Mattsson investigates the meaning of vulnerability by drawing on Martha Albertson Fineman's vulnerability theory as a starting point for the discussion of how the concept alternatively may be used by researchers as well as policy makers dealing with age-related legal issues in order to maximize the social rights potential for older people. The point of departure for the discussion is the Disability Act in Sweden, which limits disability benefits for those over 65 years old who have disabilities that are considered being part of "normal ageing".

Part I closes with the chapter by Gerard Quinn, Ayelet Gur and Joanne Watson, which looks at new developments in communications theory which potentially unlock – and reveal – the will and preference of people (including older people) who have been hitherto deemed unreachable because of their cognitive impairments. It goes further by looking at emerging evidence about the importance of social capital as a form of support to enable people to remain in control of their own lives. Finally, this chapter emphasizes the importance of community living as a way to break down ageism, and of supporting older persons to be, and remain, in charge of their own lives and as well as life choices.

The second part of the book moves from the theoretical perspective into the more empirical and descriptive perspective of the interaction between law, ageing and ageism.

The first chapter in this part is by Barbara Mikołajczyk, who describes how the participation of older persons in social life has so far been examined predominantly from the sociological, medical, psychological and economic perspective. Lawyers, apart from labour lawyers, have seldom taken on this issue. The chapter continues by arguing that it has been even more uncommon for international lawyers to touch upon active ageing. In order to fill this gap, this chapter examines whether Europe's two most important organizations, the Council of Europe and the European Union, have adopted effective legal instruments promoting active ageing of Europeans. Therefore, this chapter analyzes regional international law acts (both hard and soft law) of the Council of Europe, as well as the EU legal acts, strategies and programmes, and the ways in which they address ageism.

The next chapter is by Ann Numhauser-Henning, which shows how ageism in working life is a central concern when it comes to active ageing. More specifically, this chapter aims to discuss the relation between the EU ban on age discrimination, European employment law and active ageing strategies. In doing so it draws heavily on some earlier works of Professor Numhauser-Henning and on the premise that there is a special and close connection between ageism – the overall theme of this book – and non-discrimination regulation on the grounds of age. Discrimination – or discriminatory behaviour – is thus an integral part of most definitions of ageism.

Numhuaser-Henning's chapter is followed by Eugenio Mantovani, Paul Quinn and Paul de Hert, who comment in this chapter on the so-called 2014 Chicago Declaration on the Rights of Older Persons, one of the most recent efforts to establish the human rights status of older persons, and the way it tackles stereotyping, stigmatization and discrimination of older persons. To this end, the authors analyze a series of selected cases drawn from the case law of the ECHR with a view to (trying to) anticipate what a judge, confronted with a controversy involving ageism, would decide. The legal analysis, focused on Articles 14 (Prohibition of discrimination) Article 10 (Freedom of expression), and Article 8 (Right to private and family life). This analysis lends support to the claim that stereotyping and stigmatization are only partially open to influence from human rights law. The force of the law appears otherwise to be limited in contrasting the social manifestation of ageism in stigmatizing expressions and stereotypes.

The next chapter is an empirical analysis made by Benny Spanier and Israel (Issi) Doron. In this chapter, the authors examine the socio-legal status of older persons in the Council of Europe Member States, as reported by the States themselves. This is made possible by the European Social Charter (Revised), and by the European Committee of Social Rights, which supervizes the reports of the States' compliance with the Charter. The chapter presents the first of its kind quantitative empirical analysis of the Committee's decisions regarding older persons, and provides some insights regarding ageism and the social construction of older persons under the ESC.

The book ends with the chapter by Marijke de Pauw, Bridget Sleap and Nena Georgantzi, which describes how ageism and age discrimination lie at the root of many human rights violations faced by older persons worldwide. The authors argue that addressing these issues is thus essential in ensuring the effective protection of older persons' rights. This chapter therefore explores the link between ageism, age discrimination and the rights of older persons at a practical level. The chapter then identifies the position and recognition of ageism in international policy documents and human rights instruments, as well as within ongoing negotiations on a new international binding treaty that focuses on older persons. It thus aims to demonstrate the lack of attention for the phenomenon that negatively affects older persons, and to provide recommendations on how to strengthen an anti-ageist approach in a potential new UN convention on older persons' rights.

Clearly this book does not cover all the rich and diverse interactions between law, ageing and ageism. However, it provides a rich and diverse picture on various elements of these interactions, both at the European and the international level. In many ways it invites further research and more scientific action in this field. Finally, it will hopefully serve as another support for the promotion of future international binding human rights instruments for older persons.

Acknowledgment

This publication is based upon work from COST Action on Ageism – A multi-national, interdisciplinary perspective (IS1402), supported by COST (European Cooperation in Science and Technology).

Weblink: www.cost.eu

REFERENCES

Bodner, E. (2009). On the origins of ageism among older and younger adults. *International Psychogeriatrics*, **21**(6), 1003–14.

Burke, B.L., Martens, A. and Faucher, E.H. (2010). Two decades of terror management theory: a meta-analysis of mortality salience research. *Personality and Social Psychology Review*, **14**(2), 155–95.

Butler, R.N. (1969). Age-ism: Another form of bigotry. *The Gerontologist*, **9**(4), 243–6.

Doron, I. (1998). From lunacy to incapacity and beyond. *Health Law in Canada*, **19**(4), 95–114.

Doron, I. (2004). Aging in the shadow of the law: the case of elder guardianship in Israel. *Journal of Aging & Social Policy*, **16**(4), 59–77.

Doron, I. (2006). Bringing the law to the gerontological stage: a different look at movies and old age. *International Journal of Aging & Human Development*, **62**(3), 237–54.

Doron, I. (2008). *Theories on Law and Ageing: The Jurisprudence of Elder Law*. Berlin: Springer.

Doron, I. (2013). Older Europeans and the European Court of Justice. *Age and Ageing*, **42**(5), 604–608.

Doron, I. and Apter, I. (2010). The debate around the need for an international convention on the rights of older persons. *The Gerontologist*, **50**(5), 586–93.

Doron, I., Werner, P., Spanier, B. and Lazar, O. (2018, forthcoming). The meaning of dementia in Israeli court cases: A qualitative analysis. *Dementia: the International Journal of Social Research and Practice*.

Fitzgerald, J.M. (2000). Younger and older jurors: The influence of environmental supports on memory performance and decision making in complex trials. *The Journal of Gerontology – Series B*, **55**(6), 323–31.

Foster, C., Herring, J. and Doron, I. (2014). *The Law and Ethics of Dementia*. Bloomsbury Publishing.

Frolik, L.A. (1993). The developing field of elder law: a historical perspective. *The Elder Law Journal*, **1**, 1–18.

Hagestad, G.O. and Uhlenberg, P. (2005). The social separation of old and young: a root of ageism. *Journal of Social Issues*, **61**(2), 343–60.

Herring, J. (2016). *Vulnerable Adults and the Law*. Oxford: Oxford University Press.

Inbar, N., Doron, I. and Ohry, A. (2012). Physiotherapists' attitudes towards old and young patients in persistent vegetative state (PVS). *Quality in Ageing and Older Adults*, **13**(2), 111–24.

Iversen, T.N., Larsen, L. and Solem, P.E. (2009). A conceptual analysis of ageism. *Nordic Psychology*, **61**(3), 4–22.

Kalache, A., Barreto, S.M. and Keller, I. (2005). *Global Ageing: The Demographic Revolution in all Cultures and Societies*. In M.L. Johnson (ed.), *The Cambridge Handbook of Age and Ageing* (pp. 30–46). Cambridge: Cambridge University Press.

Katvan, E., Doron, I., Ashkenazi, T., Boas, H., Carmiel-Haggai, M., Elhalel, M.D., Schnoor, B. et al. (2017). Age limitation for organ transplantation: the Israeli example. *Age and Ageing*, **46**(1), 8–10.

Kwong See, S.T., Hoffman, H.G. and Wood, T.L. (2001). Perceptions of an old female eyewitness: Is the older eyewitness believable? *Psychology and Aging*, **16**(2), 346–50.

Mikołajczyk, B. (2013). Is the ECHR ready for global ageing? *The International Journal of Human Rights*, **17**(4), 511–29.

Mueller-Johnson, K., Toglia, M.P., Sweeney, C.D. and Ceci, S.J. (2007). The perceived credibility of older adults as witnesses and its relation to ageism. *Behavioral Sciences & the Law*, **25**(3), 355–75.

Numhauser-Henning, A. (2013a). The EU ban on age-discrimination and older workers: Potentials and pitfalls. *International Journal of Comparative Labor Law and Industrial Relations*, **29**, 391–423.

Numhauser-Henning, A. (2013b). An introduction to elder law and the Norma Elder Law Research Environment. *European Journal of Social Law*, **2013**(3), 235–52.

Ohayon-Glicksman, H. (2018). *Grey Divorce: The Divorce Experience of Older Women Under Israeli Family Law*. Thesis submitted for Master's degree in Gerontology [Hebrew]. University of Haifa, Haifa.

Ontzik-Heilburn, I. and Or-Chen, K. (2014). Approach to elderly clients among lawyers in Israel: Attitude towards the elderly and knowledge concerning the elderly among lawyers [Hebrew]. *Gerontology & Geriatrics*, **41**(3), 31–49.

Rodriguez-Pinzon, D. and Martin, C. (2002). The international human rights status of elderly persons. *The American University International Law Review*, **18**, 915–1008.

Sciubba, J.D. (2014). Explaining campaign timing and support for a UN Convention on the Rights of Older People. *The International Journal of Human Rights*, **18**(4–5), 462–78.

Soden, A. (2005). *Advising the Older Client*. Markham, Ontario: LexisNexis Butterworths.

Spanier, B., Doron, I. and Milman-Sivan, F. (2013). Older persons' use of the European Court of Human Rights. *Journal of Cross-Cultural Gerontology*, **28**(4), 407–20.

Topaz, M. and Doron, I. (2013). Nurses' attitudes toward older patients in acute care in Israel. *Online Journal of Issues in Nursing*, **18**(2).

PART I

Theories and concepts

1. Equality, social justice and older people

Rosie Harding

In this chapter I explore the concepts of equality and social justice for older people in the context of arguments for and against the need for a new Convention on the Rights of Older Persons. I interrogate the effectiveness of different theoretical approaches to equality (equality of resources, equality of recognition, equality of power and equality of condition) that could underpin arguments about the need for new international human rights protection for older people. In evaluating each of these "equality"-based approaches, I demonstrate why each falls short as a justification for a new convention. In response to the limitations of an equality approach, I argue that we need to turn towards an understanding of social justice for older people, and suggest that a capabilities approach, building on the work of Amartya Sen and Martha Nussbaum, offers the most persuasive conceptual basis for a new convention. I argue that the capabilities approach, which requires not only the discursive and rhetorical enunciation of rights but also their substantive realization, is the most effective way to understand both equality and social justice for older people.

I develop my argument in three sections. In the first section, I provide a brief introduction to the social and legal arguments for a Convention on the Rights of Older Persons, demonstrating the central place that equality and social justice aims hold within the movement for older people's rights. In the second section, I explore different conceptualizations of equality and measure each of these against the arguments in favour of a new convention. I turn, in the third section, to explore the utility of the "capabilities approach" developed by Sen (1985; 1995; 1999; 2010) and Nussbaum (1999; 2007; 2013) as a rationale for older people's rights. I argue for the need to shift from equality arguments towards social justice, building on the capabilities approach to make the case for a new convention on older people's rights.

TOWARDS AN INTERNATIONAL CONVENTION ON OLDER PERSONS' RIGHTS

Social, legal and political movements towards a new international Convention on the Rights of Older Persons have emerged since the beginning of the twenty-first century (Rodriguez-Pinzon and Martin, 2003), with momentum gathering apace since around 2010. Reasons for the emergence and escalation in calls for a new international legal instrument may include increased awareness of the human rights issues facing older people, following a range of "soft law" international agreements; the success of the UN Convention on the Rights of Persons with Disabilities (CRPD); and the emergence of a range of national and international Non-Governmental Organizations (NGOs) focused on older people's rights (Doron and Apter, 2010).

The earliest United Nations (UN) activities on the topic of ageing can be traced back as far as the World Assembly on Ageing in Vienna in 1982, which led to the Vienna International Plan of Action on Aging (United Nations, 1983). This initial plan on tackling the challenges of ageing in the international context grew from the work of the Economic and Social Council on issues to do with age and ageing (United Nations, 1982). These historical foundations go some way towards explaining why older people's rights have (largely, though not exclusively, in the past) been more often considered economic, social and cultural rights (ESCR), rather than substantive civil and political rights. This then generates "the perception that these 'rights' are only aims or goals" (Rodriguez-Pinzon and Martin, 2003: 921).

The Second World Assembly on Ageing, which took place in Madrid in April 2002, led to the replacement *Madrid International Plan of Action on Ageing* (United Nations, 2002). This new international plan shifted the focus from humanitarian aspects of ageing in developed countries, to responding to the challenges posed by ageing in the developing world (Sidorenko and Walker, 2004). The Madrid plan significantly expanded the scope of recommendations and priority areas for action. As Sidorenko and Walker (2004) argue, this change in emphasis and expansion of the scope of the plan "indicates the replacement of 'compassionate ageism', which regards older people as a 'deserving' group, with the acceptance of their rights to equal treatment and self-determination" (Sidorenko and Walker, 2004: 153). The explicit acknowledgement of older people's human rights in the Madrid plan arguably paved the way towards the 2009 Expert Group Meeting on the "Rights of Older Persons" in Bonn, organized by the Division for Social Policy and Development of the UN

Department of Economic and Social Affairs (UN DESA, 2009). The Expert Group meeting agreed that both normative gaps and implementation gaps had been generated by the complex and piecemeal coverage of age within existing (soft and hard) international law. Possibilities for closing these gaps and strengthening rights protections for older people that were proposed by the expert group included the appointment of a special rapporteur on older people's rights, and a new international convention, which "could create new principles that would empower older persons, provide older persons with greater visibility and recognition, both nationally and internationally and provide the foundational basis for advocacy, public awareness and education on the rights of older persons" (UN DESA, 2009: 18). Whilst neither of these substantive recommendations from the expert group were immediately acted upon, they undoubtedly provided the impetus for escalating work on older people's rights in the last decade, and specifically in the establishment of the Open-Ended Working Group on older persons' human rights (Doron, 2015).

Several substantive gaps in international protections of older people's human rights were identified in the Report of the UN High Commissioner for Human Rights to the Economic and Social Council (UNHCHR, 2012). These gaps included: ageism and age-based discrimination; the challenge of ensuring older people are afforded their rights to legal capacity and equal recognition under the law; rights associated with long-term care, including rights to liberty and security of the person, privacy, freedom of movement, freedom of expression, and freedom from torture and inhuman or degrading treatment; and rights to an adequate standard of living and the highest attainable standard of physical and mental health. The increased risk of violence and abuse that older people face, particularly those reliant on others for care and support, and the challenges of access to justice when older people experience abuse were also identified as problems, as were the challenges that older age generates in access to work, food security and housing. Rights to social protection and social security were highlighted as generating particular issues for older people. Finally, protection gaps were identified in relation to the right to access an adequate standard of healthcare, including access to appropriate palliative and end-of-life care. More recently, these concerns were reiterated by the Independent Expert on the enjoyment of all human rights by older persons, Rosa Kornfeld-Matte, in her report to the UN Human Rights Council (Kornfeld-Matte, 2016).

The sheer breadth of these gaps in the international human rights protection regime as it relates to older people provides an important baseline for thinking about the arguments for and against a new Convention on the Rights of Older People. Doron and Apter (2010) suggest that the two key arguments for a new convention are simply that these gaps exist, and that the creation of a convention would operate as "an effective legal tool to promote and advance the social position of older persons in the future" (Doron and Apter, 2010: 588). Arguably, the discursive shift towards thinking of older people as holders of substantive rights that has been catalyzed by the social movements and legal discussions around the creation of a new convention would also help to shift understandings of ageing, and go some way towards challenging the current gap in human rights protection. These are strong arguments, and yet there are also a range of convincing arguments against the need for a specific convention for older people. One of the main arguments against is that older people's rights are fully covered by the universal guarantees in the existing international human rights framework. Instead of focusing energies on the legal and political process that would lead to a new convention, the energy of social movement activists might be better expended making arguments for better substantive protection and implementation of the existing international human rights protections. Relatedly, there are arguments to suggest that previous "specific" conventions, notably the Convention on the Elimination of Discrimination against Women (CEDAW) and the Convention on the Rights of the Child (CRC), have not actually generated significant international shifts in the human rights protection of women or children. Indeed, some commentators argue that these specific rights instruments have made the situation worse, rather than better, even indirectly legitimizing some human rights infringements (Doron and Apter, 2010).

The aim of this chapter is to take one step back from these political and legal arguments around whether a convention on the rights of older persons is appropriate, desirable or necessary, in order to explore what the conceptual basis for such a convention would be. In the simplest of terms, we might understand the need for human rights protections for a group of people (older people) as a means to addressing their different treatment, as compared to the norm. So, if we understand older people as the non-normative group, the normative group we would contrast them with would be people who are younger, or of middle age.[1] Addressing systematic disadvantage experienced by the non-normative group means addressing the multiple inequalities and/or social injustices that they experience in their everyday lives. In this chapter, I seek to argue that a social justice approach, such as that provided by the "capabilities approach" (Sen, 1985; 1995; 1999; 2010; Nussbaum, 1999; 2007; 2013) offers a more robust justification for a new convention than an equalities approach, even though exploring the gaps in human rights protection for older persons exposes a range of pressing inequalities across multiple domains.

THE POTENTIAL AND LIMITS OF EQUALITY AS A RATIONALE FOR OLDER PERSONS' RIGHTS

Despite being a fundamental value of many national constitutions, and a core normative principle with ancient roots (such as the Aristotelian edict that likes should be treated alike), equality remains an awkward concept. It is difficult to find agreement on a definition of what equality means in any detailed and functional sense, beyond the very simple core of like-alike-ness. Notwithstanding that most would agree that at the very least, all human beings have "equal worth and importance, and are therefore equally worthy of concern and respect" (Baker et al., 2004: 23), equality has been described as a myth, because it has "no independent meaning or definition and can be understood in conflicting and incompatible ways" (Fineman, 2004: 25–6).

The heart of the problem that equality presents is that the object of equality, sometimes referred to as equality's "what", has been given wildly different content by different theorists. As Amartya Sen has noted, theoretical engagements with the concept of equality look to what equality is attempting to achieve, and "every normative theory of social arrangement that has at all stood the test of time seems to demand equality of *something*" (Sen, 1995: 12). Various different conceptions of what the "something" is that is necessary for equality have been propounded: examples include equality of resources (for example, Dworkin, 2002), equality of recognition (for example, Fraser, 1997), equality of condition (Baker et al., 2004) and equality of power (for example, Cooper, 2004). In the context of arguments for a new convention on the rights of older people, as I will demonstrate, these different approaches to equality's object can each help to support arguments for addressing some of the gaps in international human rights protections, but none can offer comprehensive solutions to the identified normative and implementation gaps.

Resources

Equal distribution of resources has always been a central idea within theoretical approaches to equality. It is most commonly used to refer to equal distribution of financial resources such as income and wealth

(Baker et al., 2004). Theoretical engagements with how to ensure the equal distribution of resources tend to take private property (or "things" which can be divided up between individuals) as the starting point of discussion. Perhaps the most well-known proponent of "resources" as the best way to conceptualize equality's "what" is Ronald Dworkin (1977; 2002), whose equal auction example provides a persuasive argument in favour of resource distribution from a social starting point of zero.

Aside from the impossibility of restarting the distribution of resources from a starting point of everyone having nothing, perhaps the most problematic aspect of Dworkin's (2002) conceptualization of equality of resources is his apparent belief in the ability of "the market" to provide a fair distribution of resources. The limitations of this belief become plainly evident in the increasing gap between rich and poor in late capitalist economies. Thinking back to the gaps identified by the UN High Commissioner for Human Rights (UNHCHR, 2012), inequality of resources is clearly a significant factor in issues relating to access to an adequate standard of living for older people, food security, access to appropriate housing, and access to quality palliative and end-of-life care. Additional redistribution of financial and practical resources to those in need should, in theory, resolve inequalities in access to these social goods. The problem, however, lies in the inadequacy of redistributive welfare systems in late capitalist societies.

Consider, as an example, the problem of access to quality, affordable care services to support the activities of daily living for older persons living in the community.[2] Gerontological research has clearly identified a preference by older people to "age in place" (Callahan, 1992; Vasunilas-horn et al., 2011). Most people would prefer to have care services they require provided to them in their own homes than move into residential or nursing care environments. Yet access to this kind of care and support requires the means to pay for it. State-funded care is available in England, through means testing, to those with the highest level of need and the lowest level of resources. Yet the current financial position of social care funding means that not only will there be an anticipated funding gap of £5.8 billion by 2020 in England (Local Government Association, 2017), but UK government spending on social care is estimated to fall to less than 1 per cent of GDP by 2020 (Nuffield Trust et al., 2016). The funding gap in social care that has arisen as a result of year-on-year cuts to local authority budgets since 2010 (totalling some 30 per cent of local government budgets) has meant an overall reduction in the numbers of people accessing publicly funded social care by 26 per cent. This reduction in state-provided care does not remove the care needs that were previously being supported. Instead, given the relational context that care is provided in and through (Harding, 2017), the lack of governmental will to provide resources for care pushes the cost of providing that care onto the person who requires care, and their families and carers. It can, for example, force family carers to give up paid employment to provide care, which then in turn generates future resource problems if people of working age are unable to earn sufficient income to save for their own older age (Harding, 2017). This privatization of care also has an uneven effect, exacerbating gendered inequalities, because women are still more likely than men to provide care to family members; and increasing the stigma of disability and illness in older age, because older people do not want to be a "burden" on their families.

A second limitation of an equality of resources approach to protecting the human rights of older persons is that if older persons' rights are primarily expressed in terms of socioeconomic rights, rather than civil and political rights, then the potential for relatively weak enforcement mechanisms and wide-ranging limitations or derogations may increase. Prior to the global economic crisis, there had been a move away from considering "civil and political rights" and "economic, social and cultural rights" as distinct groupings of rights, and recognizing the interrelationships between them (UNHCHR, 2008). Yet the response of the Committee on Economic, Social and Cultural Rights (CESCR) to the international economic crisis suggests a move back towards understanding socioeconomic rights as substantively different from civil and political rights, and allowing states to resile from them in times of economic emergency. In a letter to states, the CESCR effectively offered a new accommodations model for the times of economic crisis, disrupting the development of the doctrine of non-retrogression, and making it easier for states to roll back socioeconomic rights (Warwick, 2016). This, in turn, retrenches the "traditional message that only socio-economic rights have economic consequences (and thus that economic emergencies are only relevant to those rights)" (Warwick, 2016: 261).

Reliance on a resource equality perspective as the foundation for a new convention on the rights of older persons may not, therefore, provide enough of a rationale to remove the currently existing implementation gaps in relation to, for example, standard of living, access to social security, housing or food that older persons experience. Further, grounding older persons' rights in a resource equality context would need to address the fundamental challenges posed by the late capitalist (neoliberal) economic system, which perpetuates socioeconomic inequality through exploitation, marginalization and deprivation (Fraser, 1997). Redistribution of resources in our current economic climate cannot happen as a one-off measure, but rather must continue in an ongoing fashion in order to even begin to address the realities of unequal distribution of resources. Ongoing redistribution through means-tested political approaches does not, however, do anything to challenge the structures which generate or support resource inequality, nor is it capable of removing economic inequalities (Fraser, 1997: 25).

Turning back to the example of social care services, the market in these services is essentially dysfunctional. The provision of care services requires resources. The limited resources that are allocated to the system, alongside the market ideology that underpins it, mean that it is unable to respond to need. The private enterprise nature of care service providers requires that companies and agencies providing care are profitable (if they are not, then they fold, leading to failures of care and neglect). In order to be profitable, social care service providers must pay low wages, rely on zero hours contracts and other forms of precarious labour, and offer poor working conditions to care staff (Hayes, 2017), which then perpetuates cycles of resource inequality into the future. Governmental interventions that seek to increase wages for the lowest paid (such as the planned increases to the UK national minimum wage in the coming years) can only work where they are backed up with appropriate investment. In the context of care, ongoing cuts to local authority budgets simply mean that fewer people will have access to state support to pay for care, which means that a greater proportion of care needs will have to be provided for privately. That private funding will either operate, as it does currently, to subsidize state provision if it is paid for by self-funding recipients, or will (again) force family members to choose between their own paid employment and paying for care, or providing that care themselves (Harding, 2017). Either way, the costs of caring are reprivatized, and continue the cycle of redistribution into the future. Distributive justice is, and will continue to be, a fundamental aspect of inequality, and one of the major problems associated with ageing. Yet it is clear that equality of resources is insufficient as a conceptual rationale for a new Convention on the Rights of Older Persons, because addressing maldistribution alone will not address the systemic problems associated with the undervaluing of care and support in society (Harding et al., 2017).

Recognition

One of the great debates in equality theory has been between those who argue that the correct object of equality is resources, and those who see the target of equality as more appropriately addressing misrecognition of particular groups. Of all the different approaches to "equality of what" that have been put forward, equality of recognition seems, at first glance, to be the "what" of equality that is most relevant to challenging ageism or other forms of discrimination against marginalized groups. Arguments for equality of recognition may offer additional justifications for a Convention on the Rights of Older Persons (Doron, 2015). Whereas the redistribution of tangible resources may well enable older persons to access a higher standard of living, through access to better health, food, housing and care by being facilitated to pay more for such goods, viewing equality through the lens of recognition may offer different solutions to other gaps in contemporary human rights protections for older people. Ageism and age discrimination, which build on stereotypes of older people as incapacitated, disabled, in ill health and past their social usefulness, would, for example, be effectively challenged through equality of recognition for older persons. Recognizing that chronological age is not a determinant of capacity or ability to work or to contribute to society in other ways, would arguably catalyze significant gains for older people.

Nancy Fraser (1997) distinguished cultural or symbolic injustice from socioeconomic inequalities, arguing that cultural domination, non-recognition and disrespect create distinct forms of inequality that recognition would address. It is important to note that this distinction between redistribution and recognition is a theoretical one, which does not presume that in practice the two are entirely separate problems as "economic injustice and cultural injustice are usually interimbricated so as to reinforce each other dialectically" (Fraser, 1997: 15). Fraser uses the operation of heterosexism and homophobia to devalue lesbian and gay sexuality as an example of inequality that is rooted in an "unjust cultural-valuational structure" (1997: 18), arguing that if lesbian and gay sexuality were re-valued as equally respectable to heterosexuality, then the problem of lesbian/gay inequality would be solved. Although Fraser prefaces her theoretical argument with a disclaimer that in reality cultural and socioeconomic inequalities are linked and supportive of each other, she uses the example of lesbian/gay sexuality as one where any economic inequalities would also be resolved through the recognition and re-valuation of non-heterosexual sexuality. This example, and Butler's (1998) response to it, can be extended to consider whether equality of recognition would provide an effective conceptual basis for a new Convention on the Rights of Older Persons.

In her critique of Fraser's location of lesbian and gay sexuality exclusively within the cultural sphere, Butler (1998) highlighted the ways in which heteronormativity works to support the economic system, through the sexual division of labour and the "reproduction of the normative family" (Butler, 1998: 40). Thus, she argues, the labelling of

homophobia and heterosexism as "merely cultural" removes and con-
founds the relationship between the regulation of sexuality and modes of
production in a capitalist economic system. Crucially, however, heteronormativity does not only produce effects on sexuality, and the hetero-
normative ordering of society also works to generate particular patterns
of stereotypes about ageing. Historical patterns of employment, alongside
the gendered allocation of childcare and household labour, are also
embedded in heteronormativity.

Consider, for example, the ways in which women's working patterns
alongside differential compulsory retirement ages have historically
worked to create socioeconomic disadvantage for older women. In the
UK, despite women's life expectancy being consistently longer than
men's (ONS, 2016), historically, state retirement ages for women were
set at 60, whereas men were unable to retire until the age of 65. This
difference, combined with the greater likelihood of women either giving
up paid employment entirely for a period of time to care for children, or
working part time, has made it more difficult for women to save for
retirement, to build up sufficient national insurance contributions to be
entitled to a full state pension, or to access employers' pensions. The
persistent gender pay gap, even in full-time employment, compounds this
difference (Costa Dias et al., 2016). Whilst changes have been made in
recent years, including the removal of mandatory retirement ages and an
increase in the age at which women are entitled to receive a state pension
in the UK, this has not necessarily been either intended to address the
historical disadvantages experienced by women, nor has it had that effect.
Rather, increases in the state pension age have been intended to reduce
the pension bill and implemented as part of a range of "austerity" cuts,
and have generated significant financial problems for many older women.
Various policies have been introduced at different points as a mechanism
for introducing post hoc amelioration for these kinds of income inequalities in older age, including through redistribution of wealth through state
benefits like Pension Credit. Yet finding a long-term solution to income
disparity between older men and women requires a combination of both
equality of resources and substantive gender equality, with changes to
patterns of domestic labour, childcare, and closing the gender pay gap in
both employment and retirement. Whilst some progress has been made in
some of these areas, despite the formal prohibition of sex discrimination
in employment over 40 years ago,[3] more than two-thirds of pensioners
living in poverty in the UK are women, and the income of older women
is, on average, 15 per cent less than that of men (Turner, 2016). It is clear
that equality of recognition and equality of resources are substantially

interlinked. Neither approach, therefore, can offer a complete solution to the disadvantages experienced by older persons.

Power, Condition

In response to the limitations of the resources versus recognition dynamic in equality studies, some commentators have suggested more all-encompassing approaches to equality's object. Davina Cooper (2000; 2004) argues for a conception of "equality of what", that moves away from the difficulties of a dichotomous emphasis on resources and recognition, towards equality as nobody having "an inherent right to impact more on their social and physical environment than anyone else" (Cooper, 2004: 77–8). Unlike conceptions of equality of resources or recognition, which are rooted in group-based identifications, equality of power takes the "moral equality of living humans" (Cooper, 2004: 68) as the subject of equality. Unlike the conception of equality of power as restricted to political power (see for example, Dworkin, 2002: 184–210), this version of equality of power extends to the social world as well as to the exercise of power within the operation of the state.

In Dworkin's (2002) conception of equality of power, he considered power solely in terms of political power, situated in ideas of democracy and the distribution of political power within a community, both horizontally (between individuals) and vertically (between individuals and state officials) (Dworkin, 2002: 190–91). Dworkin (2002) also saw the distinction between influence and impact, where impact refers to the difference an individual can make on their own, and influence refers to the ways in which an individual can induce others to believe or choose in the same way as essential to his or her conception of equality of power (Dworkin, 2002: 191). Dworkin argues in favour of influence over impact, but then argues that equal influence is not an achievable possibility in a democracy, and that it should simply be positioned as an ideal, within a system of representative democracy, where majoritarian views will take precedence over true equality of power within a political system (Dworkin, 2002: 194–200). An important difference, then, is between the ways in which equality of power is conceived as a purely political ideal (Dworkin, 2002) and where it is thought of as also encompassing social, cultural and economic aspects of life (Cooper, 2004).

In contrast, Cooper's (2000; 2004) approach to equality of power argues that all people should have the same capacity to impact their environment, whilst recognizing that interests, desires and goals will vary. This version of equality of power takes the individual as the "who" of equality, but it does so without relying on the problematic assumptions of liberal "sameness" models of the individual, through an explicit recognition of the ways in which nobody actually belongs to a single "group" and the problems of intersectionality (Cooper, 2000: 257). The most fundamental way in which Cooper's (2004) conception of equality of power differs from that espoused by Dworkin (2002) is that rather than taking a conventional definition of power as a "right" which is exercized, Cooper uses Foucault's (1980) conception of power as net-like, where power is concerned with the production of effects.

Here again, however, the focus on equality of "what" leads to a difficulty within theorizing equality – that in order for individuals to have equal power, or equal capacity to produce effects, there must already be some form of parity between individuals in relation to (at least) resources and recognition. In theoretical terms, taking power as the object of equality is difficult to fault, but when considering the exercise of power, or rather, individuals' capacities to produce effects through their actions, inequalities of resources, opportunity and recognition seem to complicate the picture. Where, for example, an individual is disadvantaged by a lack of resources, they may not physically be able to get themselves to the place where their voice may be heard, or where they can exercize power to produce effects. Similarly, those disadvantaged through a lack of knowledge or ability to express themselves, perhaps caused by the effects of inequality of opportunity on their education, may find that they are disadvantaged in that they are unsure of where to turn to impact their environment. If some groups are inherently undervalued or "misrecognized", as older people often are, their voices are less likely to be heard, or their impact less likely to be felt, because their concerns may not be understandable to those around them – especially if their concerns are far removed from the wishes and desires of the "majority". In essence, it is necessary to dismantle social, cultural, religious and structural barriers, such as the regulation of the family, and differential access to healthcare, education and employment, before it can begin to be possible for all individuals to have the same power to impact their environment.

Another all-encompassing theory of the object of equality, proposed by Baker et al. (2004), is equality of condition. This has similar aims to equality of power, in that it seeks a solution that is not concentrated on a singular area of inequality (for example, resource, opportunity, recognition) but rather focuses on the practical dimensions of life where change is needed to achieve equality in a substantive, material sense. The distinctive element of their "equality of condition" approach is that it explicitly includes the affective domain, through equality of love, care and solidarity, as well as the more usual objects of equality (like resources, opportunity, recognition). They argue that all humans have "both a need and a capacity for intimacy, attachment and caring relationships" (Baker et al., 2004: 37). Consequently, they argue that "In caring for others, we act to meet their needs in a way that involves an attitude of concern or even love ... . Love involves acting for those we love, not just feeling for them. Solidarity involves active support for others, not just passive empathy." (Baker et al., 2004: 37)

This aspect of equality's "what" is often neglected in economically focused approaches to equality, yet is vital to thinking about equality for older people. It highlights the ways in which certain relationships of love, care and solidarity are prioritized over others. Caretaking (whether for children or for older or disabled people) is often argued to be a neglected or invisible but still fundamental and essential component of society, as well as one which operates to keep women subordinated to men (see for example, Fineman, 2004). Importantly, not all relationships of love, care and solidarity are given equal value or respect in society. When caretaking and dependency relationships are considered, for example, it is the relationship between parents and young children which most obviously springs to mind, rather than issues of caring for the older persons or adults with disabilities. Whether within institutionalized care settings or within the context of "the family", these caring relationships are arguably of the utmost importance, as these forms of dependency and caretaking are less normative and yet can be at least as longstanding, if not more so, as the caring/depending relationship between parent and child. When an older person (or someone affected by a debilitating illness) becomes unable to care for themselves, the responsibility for care tends to fall on family members – in particular on women, which brings us back, again, to the problems generated by inequalities of both resources and recognition which would also need to be addressed in order to make any practical or substantive move towards equality of condition for older people.

Equality Theory and the Case for a New Convention

In this section I have given a brief overview of some of the main theories of the object of equality. I have discussed resources, recognition, power and condition as possible focuses of equality, and highlighted the limitations of each of these in relation to addressing systemic problems of injustice faced by older people. The key problem, it seems, with equality-based arguments, is that putting in place practical measures to address inequality in one domain can either generate new or additional inequalities in other domains, or can be dependent on further shifts in other domains relating to both the subject and object of equality. So, for example, addressing income inequality in older age requires not only redistributive welfare-based models, but also substantive changes in working patterns across the life course. Yet such changes would impact on caring labour and choices in the affective domain. It seems that whilst it is vital that we address inequalities of condition, and we introduce law and policy at national and international levels that seek to address them, equality as a conceptual justification for a new convention on the rights of older persons falls short because of the challenge of identifying what the object of equality should be. For older persons, we can see that equality of power, of resources, of recognition, of love, care and solidarity and of condition are all important. Any convention on older persons' rights will inevitably have egalitarian aims, and when it is introduced its success will be measured on the basis of certain spaces of equality (Sen, 1995).

Looking back to the "gaps" identified above, we can see that issues of ageism, age discrimination, equal recognition before the law and the right to enjoy legal capacity, access to appropriate care and to work might all be addressed by a convention based on understandings of equality of recognition for older people. Mechanisms to address resource inequality in older age might ensure an adequate standard of living, of health, of food and nutrition, of housing, and quality care services. Alongside these, equality of condition might provide justifications for the need for quality palliative and end-of-life care, access to work and leisure pursuits in older age. Equality of power might offer solutions to problems associated with deprivation of liberty, invasions of privacy, protection from violence and abuse, or freedoms of movement and expression. These different dimensions of equality each speak to different parts of the injustices faced by older people. To argue for a convention on the basis of inequalities experienced by older people would, therefore, require the engagement of all of these complex theoretical justifications for equality. Unfortunately, these nuanced understandings of equality are always in danger of being erased in political and social movement discourse. Equality arguments often fall back to their simplest version, based on the Aristotelian idea of "like should be treated alike", which can make it difficult to argue effectively for extra support or resources for particular individuals or marginalized groups. Whilst it is essential, therefore, that inequality is appropriately attended to in discourse around the need for a new convention, it may be that a move away from equality discourse in the direction of a broader concept of social justice could be more effective as a baseline justification for increased human rights protections.

CAPABILITIES AND OLDER PEOPLE: AN ALTERNATIVE SOCIAL JUSTICE ARGUMENT FOR AN OLDER PERSON'S CONVENTION?

As the above discussion has demonstrated, equality arguments require a (more or less) specific object. The capabilities approach, as developed by Sen (1985; 1995; 1999; 2010) and Nussbaum (1999; 2007; 2013), in contrast, offers a different conceptual rationale for social, legal and political action towards justice. In this section I offer an argument that the capabilities approach provides a more coherent and persuasive justification for the need for a new supranational convention on the rights of older persons than equality theory.

Sen (1995) recognized the limitations of theories of "equality of what" and proposed a different model of understanding the conceptual justification for social justice through the capabilities approach. In Sen's words, "the capability approach points to the need to examine freedom to achieve in general and capabilities to function in particular" (Sen, 1995: 129). In this approach, rather than focusing on (in)equality as the locus of regulatory or governmental action, Sen shifts attention to ask what people need in order to have the freedom to *be* and to *do* what they choose or value. A second dimension to Sen's capabilities approach is the prominence that he gives to public reasoning in identifying and debating capabilities and functionings. He argues that the capabilities approach requires public discussion, because this "can lead to a better understanding of the role, reach and significance of particular functionings and their combinations" (Sen, 2010: 242). This dual focus (looking at what is required to enable people to live their lives in ways which respect and support their values and choices about what they prefer to do and to be, and giving space for public discussion of capabilities and functionings) generates opportunities to think differently about both national and international regulatory frameworks and human rights instruments.

One of the main impacts of Sen's work on capabilities has been the establishment of the Human Development Index, to provide an alternative method of measuring prosperity at a national level, rather than the neoliberal, capitalist-focused measure of Gross Domestic Product (GDP) per capita that is more often used. Sen (1999) argues convincingly that GDP per capita is both ineffective and misleading as a measure of the quality of life for all in a political state or area. This is because it cannot demonstrate how GDP is distributed across society (it is an average figure), leading to countries with vast inequalities scoring higher than they otherwise would (or should). The Human Development Reports, which are produced by the UN Development Programme with the aim of improving human well-being, regularly draw attention to the particular difficulties and challenges faced by older people. For example, the focus of the 2014 Human Development Report (UNDP, 2014) was "reducing vulnerabilities and building resilience", and included multiple references to the ways in which older people are structurally disadvantaged, or made more vulnerable by patterns of labour, and regulatory and economic choices. Sen's work on capabilities is, therefore, already shaping the international response to the challenges of supporting and respecting older people.

The second major theorist in the capabilities approach has been Martha Nussbaum. Unlike Sen, whose focus is on economic aspects of social justice through capabilities, Nussbaum's approach is founded in national and international constitutional law, including human rights law. In offering her version of the capabilities approach, Nussbaum (1999, 2013) has generated a list of "central capabilities" which she considers to be essential to "a dignified and minimally flourishing life" (2013: 32). Some of these capabilities are uncontroversial and well protected in existing international human rights documents. For example, "life", Nussbaum's first central capability, is protected through the "right to life" provisions in any number of national and international rights documents.[4] The simple fact that "life" is already protected in such instruments does not, however, necessarily mean that *all* lives are as fully protected as they could or should be. Too often, the lives of older persons can be considered less important or less worthy of investment in, for example, health and social care, than the lives of younger people. Consider the example of the Quality Adjusted Life Years (QALY) measure used by the UK's National Institute for Health and Care Excellence (NICE). This tool is used to measure the cost effectiveness of possible treatments on the basis of the number of life years they add, adjusted by quality. The methodology, which is used to inform decisions about which treatments should be authorized to be given to NHS patients (Stevens et al., 2012), has been accused of ageism because it places a greater QALY value on outcomes for younger people than on older people (Harris and Regmi, 2012). Discrimination appears because the QALY includes a measurement of the number of life years that are added by a treatment, and an appraisal of their quality (with "healthy" years being more valuable and valued that "disabled" years), in combination with the cost of treatment to create the value which is used for deliberative purposes. So, for example, a treatment that cost £500 000 which would provide normal life expectancy without disability for a 20-year-old would cost £9000 per year; a 45-year-old £14 200 per year; and a 70-year-old £33 000 per year.[5]

Nussbaum's articulation of life as a central capability includes "being able to live to the end of a human life of normal length; not dying prematurely" (Nussbaum, 2013: 33). Yet this raises a number of further questions about how we estimate the length of a "normal" human life, given the wide disparities in life expectancy between and across different geographical and socioeconomic spaces. Longevity varies from continent to continent, country to country and individual to individual. Reasons why person A might live longer than person B include complex inter- plays of genetics, social and cultural contexts and choices, geographical location, as well as religious and political factors. The creation of a new convention on the rights of older persons would not change the inherent variability of life expectancy. It would, however, in the debates and discussions towards a new convention, offer a space for public reason, in the manner proposed by Sen (2010). This public discussion would provide space for deliberation of the justice dimension of the right to life as it applies to older persons. In doing so, it might facilitate robust public, political debate about the appropriate levels of resources required to safeguard life for older persons, and expose potentially or actually ageist methodologies, such as the QALY.

Closely related to life are Nussbaum's proposed central capabilities of bodily health and bodily integrity. Again, whilst these capabilities already find generic protection in existing legal instruments, older persons' interests require a different set of considerations from those of younger persons. For example, older persons may find that their bodily health is less resilient to poor nourishment, lack of heat or inadequate shelter than younger persons. Older people may also be more likely to find them- selves in situations where they are dependent on others for care and support, and bodily integrity may be challenged or threatened through difficulties with securing high-quality, person-centred care that supports them in realizing their capabilities. If care assistants only visit at specific times during the day, this may, for example, limit the choices that older people have; or if older people are subjected to abuse and/or violence by those they depend on for care, this will inevitably limit their functionings. The central capabilities of bodily health and bodily integrity are therefore extremely important to older people in ways which may not be fully supported by current international human rights protections.

Nussbaum's fourth central capability highlights the importance of the senses, imagination and thought. Again, whilst freedom of conscience and expression are generally well protected in existing human rights law, the specific dimensions of these for older people are rarely considered. Public debate about the place of these capabilities might facilitate discussion of how access to religious services or rituals may be limited if an older person has restrictions on movement, or impaired mobility as a result of poor health or care needs. It may also, through the individual (rather than group) focus of the capabilities approach, draw attention to the ways that responsibilities for supporting older people in being and doing as they choose to do in these areas might fall unevenly onto family members (particularly women), rather than through public support. Public discussion of how to secure these capabilities for older people may help to generate persuasive arguments for a new convention by enabling the articulation of the normative and implementation gaps that currently exist in the rights of older persons not only to express and engage their religious and cultural preferences, but also to access the arts of their choosing, or to enjoy other entertainment like play.[6]

Nussbaum lists several other central capabilities, but there is not the space in this chapter to engage in depth with them all.[7] Importantly, the work of discussing the capabilities that are most crucial to older people would be a vital element of preparatory discussions for a new convention on older persons' rights, and in the future interpretation by national and international bodies of the rights included in any such convention. Arguing for a new convention on the basis of the capabilities approach will not solve the dilemmas about where to draw the line on the redistribution of resources. Nor will it solve the dilemmas posed by equality theory about which domain of (in)equality requires the most pressing attention. The capabilities approach does, however, in both Sen's (1992; 1999; 2010) economically focused version and Nussbaum's (1999; 2007; 2013) list of central capabilities offer a discourse within which to ground activism and arguments towards a new Convention on the Rights of Older Persons. By shifting the focus of discourse away from considering how older people are disadvantaged, or especially vulnerable,[8] a capabilities approach offers the starting point of considering what older people need in order to choose the "beings and doings" they value.

CONCLUDING REMARKS

The aim of this chapter has been to explore alternative conceptual rationales that could underpin activism and argument towards a new convention on the rights of older persons, if we were to shift our focus from the inequalities experienced by older people towards a capabilities approach. My aim has been to highlight some of the ways that public discourse around the rights of older people may be limited by a conceptual and rhetorical focus on (in)equality. I have offered the groundwork for an argument that the capabilities approach has the potential to offer a more coherent and persuasive conceptual basis for a new convention than arguments based on equality theory.

I have not, in this chapter, offered an argument for a new convention that builds from the capabilities approach. Indeed, the work in developing the arguments that could help in the movement towards a new convention is part of the ongoing project of challenging ageism and supporting the rights of older people. As activism, social movements and legal debate move us further towards the social and political conditions necessary to begin the work of constructing a convention on the rights of older persons, my argument is that a social justice focus, drawing on the capabilities approach, provides us with a set of persuasive discursive, rhetorical and legal tools to make the case for a new convention. I have, therefore, offered an argument that the capabilities approach can provide the necessary conceptual space for articulating why a new convention is required to address older persons' rights. I have demonstrated that it also provides both a necessary justification and conceptual basis for the need for public engagement, debate and discourse about older persons' rights.

NOTES

1. It would be easier to express this differential in terms of persons above or below a specific chronological age (for example, 60), but the use of chronological age in this way paradoxically contributes to ageism and age discrimination. If, for example, we say everyone over the age of 60 is 'older' we include many people who are of chronological ages greater than 60, but who do not experience infringements of their human rights on that basis, but simultaneously exclude many others who are chronologically younger than 60 years old, but for whom ageing has already had a great impact on their rights. Chronological age is therefore only ever a proxy, which is modified and mediated by a range of intersectional axes of privilege and oppression (including for example, gender, ethnicity, disability, sexuality, religious beliefs, education level, socioeconomic resources, geographical location and other variables).
2. The examples provided here are from England, but the move away from social welfare towards private provision of care services is by no means limited to the English context.
3. Sex Discrimination Act 1975; Equal Pay Act 1970.
4. Some examples would include: the Universal Declaration of Human Rights, Article 3; the European Convention on Human Rights, Article 2; and the International Covenant on Civil and Political Rights, Article 6.
5. This calculation is based upon the figures used by Stevens et al. (2012). In that article, Stevens et al. argue that there is no inherent ageism within the QALY, using a treatment cost of £450 000, and demonstrating that there would be no difference between the different exemplar age groups. There is not the space here to fully deconstruct their methodology –

suffice to say the mathematical basis of the QALY is, in fact, inherently ageist (Harris, 2005), and ableist.
6. Play is another of Nussbaum's (2013) central capabilities. For an interesting discussion of the normative gap in the right to leisure in old age, see Karev and Doron (2017).
7. These include emotions, practical reason, affiliation both in relationships and in the sense of dignity; control over one's environment in both political and material terms; and the capability to live "with concern for and in relation to animals, plants and the world of nature" (p. 34).
8. For an argument about the potential of vulnerability theory in the context of older persons' rights, see Chapter 2 by Titti Mattsson.

REFERENCES

Baker, J., Lynch, K., Cantillon, S. and Walsh, J. (2004). *Equality: From Theory to Action*. Basingstoke: Palgrave Macmillan.

Butler, J. (1998). Merely cultural. *New Left Review*, **I**/227: 33–44.

Callahan, J.J. (1992). *Aging in Place*. Amityville, NY: Baywood Publishing Company.

Cooper, D. (2000). "And you can't find me nowhere": Relocating identity and structure within equality jurisprudence. *Journal of Law and Society*, **27**(2): 249–72.

Cooper, D. (2004). *Challenging Diversity: Rethinking Equality and the Value of Difference*. Cambridge: Cambridge University Press.

Costa Dias, M., Elming, W. and Joyce, R. (2016). *The Gender Wage Gap*. London: Institute for Fiscal Studies. Accessed on 20 December 2016 at https://www.ifs.org.uk/uploads/publications/bns/bn186.pdf.

Doron, I. (2015). Ithaka: On the journey to a new international human rights convention for the rights of older persons, in R. Ruebner, T. Do and A. Taylor (eds), *International and Comparative Law on the Rights of Older Persons*, pp. 18–34. Lake Mary, FL: Vandeplas Publishing.

Doron, I. and Apter, I. (2010). The debate around the need for an international convention on the rights of older persons. *The Gerontologist*, **50**(5): 586–93.

Dworkin, R. (1977). *Taking Rights Seriously*. Cambridge, MA: Harvard University Press.

Dworkin, R. (2002). *Sovereign Virtue: The Theory and Practice of Equality*. Cambridge, MA: Harvard University Press.

Fineman, M.A. (2004). *The Autonomy Myth: A Theory of Dependency*. New York, NY: The New Press.

Foucault, M. (1980). *Power/Knowledge: Selected Interviews and other Writings*, Colin Gordon (ed.). New York, NY: Pantheon.

Fraser, N. (1997). *Justice Interruptus: Critical Reflections of the "Postsocialist" Condition*. New York, NY: Routledge.

Harding, R. (2017). *Duties to Care: Dementia, Relationality and Law*. Cambridge: Cambridge University Press.

Harding, R., Fletcher, R. and Beasley, C. (eds) (2017). *ReValuing Care in Theory, Law and Policy: Cycles and Connections*. Abingdon: Routledge.

Harris, J. (2005). It's not NICE to discriminate. *Journal of Medical Ethics*, **31**: 373–5.

Harris, J. and Regmi, S. (2012). Ageism and equality. *Journal of Medical Ethics,* **38**(5): 263–6.

Hayes, L.J.B. (2017). *Stories of Care: Gender and Class at Work.* London: Palgrave.

Karev, I. and Doron, I. (2017). The human right to leisure in old age: Reinforcement of the rights of an aging population. *Journal of Aging & Social Policy,* **29**(3): 276–95.

Kornfeld-Matte, R. (2016). Report of the Independent Expert on the enjoyment of human rights by older persons A/HRC/33/44. Accessed on 26 January 2017 at http://ap.ohchr.org/documents/alldocs.aspx?doc_id=26860.

Local Government Association (2017). *Adult Social Care Funding: State of the Nation 2017.* London: Local Government Association. Accessed on 27 February 2018 at https://www.local.gov.uk/sites/default/files/documents/1.69% 20Adult%20social%20care%20funding-%202017%20state%20of%20the%20 nation_07_WEB.pdf.

Nuffield Trust, Health Foundation and King's Fund (2016). *The Autumn Statement: Joint Statement on Health and Social Care.* Accessed on 2 December 2016 at https://www.kingsfund.org.uk/sites/files/kf/field/field_publication_file/ Autumn_Statement_Kings_Fund_Nov_2016_3.pdf.

Nussbaum, M.C. (1999). Women and equality: The capabilities approach. *International Labour Review,* **138**(3): 227–45.

Nussbaum, M.C. (2007). *Frontiers of Justice: Disability, Nationality, Species Membership.* Cambridge, MA: Harvard University Press.

Nussbaum, M.C. (2013). *Creating Capabilities: The Human Development Approach.* Cambridge, MA: Harvard University Press.

Office of National Statistics (2016). National Life Tables, UK: 2013–2015. Accessed on 15 December 2016 at https://www.ons.gov.uk/peoplepopulation andcommunity/birthsdeathsandmarriages/lifeexpectancies/bulletins/nationallife tablesunitedkingdom/20132015.

Rodriguez-Pinzon, D and Martin, C. (2003). The international human rights status of elderly persons. *American University International Law Review,* **18**(4): 915–1008.

Sen, A. (1985). *Commodities and Capabilities.* Oxford: Oxford University Press.

Sen, A. (1995). *Inequality Reexamined.* Oxford: Oxford University Press.

Sen, A. (1999). *Development as Freedom.* Oxford: Oxford University Press.

Sen, A. (2010). *The Idea of Justice.* London: Penguin Books.

Sidorenko, A. and Walker, A. (2004). *The Madrid International Plan of Action on Ageing*: From conception to implementation. *Ageing & Society,* **24**(2): 147–65.

Stevens, A., Doyle, N., Littlejohns, P. and Docherty, M. (2012). National Institute for Health and Clinical Excellence appraisal and ageism. *Journal of Medical Ethics,* **38**(5)**:** 258–62.

Turner, C. (2016). The gender pay gap means that more women will be in poverty later in life – but there is something the government can do. *The Independent,* 26 August. Accessed on 20 December 2016 at http://www. independent.co.uk/voices/gender-pay-gap-women-will-be-in-poverty-late-in-life- but-there-is-something-the-government-can-do-a7210931.html.

United Nations (1982). *Report of the World Assembly on Aging.* New York, NY: United Nations. Accessed on 27 February 2018 at https://www.un.org/development/desa/ageing/resources/vienna-international-plan-of-action.html.

United Nations (1983). *Vienna International Plan of Action on Aging.* New York, NY: United Nations. Accessed on 27 February 2018 at http://www.un.org/es/globalissues/ageing/docs/vipaa.pdf.

United Nations (2002). *Madrid International Plan of Action on Ageing.* New York, NY: United Nations. Accessed on 27 February 2018 at https://www.un.org/development/desa/ageing/madrid-plan-of-action-and-its-implementation.html.

UN DESA (2009). Report of the ExpertGroup Meeting "Rights of Older Persons". Accessed on 27 February 2018 at http://www.un.org/esa/socdev/ageing/documents/egm/bonn09/report.pdf.

UN DP (2014). Sustaining Human Progress: Reducing vulnerabilities and building resilience. *Human Development Report 2014.* New York, NY: UNDP. Accessed on 26 January 2017 at http://hdr.undp.org/en/content/human-development-report-2014.

UNHCHR (2008). *Frequently Asked Questions on Economic and Social Rights: Factsheet No. 33.* New York, NY: Office of the UN HCHR. Accessed on 26 January 2017 at http://www.ohchr.org/EN/Issues/ESCR/Pages/ESCRIndex.aspx.

UNHCHR (2012). Report of the United Nations High Commissioner for Human Rights (GE12-42071, E/2012/51). Accessed on 26 January 2017 at http://www.un.org/ga/search/view_doc.asp?symbol=E/2012/51.

Vasunilashorn, S., Steinman, B.A., Liebig, P.S. and Pynoos, J. (2011). Aging in place: Evolution of a research topic whose time has come. *Journal of Aging Research*, **2012**, doi:10.1155/2012/120952.

Warwick, B.T.C. (2016). Socio-economic rights during economic crises: A changed approach to non-regression. *International & Comparative Law Quarterly*, **65**(1): 249–65.

2. Age, vulnerability and disability

Titti Mattsson

INTRODUCTION

Age is a ground for distinctions among individuals in Swedish as well as many other countries' regulatory frameworks, and in some cases legitimately so. However, among the problems with age as an organizing principle is that the original political or policy basis for the existing age limits too often remains unremembered and unexamined, even as circumstances change. Many age limits were in fact set years or even decades ago in a different cultural and political context with different health statuses and life expectancy as well as different societal possibilities and obligations. At the same time, age limits inevitably raise questions about how to allocate rights and obligations, and they involve problems that need to be handled politically. Finally, but not least, they also involve problems with the risk of ageism.

The issue of age, along with the issue of legitimate justification for age limits in national regulation, are becoming urgent matters to discuss in many parts of the world, as we are living longer than before. One of the major achievements in the last century has been a dramatic increase in life expectancy. Because of rising living standards, better working conditions and significant medical advances, average life expectancy has increased and is expected to continue to do so. This development brings many benefits for both the individual and society as a whole. However, it is often stated that the same development brings challenges as well. One of them is the major demographic change in many parts of the world towards an ageing society, with expected substantial social, economic and political consequences. Response to population ageing is a policy priority worldwide and is often referred to as a "grand challenge" (for example, EC, 2009). The EU 2015 Ageing Report analyzed the economic and budgetary impact of an ageing population over the long term and forecast increasing expenditures to cover pensions, unemployment, healthcare, long-term care, and education transfers for the Member States (EC, 2015). Different ways to meet the challenges of an ageing population with various social solutions are currently under discussion. For example, the EU has developed Europe 2020, a strategy that, among other things, strives to keep older people as long as possible inside the labour market. The term "active ageing" is central in this strategy document and refers, broadly, to the idea that older people should get opportunities to stay active as workers, consumers, carers, volunteers and citizens.

The law is considered to play a key role in achieving the relevant structural changes. In particular, legal questions that have to do with the labour market in one way or another – such as age discrimination, workplace-related issues and social security issues (pensions, unemployment benefits, economic assistance) – have in recent years been the subject of many national policy discussions and research, as well as those concerning good healthcare and social welfare services.[1] Increasingly, other challenges related to this demographic development are being discussed as well. For example, housing in old age is a burning issue in Sweden and other countries (Swedish Agency for Health and Care Services Analysis, 2015) along with the legal, social and ethical consequences of an increasingly globalized, digitalized and privatized health care (Mattsson et al., 2017).

Activity within the EU and in many national regimes to find solutions for the demographic changes is based on the assumption that the population in general will become increasingly dependent on society's resources and common goods, without an easy way of accessing those resources. Thus, concerns about increasing age in the population are often combined with discussions about dependency, vulnerability and similar concepts signalling increasing demands and costs for society. Seldom, however, is it questioned under what circumstances a certain group is considered to be particularly vulnerable, or to what extent vulnerability is a relevant concept for the discussion of the distribution of societal resources. I will argue that this is a relevant issue and that it may have consequences for the distribution of society's resources as well as the outcome of the individual's claim for support.

The aim of this chapter is to challenge the traditional perception of who is a vulnerable older person by discussing the concept from a theoretical standpoint that basically accepts vulnerability as a universal state of being for everybody and does not accept definitions of vulnerability that are based on classifications derived only from age. I want to discuss the risk that the distribution of public services for older people ends up being based on age absent considered rationale or practical or policy benefits, which in practice becomes an ageist approach. I will particularly focus on the risk of ageism when using age limits in social welfare legislation. Sweden will be used to illustrate this problem.

This chapter uses Martha Albertson Fineman's Vulnerability Theory as a starting point for the discussion of how the concept of "vulnerability" may be used effectively by researchers as well as policy makers dealing with age-related legal issues to avoid an ageist approach to older persons.[2] The specific point of departure for the discussion of the Swedish example is based in social welfare regulation in Sweden, more precisely the Disability Act, which limits disability benefits available to those over 65 years old who have disabilities that are considered to be part of "normal ageing".

A brief description of the Swedish regulation follows below. The subsequent section lays out an overview of the key elements of Vulnerability Theory. The final section of this chapter proposes arguments for why and how this theory could provide an effective framework for analysis of societal arrangements concerning aging, and applies this theoretical framework to the national example.

DISABILITY REGULATION FOR OLDER PERSONS IN SWEDEN: AN EXAMPLE OF AN AGE-BASED REGULATION

In Sweden, there are two systems for providing social services and other support to individuals with mental or physical impairments. Which one individuals access is, in part, determined by age, as one of them applies to persons suffering from "age-related impairments" while the other deals with disabilities more generally. The impact on an individual being placed into one system or the other is high, as the systems vary in the level of assistance that they provide.

Support for older people with impairments comes legislatively through the general Social Services Act, whose goal is to provide "decent living conditions". This broad piece of Swedish social welfare legislation aims to promote security, participation, inclusion and opportunities for people to "live as others" (Social Services Act Ch. 1 Sec 1, cf. SOU 2008: 77). These social welfare principles in the Swedish legislation are reflected and made concrete in legal requirements for the social welfare services to offer a variety of social services depending on the needs and wishes of each individual. Among these required services are support for those experiencing age-related impairments, as mentioned above.

Whereas the Social Services Act is a general law that offers basic social assistance and support, the Disability Act – the Act to Regulate Support and Services for Persons with Certain Functional Disabilities

(1993: 387) – is a *lex specialis* legislation which offers special and high-quality assistance for different forms of disability of the individual, such as a personal assistant. Services for younger people with functional impairments are provided under the Disability Act which is designed to ensure "good living conditions" as opposed to the "decent living conditions" of the Social Services Act. The most costly and personalized form of help, personal assistance, can only be granted to people according to the Disability Act before they reach the age of 65. The benefit "personal assistance" is one of the central benefits derived from the Act and is a very extensive service. This and other services, such as a contact person or a companion who facilitates social or practical activities, may be granted to older people with severe, long-lasting impairments only when "obviously not caused by normal ageing".

Thus, Sweden's social legislation has the consequence that one can become "too old" for a social welfare benefit for assistance due to a disability arising in old age. Persons over 65 years of age whose disability is considered to have been caused by "normal ageing" are not eligible for several central social assistance benefits under the Disability Act. The provision does not constitute an absolute obstacle for aid after 65; older people with disabilities that are *not age-related* can still fall within the personal scope and thus be eligible for benefits under the Act. It is, however, a very limited number of situations that are referred to in the legislative works (Government Bill 1992/93:159). It may, for example, be a question of a particular incident, such as a car accident, that has caused the disability. Another example is a disability that clearly is not age-related. For disability caused by "normal ageing" the legislation is substantially more limited.

It is argued in the preparatory works to the legislation that the reason for the limited possibilities to be granted assistance according to the Disability Act with increasing age is mainly financial (Government Bill 2000/01:5). The argument is also that those who are not eligible for benefits according to this Act may still receive social assistance benefits under the basic social welfare regulation, the Social Services Act. However, such benefits are not as extensive and generous as according to the Disability Act. Thus, the equality of living conditions for persons with a disability pursued may be conditional solely upon the individual's age in Sweden due to this regulation.

The fact that benefits such as personal assistance only applies to persons who became disabled before the age of 65 excludes many persons with disabilities derived from and/or arising in older age from being part of this extensive welfare benefit. A piece of legislation, such as the Disability Act, that excludes disability benefits due to age is problematic. Foremost, this is because the Act assumes that there is something as a certain ageing phase. The question is what effectively is meant by "normal ageing" in this legal context. What is normal ageing in relation to specific diseases and disorders? What was normal ageing 25 years ago is not the same today. For example, in the age group of 65–74 years old in Sweden, the proportion of severe illness decreased from 14 to 8 per cent during the years 1986–2010 (Lagergren, 2012; Jönsson and Harnett, 2015). How, then, is normal ageing assessed under such changing conditions for the same age group? In addition, according to the current text of the Act, the Swedish disability policy seems to assume that diseases and disabilities occurring after the age of 65 are exclusively caused by ageing. But there can be many other causes than increasing age. Despite this, the legislation makes the assumption that the disability or disease is age-based, which will have a large impact when the social welfare officer assesses the 65-year-old individual's claim for a benefit. Also, it is not discussed how the disability regulation is to be understood in relation to research and various policy ambitions (for example the EU active ageing policy) stating that old age is not the same as a disease. Thus, the assumption that functional impairments after the age of 65 are considered part of the "normal process of ageing" is an idea that is at odds both with the demographic development in society and the current discourse on the prolongation of the working life. At worst, it can have the effect of excluding people over 65 from daily activities.

Another problem with age as an organizing principle is that the policy basis for the existing age limits frequently seems to be forgotten. Society is continually undergoing changes, for example in relation to people's health statuses and life expectancy. Today, the reasons for several age limits may not be relevant or valid. In times of welfare challenges the historical and cultural motivation for a certain age limit needs at least to be made visible, problematized and questioned.

Also, age is so much more than the biological clock. Social constructions of certain age groups are increasingly being questioned. The concept of age has undergone major changes in recent decades, and that phenomenon previously linked to terms such as "youth" and "adult time" is no longer necessarily tied to a certain age. Music and taste in clothes, hobbies, exercise habits, leisure activities and social problems can no longer be associated with a particular phase of life in the same easy way as previously (Jönsson and Harnett, 2015). The slogan "Tear down the Age Steps" was coined by a Swedish political investigation in the 2000s (SOU, 2003: 91) to promote the premise that the life-course is increasingly unclear and consists of overlapping phases. Many researchers today claim that the category of "older" is an outdated design and that it is more correct to speak of a third age, where individuals have relatively good health and often use their time to travel, study, volunteer and in self-realization, and a fourth age, characterized by dependence, disease and severe disabilities (see, for example, Laslett, 1989; Baltes and Baltes, 1990). In addition, the risk of ageism is ever present. A regulation such as the Disability Act reinforces the risk for alienation of certain "vulnerable" groups in society.

VULNERABILITY THEORY

The term "vulnerability" is often used to categorize a certain group or part of the population in order to emphasize different commonly considered "undesirable" traits of the human condition, such as weakness, poverty, loneliness, dependency, or even old age.[3] Often it takes the shape of a claim that a certain group, including for example older persons or persons with disabilities, is "more vulnerable" than other individuals in society. I want to argue that this alienation of certain groups from the rest of the population is not without problems, especially when it occurs in policy and legislative discussions. For example, by using this type of categorization when it comes to age, there is a risk of creating unnecessary ageism. I wish to argue for an alternative use of the concept that instead accepts vulnerability as a universal state of being and not something derived from being of a certain age or belonging to some other population group. I will also argue that the alternative use can help to affect the rights, interests and needs of older people by promoting a focus on the individual's specific dependency and needs. More precisely, I will be proposing Fineman's Vulnerability Theory as a fruitful approach for researchers as well as policy makers dealing with age-related legal issues.[4] After setting out basic concepts, I will argue that the theory can be used as an effective theoretical framework for establishing new considerations on how to address the rights of older people.

According to Vulnerability Theory, regulation and policy making should not focus on older people as a group based on biological age and legal status. Instead of being a sign of solidarity, it may lead to stigmatizing older people as a "vulnerable group" and therefore using paternalistic measures without giving these individuals strong social rights and the right to participation in their own welfare or specially adapted support for decision making. Instead, an individual assessment, taking into account each person's dependencies, needs and wishes, needs to be in focus.

Fineman argues that the core of being human is to be vulnerable, and not autonomous, free and independent, as is often asserted in jurisprudence. Two theoretical questions are central in Fineman's work. First, what does it mean to be human? And second, what does our approach to that say about how we should organize our societies? The theory is not concerned with specific instances of harm or injury, but with resilience against risk and harm during the whole life-course. Vulnerability should be understood as something shared and universal. This has the consequence that comparisons should not be made between individuals based on how vulnerable they are, but between states and institutions based on how good they are at providing people with resilience to their shared vulnerability.

Inequality of resilience is at the heart of the vulnerability theory, which turns its attention to society and social institutions to compensate for this inequality. No one is born resilient. Rather, resilience is produced within and through institutions and relationships that confer privilege and power. Generally, the concept of the legal subject needs to reflect this complexity and to guide how we define individual and state responsibilities. Currently, the legal subject too often exists as an all-inclusive and universal construct – the "idealized ordinary". The laws we craft reflect the assumed needs, capabilities and characteristics of that contrived subject and form the social institutions and relationships that meet those needs. An alternative conceptualization of the legal subject would be a greater acceptance of the individual traits of each individual, to the context within which each person lives and to the dependency that all people share. A vulnerability approach therefore argues that the state must be responsive to the realities of human vulnerability in regulation and policy-making concerning the institutions in society that deal with our social dependency. Fineman makes the point that a group approach ignores the universal vulnerability we all experience throughout life and creates the risk of unnecessary competition among different groups in society.

When it comes to older people, they are in many ways "caught" as a "vulnerable" group. This becomes obvious in times of demographic changes and demands policy-making attention to these changes. Unfortunately, the debate still tends to reflect certain stereotyped portraits of who older people are and what they need. Fineman highlights difficulties in the political discussions of the older population in the United States that are similar to those we can see in European discussions (Mattsson, 2013). Older people often seem to be portrayed as either constantly dependent – in need of state protection because of illness, weakness, loneliness and sometimes lack of money – or not dependent at all, being in good health and with a financial and private situation that enables them to handle their daily lives by themselves. In their situation of being considered vulnerable, society is not demanding self-sufficiency and independence of older people. Instead, the older people are perceived as needing protection, and society's response is guided by paternalism. This deprives older people of agency. As a result, capacity becomes something that may even be disregarded among older persons. They are thus positioned as needing intervention to enable independence. When a group is thus constructed as a "vulnerable group", a stigma is created as well as a border between different groups of people.

Vulnerability theory problematizes the conceptualization of age groups, such as older people, which is an important task for any criticism of age and group classifications. According to this way of viewing the different life stages, ageing is more a part of life than the characteristic of a distinct group of (older) persons. Older people, like everyone else, are persons who live with present and future changing needs and circumstances on a daily basis. This makes their needs as varying as the individuals themselves. The relationship between (old) age and vulnerability therefore needs to be analyzed in order to challenge the idea of age as a central categorization of the population in the society.

AGE CLASSIFICATIONS AND AGE LIMITS

Age classification in the law regulating national welfare systems in Europe is a way to create specific benefits for members of certain age groups in society. Earlier in this chapter, the age limits in the Disability Act were highlighted. Another example in Sweden is the old-age pension system, where you can receive a general pension after a certain age, usually 61 years. However, it is also a way to limit the same benefits for members of other age groups. For example, after the age of 18, children no longer have free health and dental care in Sweden.[5] Also, after the age of 65, local governments no longer provide social assistance to individuals without income. Instead, these individuals may apply for old-age support from the Pension Authority (a national institution) in the case of an absent or insufficient retirement pension.

An argument *for* age-based (or equivalent) assessments is that they can help to ensure everyone is treated equally, as compared to the individual's risky position in any administration of public services that relies on individual assessments and decision-making. A legal framework that clarifies the criteria for an applicant to be entitled to a certain benefit may offer a higher degree of transparency than often locally-varying assessment criteria. The equality principle stipulates that everyone should be treated according to the same conditions. The argument for using this principle as the dominant one in creating regulatory works is that, in addition to the protection from subjective judgement, it also helps to ensure that the applicant need not fear disadvantages based on age, sex, ethnicity, or other possibly discriminatory practices.

However, the equal-treatment argument has some flaws that ought to be considered. As discussed by Rosie Harding in Chapter 1 of this volume, it is based on the interpretation of equality as sameness-of-treatment. The problem with this understanding is that it ignores differences in circumstances and abilities of the individual.[6] Treating everybody the same may, at worst, fosters unequal treatment. For example, an individual's health, disability or financial conditions may be different from those for the rest of the population. When this is not considered, that individual may come out worse than the rest of the population due to having been treated the same as everyone else. There is a strong argument to be made that professionals at all levels need to develop alternative approaches to equal treatment that include the context of the person (see Brodin and Mattsson, 2014). Such approaches often demand individual and personal contact with the client, patient or other user of public services.

Age limits are useful in creating foreseeability, a central ingredient in the concept of legal security and the notion of justice. Certain ages for starting school, driving, drinking, getting married, receiving a pension and so on are practical and equal for all. Even if they create other problems (for example that there is no high-standard method of deciding age in unclear cases[7] or that individual levels of maturity make same-age arguments of fairness and equality weak) it is often the fact that alternatives may be even more problematic. Thus, certain kinds of ageism will have to be accepted. Also, it is a fact that a great deal of regulation directed to older people, for example benefits such as old age pensions at a certain age, is ageist in the sense that it is only available for persons of a certain age. Even elder law as a discipline can be proclaimed to be an ageist approach. There are obviously circumstances where an age limit is the only – and even the best – solution.

However, as already noted, age is also used as a way to restrict the use of society's resources in different ways and to limit the distribution to some. It is therefore relevant to highlight the important role of age for the social life conditions for the population as a whole and the distribution of public services to fulfill social rights of individuals. One can argue that

age limits may constitute ageism. Still, age limits are often not considered discriminatory to the same extent as other categorizations of people.
For example, there is a basic idea in many national regulations that law
should not be guided by stereotypes such as gender and ethnicity. With
age it is a somewhat different story; here, it is often considered
acceptable to distinguish between different age groups. Age is sometimes
even used as a standard way of categorizing individuals and distributing
welfare in national regulation. The arguments for regulating distribution
by age are mainly of a practical nature. It is for example argued that
people's needs differ naturally over the life-course and that many of those
needs are age-related. Thus, it is argued, there may be good reasons to
take age and phases of life as the basis of assessments related to social
services and other public support. Another argument is that the distribution of scarce resources has to be limited in some way and that age limits
are a straightforward and efficient way of distributing services, without
any time-consuming needs-based assessments.

THE RELATION BETWEEN AGE AND VULNERABILITY

In Sweden, as well as in most countries, age is an attractive and
often-used tool in governmental practice. Citizens are ascribed certain
needs, behaviours, bodily functions, abilities and competences on the
basis of their age. A broad spectrum of civil rights and obligations,
resources and responsibilities, are tied to different ages, in various ways
enabling and limiting the lives of the citizens. As we pass through the
stages of the life-course, legal age limits and age categorizations generally do not stand out as discriminatory.

By necessity, ageing is a basic human condition which influences the
relationship between the state and the individual in different ways.
However, ageing is not a measurable account for individuals' needs and
capacities. Age classifications, such as certain age limits or prerequisites
such as "normal ageing", are blunt simplifiers to use to categorize who
should have and who should have not. In addition, such approaches in
policy-making for older people risk being stigmatizing or paternalistic.

The Disability Act in Sweden, with its exclusion of disabilities related
to "normal ageing", provides unnecessary ageist applications that do not
seem to have a convincing explanation. A vulnerability analysis pro-
claims that equal opportunities can be achieved only by offering different
ways in which vulnerable situations can be overcome by institutional
frameworks (Fineman, 2008). The conclusion of the theoretical approach

that I propose in this chapter is therefore, instead, an emphasis on the need for respecting difference and diversity among persons and during their lifespan (cf. Fineman, 2012). A needs-based approach for distributing services becomes a more justified way than age (or age-related terms such as "normal ageing") to decide who should get and who should not get access to public resources.

To be in line with the vulnerability theory, regulation and policy making should not focus on older people as a group based on biological age and associated legal status in the way that the Swedish regulation does. It may lead to stigmatizing older people and therefore using paternalistic measures without giving these individuals strong social rights and the right to participation in their own welfare. At the same time it excludes those in need of the support. In sum, it leads to ageism in legislation as well as in practice.

Having a life-course perspective on older people, as argued in this chapter, would mean not positioning old age as a separate category of human existence, and instead recognizing it as one end of a continuum of the life of a human being. Such a perspective highlights that older people's needs will differ and develop as their circumstances change, just as for anyone. Therefore the person's unique needs and the level and amount of support should be evaluated individually. The life-course perspective also highlights that society cannot focus only on the situation of individuals who are already older persons. Every society must also take into account those younger individuals who will enter the category eventually, as well as those who may experience dependency and need care even though they are young.

CONCLUSION

The law needs to recognize the different ways in which actual human lives are socially and materially dynamic, as age-related restrictions often do not. Since we are universally vulnerable to changes during our lives, both positive and negative, an important task of law and policy should be to explore the strategies by which we can respond to human vulnerability. A central insight from this perspective is that human beings are not more or less vulnerable because of certain characteristics or at various stages in their lives. Individuals do, however, experience the world with differing levels of resilience. Therefore, there is a need to develop legal and policy approaches aimed at fostering individual resilience for older people as well as for people of all other ages.

NOTES

1. For research in a Swedish context, see Ann Numhauser-Henning (2017).
2. Fineman's Vulnerability Theory is the basis for several research centres in Europe and the United States, including the VHC Initiative at Emory, the VHC hub at the Centre for Law & Social Justice at Leeds University and the Law and Vulnerability Research Programme at Lund University and is used increasingly as a basis for research and practice communities, including the programme at Lund University. The theory is also an integrated part of the Norma Elder Law Research Environment at Lund University.
3. Note that this use of "vulnerability" sometimes also refers to membership in groups where there is nothing "undesirable" about the group itself, but rather what is undesirable is the actions of others vis-à-vis that group, for example vulnerability due to minority status in a society.
4. Fineman's core concepts, on which this discussion draws, are laid in a series of publications including *The Vulnerable Subject: Anchoring Equality in the Human Condition* (2013); "'Elderly' as Vulnerable: Rethinking the Nature of Individual and Societal Responsibility" (2012a); "Grappling with Equality: One Feminist Journey" in Fineman (ed.) *Transcending the Boundaries of Law: Generations of Feminism and Legal Theory* (2011); "The Vulnerable Subject and the Responsive State" (2010); "The Vulnerable Subject: Anchoring Equality in the Human Condition" (2008); and *The Autonomy Myth: A Theory of Dependency* (2004). An overview of the theory can also be found in Mattsson and Katzin (2017).
5. They are, however, still eligible for the almost-free health care provided to residents in Sweden.
6. For a discussion of this from the Vulnerability Theory perspective, see Fineman (2017).
7. This is a major topic in Europe just now, where those coming to the continent to flee war or other circumstances receive sharply different services depending on whether or not they are under 18, but do not always have evidence of age.

REFERENCES

Baltes, P.B. and Baltes, M.M. (eds) (1990). *Successful Aging: Perspectives from the Behavioural Sciences*, Cambridge: Cambridge University Press.

Brodin, H. and Mattsson, T. (2014). "Lägst ner på skalan? Hälso- och sjukvårdens bemötande av äldre kvinnor som migrerat till Sverige", *Socialvetenskaplig Tidskrift*, **21**(3–4), 372–91.

European Commission (2009). "The Lund Declaration", available at http://www.vr.se/download/18.7dac901212646d84fd38000336/.

European Commission (2015). "The 2015 Ageing Report: Economic and budgetary projections for the 28 EU Member States (2013–2060)", *European Economy*, 3/2015, May.

Fineman, M.A. (2004). *The Autonomy Myth: A Theory of Dependency*, New York, NY: The New Press.

Fineman, M.A. (2008). "The Vulnerable Subject: Anchoring Equality in the Human Condition", *Yale Journal of Law & Feminism*, **20**(1), 1.

Fineman, M.A. (2010). "The Vulnerable Subject and the Responsive State", *Emory Law Journal*, **60**(2), 251–76.

Fineman, M.A. (2011). "Grappling With Equality: One Feminist Journey", in Martha Albertson Fineman (ed.), *Transcending the Boundaries of Law: Generations of Feminism and Legal Theory*, Abingdon: Routledge Press.

Fineman, M.A. (2012a). "'Elderly' as Vulnerable: Rethinking the Nature of Individual and Societal Responsibility", *The Elder Law Journal*, **20**(1), 71–111.

Fineman, M.A. (2012b). "Beyond Identities: The Limits of an Antidiscrimination Approach to Equality", *Boston University Law Review*, **92**(6), 1713–79.

Fineman, M.A. (2013). *The Vulnerable Subject: Anchoring Equality in the Human Condition*, Princeton University Press: Princeton University Press.

Fineman, M.A. (2017). "Vulnerability and inevitable inequality", *Oslo Law Review*, **4**(3), 133–49.

Government Bill (1992/93). "Om stöd och service till vissa funktionshindrade" (1992/93:159).

Government Bill (2000/01). "Personlig assistans till personer över 65 år" (2000/01:5).

Jönsson, H. and Harnett, T. (2015). *Socialt Arbete med Äldre*, Stockholm: Natur och Kultur.

Lagergren, M. (2012). *Vad har hänt med Resurserna för Äldreomsorgen?* Socialdepartementet.

Laslett, P. (1989). *A Fresh Map of Life*, Cambridge, MA: Harvard University Press.

Mattsson, T. (2013). "National Ombudsman for the Elderly: A Solution for a More Responsive Welfare State?", *Retfaerd*, **36**(3), 9–24.

Mattsson, T. and Katzin, M. (2017). "Vulnerabilty and ageing", in Ann Numhauser-Henning (ed.), *Elder Law: Evolving European Perspectives*, Cheltenham, UK and Northampton, MA, USA: Edward Elgar Publishing, pp. 113–31.

Mattsson, T., Axmin, A. and Holm, E. (2017), "Perspectives on solidarity in social security, healthcare, and medical research", in Ann Numhauser-Henning (ed.), *Elder Law: Evolving European Perspectives*, Cheltenham, UK and Northampton, MA, USA: Edward Elgar Publishing, pp. 309–34.

Numhauser-Henning, A. (ed.) (2017). *Elder Law: Evolving European Perspectives*, Cheltenham, UK and Northampton, MA, USA: Edward Elgar Publishing.

SOU (2003). "Äldrepolitik för Framtiden: 100 Steg till Trygghet och Utveckling med en Åldrande Befolkning", 2003:91.

SOU (2008). "Möjlighet att leva som andra. Ny lag om stöd och service till vissa personer med funktionsnedsättning", 2008:77.

Swedish Agency for Health and Care Services Analysis (2015). Available at https://www.vardanalys.se/rapporter/hemtjanst-vard-och-omsorgsboende-eller-mitt-emellan/.

The Disability Act (SFS 1993:387).

The Social Services Act (SFS 2001:453).

3. Ageism, moral agency and autonomy: getting beyond guardianship in the 21st century

Gerard Quinn, Ayelet Gur and Joanne Watson

INTRODUCTION

Many older people are vulnerable to having their legal capacity to make decisions for themselves taken away. In the past, the onset of cognitive impairments meant an almost automatic loss of the right to make decisions for oneself. However, and more recently, there has been a consciousness that such a loss begs strong justification. Over the past twenty years or so this has led to a first wave of reform that has increased attention on ways and means of reducing the scope for any loss of the legal right to make decisions as well as policing the process by which decision-making power is taken away (typically through guardianship regimes). And it has meant a much closer regulation of the actions of third parties in as much as they purport to make decisions on behalf of older people. That is to say, the policy focus thus far has impliedly conceded the need for "protective" mechanisms like guardianship upon a showing of cognitive incapacity and has therefore focused on ensuring that the mechanism is applied only in instances where it is objectively required and in the "best interests" of the older person.

This first wave of reform is now giving way to a newer wave that more radically challenges the need for guardianship in the first place. The post-guardianship wave of reform is partly due to new insights about how people actually make decisions. Whereas traditional approaches have focused (perhaps fixated) on declining cognitive ability, newer approaches place cognitive capacity in a much broader context. Indeed, some (including such august bodies as the World Bank) would dispute the very centrality of cognition in human decision making. One result is that the focus of public policy enquiry is shifting away from guardianship toward a search for new tools of discovery to reveal the person and support him or her in forming and expressing their wishes.

These newer approaches create space for a new policy imagination, one that is not exclusively deficits-based and one that does not rest on ageist assumptions about the inevitability or consequences of decline. Such new approaches are already changing policy perspectives in the related field of disability as a result of the adoption of the UN Convention on the Rights of Persons with Disabilities (UN CRPD, 2007). As will be seen, the UN CRPD sets a path that is well clear of "protective" mechanisms like guardianship and instead places a presumption of autonomy (with support where needed) at its core. It is almost inevitable that something similar will gradually replace more traditional ideas about guardianship in the context of older people. It will happen simply because of reforms in the field of disability. It will happen because the scientific and other premises validating guardianship have changed for all persons.

This chapter is about ageism and guardianship and the need for a new approach to restore autonomy and legal capacity to older persons. The first section looks at the older paradigm, its fixation on cognitive ability and its reliance on "protective" measures like guardianship for those deemed not able to make their own decisions because of cognitive frailty. It will briefly examine the law and doctrine of the relatively new UN Convention on the Rights of Persons with Disabilities (UN CRPD) and its radical assumption of universal legal capacity regardless of cognitive ability.

The second section looks at the emergence of new techniques of discovery in communications theory which potentially unlock – and reveal – the will and preference of persons (including older persons) who have been hitherto deemed unreachable because of their cognitive impairments. This is important because it gives the lie to ageist assumptions that many older persons are forever "locked away" behind a façade and cannot be meaningfully reached.

The third section looks at emerging evidence about the importance of social capital and broader social inclusion strategies as a form of support to enable people to retain their autonomy. What we aim to get at is the symbiotic relationship between autonomy and social inclusion as a way of supporting older persons to retain their autonomy.

1. AUTONOMY AND AGEISM: CHANGING PARADIGMS FROM DEFICITS TO RIGHTS

1.1 Ageism and Personhood: Toward New Framings

As suggested above, many people effectively deny the full personhood of older persons. That is to say, they deny that a "person", as we normally understand the term, lurks behind the mask of age. That being so, the only course of action is to intervene in order to protect. If that intervention requires taking away the last vestiges of voice, then so be it. Or, even if we may assume that a "self" still lurks within the form of the body, we may have cause to doubt whether the "self" can make itself understood in the world, since purely formal methods of communication may be unavailing. Both postures raise a lot of questions that are usually left unaddressed in public policy debates.

1.1.1 Empirical questions about who is a human: an open-ended continuum

In approaching this one must distinguish between empirical questions about what it means to be a human, and more normative questions about what it takes to be recognized as a person in law. Empirically, it is easier to be recognized as "human" in biology than it is to be recognized as a "person" in law with full rights and responsibilities. Many traditional criteria of legal personhood are purely internal to the person (like having a body, having a mind, having consciousness, having a certain degree of cognitive capacity) and many are more outward-facing (like sociability, emotional connectedness, empathy, being able to project oneself into the future and so on). Cognitive ability is but one factor among many. Personhood is like a portal; once you are acknowledged as a person the moral and political community has some responsibilities toward you and you have rights to express and manifest yourself in civil society.

1.1.2 Normative questions about who counts as a "person": the bias in favour of cognitive ability

The "problem" is that the normative requirements – the "essentialist" characteristics you must possess before you can be acknowledged as a person in law – can be quite exclusionary in their operation (Bernstein, 1998). It is first of all within the domain of ethics that persons with cognitive impairments, whether older or not, are not altogether embraced as "persons" (Kittay and Carlson, 2010). Ethicists have long disputed whether persons with severe cognitive impairments are "morally consid-erable" or possess "full moral status" in order to be considered the fitting subjects of justice (with autonomy rights). Why? This is so for one very simple reason. The ethicists tend to consider cognitive capacity to be the key to "full moral status". That is to say, they use the indicator of cognitive ability to distinguish between those entities with "full moral status" from those with "lesser moral status" and those with no moral status at all (like a rock).

What this leads to is the assertion that the truly autonomous person – the one whom we can trust to make decisions for themselves – is the rational person capable of logically apprehending the world, capable of unpacking the natural and probable consequences of one decision over another and capable of rationally communicating their preferences to the outside world. Our main point here is that the standard account of who is a person – in ethics and in law – has tended to rest on cognitive ability. This legacy weighs down the debate about how to preserve and support autonomy and decision-making ability for many older persons.

1.1.3   Rethinking cognitive ability as the essence of personhood: new insights from the hard sciences

What we have witnessed over the past two or three decades is the unravelling of that image of the atomized rational man in the hard sciences and the consequent unravelling of the "standard account" of personhood. It is this unravelling that gives us fresh space to think anew about autonomy and decision-making for older people.

First of all, take the traditional emphasis on the atomized individual. Modern science is displaying in brilliant technicolour the true extent to which the "self" is a social construct. Much neuroscience is yielding new theories of the mind which have been conspicuously absent from orthodox debates about the "self" including decision-making. Antonio Damasio, for example, is famous for his thesis that the brain is "wired to connect" (Damasio, 2012). He does not say that the brain of only those with higher cognitive functioning is "wired to connect". He says that all brains are wired to connect. In essence the "self" emerges from these essentially social connections. Our "selves" are inter-subjective from the outset and our autonomy is fundamentally "relational". Laura Davy at the University of Sydney captures brilliantly the notion of inter-subjectivity or shared personhood in feminist legal and political thinking and applies it to the sphere of intellectual disability. Her survey of the idea of our inter-subjectivity reinforces the move toward a support paradigm – especially when one realizes that the supports occur naturally in the community (Davy, 2015). Similarly, Bruce Hood develops the idea of the "social brain" (Hood, 2014). The point is that modern neuroscience debunks the "standard account" of a hermetically sealed and disconnected mind. What it points to instead is the quality of the social connectors in our lives and especially in the life of the mind. These social connectors are exactly the things that fray into old age.

One pithy way of putting this is to say that, although the stuff of our personhood is necessarily experienced individually, it is essentially a shared phenomenon. This is another way of making sense of the support paradigm in Article 12 of the UN disability convention. Bernadette McSherry's perceptive article in the 2015 issue of *Laws* shows how the new "discovery" techniques being opened up by neuroscience have positive potential into the future to reveal formerly unknown and unknowable persons as the science evolves (McSherry, 2015).

Contemporary clinical psychology also tends to reveal the complexity of decision-making which is very far from the simple unilinear image above of consciousness, mind, rationality and decision. Decision-making is never so straightforward. Indeed many clinical psychologists question the very existence of a boundary between cognition and emotion. Much of the relevant literature casts doubts on the standard account to say the least. And of course these doubts apply to all of us – not just persons with cognitive impairments (Leher, 2009). Added to recent literature in clinical psychology is the burgeoning field of behavioural economics. The standard account of mind, consciousness and rational decision-making underpins much classical economics and animates many econometric models. Yet the explanatory power of these models has been found wanting. Contemporary economists have been reassessing the role of rationality in economic decision-making. Indeed, the famous 2015 World Development Report of the World Bank focuses on exactly this: *Mind, Society and Behavior* (World Bank, 2015). The report characterizes decision-making (for all of us) along three axes: (1) automatic decision-making; (2) social decision-making; and (3) mental decision-making models. It insists that the vast majority of decisions are made automatically with little or no in-depth deliberation. By social thinking is meant the reflex in all of us to fit with and be valorized by our group affiliation (if we are lucky enough to have one). Indeed, the report insists we "imitate the behavior of others almost automatically" (World Bank, 2015, p. 6). Lastly, the Report insists that we come to decision-making with baggage – narrow windows through which we make sense of the world (bypassing our cognitive functioning). Rational economic man hasn't disappeared – but he just got radically contextualized!

What these disciplines are telling us is that cognition is just one part of a menu of capacities that most humans possess. They are telling us that personhood is primarily shared and that it is wholly natural to focus on the dialectic between supports and threats that are integral to all of our decision-making. They are telling us that new discovery techniques are available and are evolving to enable us to divine the will and preference of the person even in circumstances where we thought they were unreachable to us. And they are telling us that the quality of our social life and connections has a direct bearing on our capacity and resilience as autonomous persons. All this should be enough to force a policy rethink. Why persist with laws and policies that rest on assumptions that are plainly at odds with new insights from the hard sciences? If ever the term "evidence-based policy-making" had any validity, then clearly our old policies on the autonomy of older persons and the case for guardianship stand in clear need of reform.

1.1.4 Building the new paradigm: searching for new forms of support to enable autonomy to flourish

In a sense the combined insights from science point to a completely new set of departure points in thinking about (and legislating for) the autonomy for older persons (as well as many others). First of all, it re-focuses attention away from "protection" toward "support" and indeed toward social inclusion in the broadest sense. That is to say, the centrality of the traditional approach which was to "protect" older people by taking away their voice (guardianship) is now displaced by a new focus: the search for ways to enable the voice of older persons to be supported and revealed. One incidental by-product of an exclusive focus on guardianship in the past was that it dis-incentivized the search for new techniques of discovery. There is a full continuum here ranging from interventions to spark a will and preference (for example, in someone whose social capital has frayed or their experience in making decisions has deteriorated) and interventions to decipher the person's will and preference through the interpretation, for example, of informal communication.

Second, it assigns a new task to "protection". It is no longer about insisting on safeguards in the process of taking rights away; it is about protecting the integrity of the process whereby the will and preference of the person is "discovered". Obviously, a new science needs to emerge about how to handle all the attendant risks. For example, how do we guard against the contamination of the process by the even unintentional interpolation of the wishes and preferences of the supporters? If the process requires more than just interpretation but actually help to reconstruct the self, then how do we guard against the "manufacturing" of the self by third parties (even unintentionally)? These are not challenges that stop the process of change, but variables that need to be calibrated as policy makers learn from experience to make change work (Quinn, 2016).

Third, as the term itself suggests, the "support" concept is closely aligned with the idea of the social dimension of the "self" and the related idea that our personhood is primarily a shared entity. The quality (or even existence) of these social relationships is in itself a key "support" to enable us to exercize our autonomy. That is why there is such a close nexus between our decision-making prowess and the quality of our social embeddedness – our sense of belonging and place.

So the emphasis in modern law and policy should now be on support and not protection, and the object of protection itself should shift away from protecting the person (perversely by taking their voice away) to protecting the process for identifying the person's will and preferences.

1.2   The Move to the New Paradigm of Support under International Law

The UN disability convention epitomizes the shift away from guardianship and is a precursor to similar law and policy moves in a web of fields including elder policy. It became quickly obvious to most during the drafting process of the UN CRPD that the dignity and autonomy rights of the person were key. In a sense the drafters had moved beyond the early 1990s' agenda of "equality of opportunities" and were focusing much more intentionally on the concept of personhood. That was because the drafters realized that it wasn't enough to create equal access to the mainstream – they had to tackle the very invisibility of persons with disabilities as persons in the first place.

1.2.1   Restoring moral agency and legal capacity despite cognitive frailty

So how does Article 12 of the UN CRPD seek to restore "moral agency" and what are its lessons for older people?[1] The first paragraph of Article 12 (12.1) states the obvious and is notable simply because it was felt necessary to state the obvious in the first place, namely that persons with disabilities have a right to recognition as "persons" before the law. Put another way, it inverts the normal assumption, which is: while persons with intellectual disabilities are indisputably human, they do not necessarily qualify as full persons in the legal sense with all the rights and privileges that attach to that.

Instead, Article 12 effectively announces a theory of universal legal capacity even in the face of severe decision-making frailties. Article 12 therefore does not rest on a view that persons with disabilities are only *contingently* persons if they pass a certain test of cognitive ability. It asserts that they are persons *simpliciter.* The second sub-paragraph (12.2) assures persons with disabilities a right to enjoy legal capacity "*on an equal basis with others*" and in all spheres of life. Of course, it is open to States' Parties to assert (and many of them strenuously do) that there are significant material differences between persons with severe intellectual disabilities and others to fully justify the withdrawal or limitation of legal capacity.[2] However, the third sub-paragraph (perhaps one of the most discussed provisions in any modern human rights treaty) points to a new departure point in the context of personhood and decision-making frailty. It speaks of a right of "access" to "supports" to enable a person to "exercise" their legal capacity. It does not, at least ostensibly, proscribe guardianship. But its overall thrust is unmistakable: at the first sign of frailty States should not resort to guardianship. Instead, the States' Parties should endeavour to promote "*access*" to a web of supports to enable a person to exercize, or continue to exercize, their inherent legal capacity.

Whether the obligation incumbent on the State is one of opening up *access* to already existing and naturally occurring supports (and regulating the same), or whether it is one of providing more direct support, it is clear that it cannot be achieved over night. In the argot of international law, it is something to be "achieved progressively".

Sub-paragraph 4 famously places the spotlight on the centrality of the "will and preferences" of the person. Most people rightly use the term "will and preferences" as a term of art that refers essentially to the choice of the person (howsoever formed) as distinct from choices imposed upon the person by a third party and even with their "best interests" in mind. Sub-paragraph 5 deals with the right to legal capacity on the context of decision-making over property and financial affairs. Strictly speaking, this was not necessary since the reference to "all aspects of life" in sub-paragraph 2 should have been sufficient to cover it. What probably moved the drafters to include a specific provision on it was the widespread prevalence of financial abuse. This is just as important for older persons as it is for persons with disabilities.

As if to underscore Article 12 as the fulcrum of the whole convention, the UN CRPD Committee chose to issue its very first General Comment on it in 2014. The General Comment asserts that "will and preferences" should replace the old theory of "best interests" (paragraph 21). In other words the process of exploring (excavating) the "self" and identifying his/her own choices is primary. The endeavour of controlling the actions of substitute decision-makers through the application of controlling notions like "best interests" is not only not secondary – it doesn't exist.

To be sure, all of the above jurisprudence of the UN Committee seems starkly ahead of State practice. If you continue to accept the assumptions behind the "standard account" of personhood (which pivots on cognitive ability), then the new jurisprudence probably doesn't make much sense. But if you have already begun to move away from the "standard account", then it begins to make sense. So, in a way the UN CRPD jurisprudence bubbles to the surface a very profound debate that actually goes beyond disability or old age: who are we as persons and are there essentialist criteria against which we measure personhood?

1.2.2 Shared personhood, social capital and the concept of support

The concept of "support" in Article 12.3 is key to any new paradigm of enabling a "civil life" as against providing for a "civil death".[3] It has to be first noted that it refers to "support" to enable a person to *exercise their legal capacity*. It bears repeating that this goes far beyond support for just decision-making. Indeed, decision-making can be seen as something at the very end of a spectrum that begins first of all with the very stuff of personhood, something that includes cognitive ability but does not necessarily revolve exclusively around it. As a recent evaluation of a South Australian pilot project on supported decision-making concludes, the building of trust in support relationships, which takes time, is key.[4]

Implicitly at least, the support concept assumes that our personhood is primarily shared, that the very stuff of our personhood emerges from and through an ongoing iterative process with others. Our sense of self congeals as we are "held" by others and reflected back. Naturally, this depends on a minimum level of social interaction, and on the existence of and our immersion into dense social networks that occur naturally for most people. Many persons with disabilities have never had this. And most older people have had this but tend to lose it as they age and as their peers decline or pass away.

Many have noted the symbiotic relationship between Article 12 and Article 19 (the right to live independently and be part of the community) in the UN CRPD. This underscores the importance of "home". Home is a place that offers repose from the world (and an opportunity to form and even mutate our identity) as well as connectedness with the world and the local community (Fox-O'Mahoney, 2006). It is part of the "scaffolding of the self". It is much more than bricks and mortar. And it is not often enjoyed by persons with cognitive impairments, including older people. It is no surprise therefore, that "supports" to enable individuals to exercize their legal capacity primarily mean putting in place social networks and connections to spark the individual's personhood which, though maybe flickering and faint, still exists. This is a form of support to enable a person to exercize legal capacity no less than a support to enable a person to make a decision.

It follows that the main role of government is to open up that zone of rich social interaction to persons with intellectual disabilities and indeed older persons. Success in embedding these kinds of supports will (it is hoped) enable the person to emerge and manifest their "self" to others. This does not necessarily mean that the person manifests as strongly or as coherently as "others" do. And it certainly does not mean that we "find" the person primarily through their rational expression or in formal communication. But it does mean that there is always a spark of their humanity hidden somewhere that stands a better chance of emerging when the social context we take for granted for everyone is layered back in. Again, this seems apt for both older people and people with disabilities.

If our personhood is shared, if "we" are to be found echoed and echoing in our close relationships and are "held" by those close to us, and if those close to us have privileged access to who we are as persons (not necessarily through rational dialogue), then it is only natural to try to find us or gain access to us (reveal our sense of self, our identity and broad preferences in the world) in those others. It is in these intimate circles of love and support that the person – otherwise unknown to the broader world – can emerge and count as a person.

2. REACHING AND REVEALING OLDER PEOPLE USING NEW TOOLS OF DISCOVERY

As discussed in section 1, the focus of policy is shifting away from mechanisms that "protect" people with cognitive disabilities by silencing their voice through guardianship, to a search for new tools of discovery to support autonomy and the restoration of legal capacity. Do these tools exist, and what is their future potential?

Building on decades of communication-based theory and practice, these new tools are indeed emerging and hold promise for many who may be considered unreachable due to declining cognitive capacity as they age. This section focuses on what can be gleaned from a body of research focused on the realization of autonomy for people with intellectual disability who communicate informally and sometimes unintentionally (Watson, 2016; 2017; Watson et al., 2017).

2.1   The Universality of Human Communication

Central to an inclusive view of communication is the acceptance that "all
people, no matter how severe their level of disability, can and do attempt
to communicate" (Mirenda et al., 1990, p. 3). This includes people who
are ageing. Human communication is described by communication
theorists and practitioners as progressing through a series of stages that
reflect a continuum from informal unintentional to intentional formal
communication (Iacono et al., 2009; Ogletree and Pierce, 2010). At one
end of the continuum, informal communication is characterized by the
use of communicative actions such as gesture, eye gaze, touch, facial
expression and body language. Further along the continuum is formal or
symbolic communication, characterized by the use of language.

Informal communication has been further categorized into two stages:
first, unintentional informal communication and, second, intentional
informal communication. In contrast to an intentional communicator, an
unintentional communicator does not generate a message with the
deliberate intent of engaging with a listener. Therefore, there is an onus
on communication partners to infer meaning from that person's behaviours and responses. These behaviours are likely to be highly idio-
syncratic, ranging from vocalizations, facial expression, behaviour
(sometimes labelled challenging) and very subtle physiological responses
such as changes in skin tone and colour, body temperature and breathing
rate.

It was not until the 1970s that communication began to be viewed as a
universal construct. Until that time, people who communicated unintentionally were viewed as non-communicators. At this time, a more
inclusive view of communication began to emerge, recognizing that all
behaviour is communicative. This view began to emerge from the work
of communication theorists such as Dunst, Bruner, Donnellan and
Mirenda. Drawing from this body of work, Dunst and colleagues
proposed a new definition of communication to encompass: "Any overt
conventional or nonconventional behaviour, whether used intentionally or
not, that has the effect of arousing in an onlooker a belief that the signal
producing organism is attempting to convey a message, make a demand,
request etc. to an onlooker" (Dunst, 1978, p. 111).

This body of work contributed to an extremely important new
paradigm from a narrow interpretation of communication to one that
acknowledges the communicative function of a broad range of human
behaviour, regardless of its formality and intentionality. This contemporary view has provided motivation to further develop listening techniques, strategies and supports for people who communicate informally

and unintentionally, to have their will and preference "voiced" and their legal capacity realized.

2.2 Supported Decision-making for People Rarely Heard: a Case Study

To understand supported decision-making for people with intellectual disability who communicate informally, an approach specifically designed to support decision-making was developed with five people and their support networks, as part of an action research study (Watson and Joseph, 2015). The approach drew together a set of key ideas and strategies for supporting someone with an intellectual disability who communicates informally and unintentionally to participate in decisions that impact their life. A group of people who care for and about a person with an intellectual disability (circle of support) was assembled, and guided through a supported decision-making process over a period of three to six months, focusing on a particular decision faced by the person at the centre. The approach was highly individualized and customized to each person and their support network. It involved a combination of on-site mentoring, observation, modelling, coaching and provision of feedback by the researcher, a speech pathologist with many years of experience supporting informal communicators. In conjunction with onsite mentoring and support, each group attended a five-hour workshop facilitated by the researcher. Embedded within the approach is a framework for supported decision-making which, consistent with an action research approach, was adapted over the course of the study (Watson, 2016). This framework is comprised of five core phases of collaborative activity: identifying a decision; listening; exploring options and building evidence; making a decision and acting on it; and documentation. An important aspect of documentation is the use of video, which allows supporters to closely attend to and interpret subtle communicative behaviours.

An important outcome of this study was the characterization of supported decision-making for people who communicate informally in terms of the existence of two distinct but interdependent roles, the roles played by: (a) the person with a disability (supported); and (b) the circle of support (supporters). The role of the person with a disability in this dynamic was unsurprisingly found to be to express their will and preference, intentionally and unintentionally, using a range of modalities (for example behaviour, vocalization, vocal pitch, muscle tone, facial expression, eye movement, self-harm, breath, unintentional physiological functions). The role of the supporter was found to be to respond to this expression of preference by acknowledging, interpreting and acting on this expression in some way. Within this decision-making dynamic, supporter responsiveness, as opposed to the supported person's expression of preference, is the component that is amenable to change, making the enablement of supporter responsiveness a crucial element in supported decision-making for people who communicate informally. Several factors characterizing supporter responsiveness were identified. One of these, the importance of relational closeness between supporters and those being supported, is discussed here.

2.3   The Role of Relational Closeness in the Realization of Autonomy

Within neoliberal cultures, autonomy is associated with being self-supporting and self-reliant, thereby excluding the role of others. Jennifer Nedelsky (1989), along with a cast of feminist theorists, views this neoliberal individualized ideal of autonomy as contradictory to the inherently social nature of human beings. They promote the idea that autonomy should be re-conceived as relational, promoting a conjoint as opposed to a disjoint model of agency whereby the self is understood interdependently in relation to others (Markus and Kitayama, 2003). The thesis of Antonio Damasio once again comes to mind: the human brain is "wired to connect" (Damasio, 2012).

As highlighted by Johnson and her colleagues, there is a lack of understanding of the mechanics of relationships for people who communicate informally (Johnson et al., 2014). Watson's (2016) study's findings not only highlight the importance of relational closeness between people with intellectual disability who communicate informally and their supporters, but also provide some insights into what a responsive relationship is likely to look like.

2.3.1   "Seeing" a person
Participants who reported intimate or very close relationships with those they support in Watson's study described a "knowing" of the person they supported beyond their disability. This notion of "seeing a person" beyond their disability has been described by Lyng (2007). Lyng suggests that a factor important in relationship closeness is knowledge or appreciation of a person beyond their disability (Lyng, 2007). To summarize the relevant findings, supporters who reported an intimate or very close relationship with those they support were more likely to be responsive to

their expression of will and preference, and additionally they demonstrated a willingness to see the person they support "beyond their disability". This data taps into the notion of perceptions of personhood, discussed previously in this chapter. Lyng's technique of encouraging supporters to see focus people "beyond their disability" illuminates the value of seeing someone as a person, rather than their disability.

2.3.2 Knowing of a person's history and life story

Participants in Watson's study who reported intimate or very close relationships with those they supported described their relationships in terms of having knowledge of a focus person's history and life story. Such information was not evident in the descriptions provided by the supporters who reported more distant relationship. A supporter who described her relationship with Kevin (not his real name) as intimate recalled Kevin's childhood, saying, "remember, no you didn't work at [institution], he used to sit in the creek ... loved that water, [he] used to sit there for hours". Neil's (not his real name) mother demonstrated her and her family's deep historical knowledge of Neil's preferences when talking about decisions that were made around his funeral:

> It was everything that we all know he wanted, coz you know, we know him love. We have known him all his life. ... And Dave reminded me, you know his cousin ... he reminded me about the jelly slice that he loved before the peg when he was teeny tiny. So we had to have that after didn't we, with a cuppa you know. He would have loved it.

In summary, Watson's study found that supporters, who report "intimate" or "very close" relationships with those they support, are likely to be knowledgeable about their history and life story. In contrast, those who reported a "distant" or "not close" relationship with those they supported articulated little knowledge of the person's history and life story. Supporters who reported a good historical knowledge did not necessarily acquire this knowledge through relationship longevity, but through stories and visual images shared about the person. That is, for supporters to have an intimate or very close relationship with a focus person, they did not necessarily need to have known them for a long time, but to have access to information from those who had.

To conclude, supporter responsiveness to the will and preference of people who communicate informally, including those who are ageing, is an essential component of supported decision-making. This responsiveness is characterized by three components: acknowledgement of a person's will and preference, interpretation of that preference, and acting on that preference (Watson, 2016; Watson et al., 2017). Watson's study has found that this responsiveness is dependent on relational closeness, characterized by both a willingness and ability to "see the person beyond their disability" and a deep historical knowledge of the person. The findings from this study are relevant to all informal communicators regardless of whether their disability is intellectual or age-related.

This section has further illustrated the role of social capital in underpinning human autonomy. Using Watson's research as a backdrop, we have illustrated its crucial role for people with intellectual disability.

3. SUPPORTING THE AUTONOMY OF OLDER PEOPLE BY BUILDING SOCIAL CAPITAL

3.1 The Importance of Social Capital for the Autonomy of Older People

A central thesis of this chapter is that autonomy is part of a broader continuum that rests vitally on a bedrock of social capital. The concept of social capital reflects a fundamental idea grounded in social theories that social participation in society-at-large is beneficial for the individual (Portes, 1998). Thus, most definitions of social capital focus on social relations that have productive benefits for individuals within the relevant social network. Burt (1992, p. 9) suggested that social capital represents "friends, colleagues, and more general contacts through whom you receive opportunities to use your financial and human capital". These networks are like scaffolds of the self: they "hold" us, they reflect us, they reaffirm us – our sense of place in the world and even our identity. Healthy networks enable us to grow, to evolve, to have a strong sense of "self" and to express it. Unhealthy networks (or even the absence of such networks) degrade our sense of "self" through time as well as our confidence and competence to navigate our own way in the world through our own decisions.

3.1.1 The general benefits of social capital

The benefits of such networks have been well documented in discrete areas such as health. The association between social relationships and health and well-being is now securely established for all (Antonucci, 2001; Kawachi and Berkman, 2001; Rose, 2000; World Health Organisation (WHO), 2004). Older persons are not exceptional (Ashida and Heaney, 2008; Cornwell and Waite, 2009; White et al., 2009). It was found that social capital and socially integrated lifestyle in late life protect against functional decline and diseases (Fratiglioni et al., 2004; Reblin and Uchino, 2008) and enable older people to maintain productive, independent and fulfilling lives (Cannuscio et al., 2003).

The most immediate social relationships may be with kin, for instance with spouses, adult children and other family members. Bubolz (2001) claimed that the family is a builder and a source of social capital. Relationships between family members establish the principles of reciprocity and exchange, meaning that family members are expected to give and receive instrumental and emotional support from one another. Within these exchanges, there is an implicit assumption that children will provide care and support for their ageing parents. Indeed, research has demonstrated the importance of kinship and family social network in shaping the lives of older adults (Bernard et al., 2001). Kin was found to be a significant source of social support among elders who were childless. Of course, the "natural" decline of family connections into old age is a factor that powerfully affects older people – leading potentially to isolation, loneliness and a degradation of a capacity to make decisions. One cannot legislate for family members to remain involved. But one might try to incentivize engagement through family leave policies.

That is why the second source of social relations – which has to do with neighbours and friends and other community members through communal organizations or religious groups – may be even more powerful sources of support into old age. Putnam (2000) claimed that as social networks of older adults "naturally" decrease, they are, by definition, more dependent on the social capital that is available within their broader communities. The non-kin social networks of elders provide practical and emotional support. For example, it was found that social capital and social cohesion within the neighbourhood contribute to the well-being of older adults (Cramm et al., 2013). Conversely, studies show that isolation and loneliness are common (Dykstra, 2009; Golden et al., 2009; Victor et al., 2008) and that older persons are at greater risk for decreased social networks by losing critical parts of their social ties.

The house – and home – are especially important indicators of support. Cannuscio et al. (2003) suggested that social ties of elders might vary with the type of housing environment. While some types are highly connected to isolation and loneliness, other types facilitate social interaction among residents and between residents and the wider community. The institutional model of nursing home care was characterized as highly regulated and depersonalized and geographically segregated from the general society. This type of housing arrangement is associated with social isolation for elders (Andersson et al., 2007; Cannuscio et al., 2003; Scocco et al., 2006).

3.1.2 Social capital, autonomy and decision-making

Less understood is the profound and real connection between preserving (or intentionally building) social networks for older people and having (or retaining) a capacity to make decisions for oneself. Older people – like all others – make decisions in a social context (Schobel et al., 2016). As social networks are central and a significant aspect of our lives, people tend to make choices and decisions through social influences from our social circles (Kilduff, 1992). Most of the influence is carried through close relationships (Cross et al. 2002). Heller et al. (2011) stated that the expression of self-determination (the architecture of choice) is shaped by opportunities created within social networks such as families, friends and community networks, educational and vocational settings and residential environments.

In other words, the social networks of older people have the power to support and expand opportunities to become more self-determined – or decisively to restrict them. For example, Hopp (2000) argued that the most common method of discussing care wishes and preferences is through informal communication with the individual's social network's members, as family members, friends, community members or other informal network members. Likewise, Fiori et al. (2006) suggested that friendships, which provide emotional intimacy and companionship, contribute to reaffirmation of self-worth and feelings of autonomy.

The onset of cognitive impairments coupled with a decline in the extent or quality of one's social networks can affect one's competence and confidence to remain in control of one's own life. There is nothing natural or inevitable in this process. Active ageing is achieved, among other things, through respecting older people's decisions and choices. Moreover, the WHO's guide for global age-friendly cities states that "There is a link between appropriate housing and access to community and social services in influencing the independence and quality of life of older people" (World Health Organization (WHO), 2007, p. 30).

3.1.3 The link between community living and autonomy

Although there is still a dearth of quantitative research and publications on factors that are associated with or predict autonomy in older people (Hwang et al., 2006), extensive research attests that long-term care facilities for elders are associated with decreased social networks and autonomy decline (Abbott et al., 2000; Choi et al., 2008). Moreover, older people, in various nursing environments, are often denied the right to independent decisions because of their perceived inability or limited competence. Hellström and Sarvimäki (2007), who explore how older people living in sheltered housing experience self-determination, concluded that it could be labelled disempowerment. This residential type did not strengthen individual self-determination, participation or control. Thus, the residents had very minimal decision-making opportunities and little influence overall. Comparing community-dwelling elders to institutionalized elders, Fry (2000) has found significant differences in their social resources and support; institutionalized elders had fewer meaningful social resources and demonstrated decreased well-being.

Abbott et al. (2000) studied experiences of older people living in sheltered residential settings. Most residents expressed some concerns about their social contact and many felt their social contact was more a matter of adjustment than of friendship. There was little evidence of friendships or intimacy. Furthermore, residents demonstrated decreased self-determination; they had very low control over their lives, with insufficient respect for their autonomy and individuality. Similarly, Choi et al. (2008) studied the causes for depressive mood among older people living in nursing homes. Many mentioned the loss of independence and autonomy and emphasized the strictly regimented routines and regulations that characterize institutional care, as well as decreased participation in social engagements and outside activities. The majority expressed their feelings of social isolation and loneliness (Choi et al., 2008).

To conclude, the social environment of older people, which may include family members, friends and community members, as well as staff in residential settings and health professionals, plays a significant role in setting expectations, providing support and enabling opportunities for self-determination.

CONCLUSIONS

What conclusions are warranted by the above? First of all, since the standard account of legal personhood has moved away from an exclusive reliance on cognitive ability, it is time to reflect on the policy and legal implications in the context of older people. The paradigm shift in the UN disability treaty away from guardianship and toward support is instructive and has broader implications far beyond the field of disability.

Secondly, unlike in the past, there now is a web of discovery techniques available and emerging that enable us to retrieve the self even when well hidden behind a veil of seeming communicative inability. It is high time to concentrate our efforts into refining and applying these techniques. While the art and science of supported decision-making is in its infancy it is well underway. The time is right to capitalize on it in the context of imagining new policies to retain and even grow the autonomy of older people.

Third, advancing autonomy for all persons including older persons is part of a broader skein of public policy approaches that specifically include a right to live independently and be included in the community (or ageing in place). Autonomy and social inclusion are mutually reinforcing. It is just as important to attend to the broader ecosystem of autonomy which includes keeping older people out of institutions as it is to the law of legal capacity.

NOTES

1. For a recent survey of relevant law reform see Bagenstos (2017).
2. The reservations, declarations and understandings made by the States' Parties to the UN CRPD are available at: https://treaties.un.org/Pages/ViewDetails.aspx?src=TREATY&mtds g_no=IV-15&chapter=4&lang=_en&clang=_en.
3. The phrase "civil death" is commonly attributed to Sir William Blackstone, who wrote in his *Commentaries on the Laws of England* that upon marriage "the very being or legal existence of the women is suspended" (Blackstone, 1765).
4. For a review of supported decision-making pilots across Australia see Department of Justice and Attorney-General (2014).

REFERENCES

Abbott, S., Fisk, M. and Forward, L. (2000). Social and democratic participation in residential settings for older people: Realities and aspirations. *Ageing and Society*, **20**(3), 327–40.

Andersson, I., Pettersson, E. and Sidenvall, B. (2007). Daily life after moving into a care home: Experiences from older people, relatives and contact persons. *Journal of Clinical Nursing*, **16**(9), 1712–18.

Antonucci, T.C. (2001). Social relations: An examination of social networks, social support, and sense of control. In J. Birren and K. Schaie (eds), *Handbook of the Psychology of Aging*. San Diego, CA: Academic Press.

Ashida, S. and Heaney, C.A. (2008). Differential associations of social support and social connectedness with structural features of social networks and the health status of older adults. *Journal of Aging and Health*, **20**(7), 872–93.

Bagenstos, S. (2017). Disability, universalism, social rights, and citizenship, *Cardozo Law Review*, **39**(2), 413–36.

Bernard, M., Ogg, J., Phillips, J. and Phillipson, C. (2001). *The Family and Community Life of Older People: Social Networks and Social Support in Three Urban Areas*. London: Routledge.

Bernstein, M. (1998). *On Moral Considerability: An Essay on Who Morally Matters*. Oxford: Oxford University Press.

Blackstone, W. (1765), Chapter XV of husband and wife, in *Book 1 on the Law of Persons*, Oxford: Clarendon Press, p. 430.

Bubolz, M. (2001). Family as source, user, and builder of social capital. *Journal of Behavioral and Experimental Economics*, **30**(2), 129–31.

Burt, R. (1992). *Structural Holes: The Social Structure of Competition*. Cambridge, MA: Harvard University Press.

Cannuscio, C., Block, J. and Kawachi, I. (2003). Social capital and successful aging: The role of senior housing. *Annals of Internal Medicine*, **139**(5 Pt 2), 395–99.

Choi, N.G., Ransom, S. and Wyllie, R.J. (2008). Depression in older nursing home residents: The influence of nursing home environmental stressors, coping, and acceptance of group and individual therapy. *Aging and Mental Health*, **12**(5), 536–47.

Cornwell, E.Y. and Waite, L.J. (2009). Social disconnectedness, perceived isolation, and health among older adults. *Journal of Health and Social Behavior*, **50**(1), 31–48.

Cramm, J.M., Van Dijk, H.M. and Nieboer, A.P. (2013). The importance of neighborhood social cohesion and social capital for the well being of older adults in the community. *Gerontologist*, **53**(1), 142–52.

Cross, R., Borgatti, S.P. and Parker, A. (2002). Making invisible work visible: Using social network analysis to support strategic collaboration. *California Management Review*, **44**(2), 25–46.

Damasio, A. (2012). *Self Comes to Mind: Constructing the Conscious Brain*. New York, NY: First Vintage Books.

Davy, L.K. (2015). Philosophical inclusive design: Intellectual disability and the limits of individiual autonomy in moral and political theory. *Hypatia*, **30**(1), 132–48.

Department of Justice and Attorney-General (2014), A journey towards autonomy? Supported decision-making in theory and practice: A review of literature, Brisbane: Office of the Public Advocate, Queensland Government.

Dunst, C.J. (1978). A cognitive-social approach for assessment of early non-verbal communicative behavior *Communication Disorders Quarterly*, **2**, 110–23.

Dykstra, P.A. (2009). Older adult loneliness: Myths and realities. *European Journal of Ageing*, **6**(2), 91–100.

Fiori, K.L., Antonucci, T.C. and Cortina, K.S. (2006). Social network typologies and mental health among older adults. *Journal of Gerontology Series B, Psychological Sciences and Social Sciences*, **61**(1), P25–32.

Fox-O'Mahoney, L. (2006). *Conceptualising Home: Theories, Laws and Policies*. Oxford: Hart Publishing.

Fratiglioni, L., Paillard-Borg, S. and Winblad, B. (2004). An active and socially integrated lifestyle in late life might protect against dementia. *Lancet Neurology*, **3**(6), 343–53.

Fry, P. (2000). Religious involvement, spirituality and personal meaning for life: Existential predictors of psychological wellbeing in community-residing and institutional care elders. *Aging & Mental Health*, **4**(4), 375–87.

Golden, J., Conroy, R.M., Bruce, I., Denihan, A., Greene, E., Kirby, M. and Lawlor, B.A. (2009). Loneliness, social support networks, mood and well-being in community-dwelling elderly. *International Journal of Geriatric Psychiatry*, **24**(7), 694–700.

Heller, T., Schindler, A., Palmer, S.B., Wehmeyer, M.L., Parent, W., Jenson, R., Abery, B.H. et al. (2011). Self-determination across the life span: Issues and gaps. *Exceptionality*, **19**(1), 31–45.

Hellström, U.W. and Sarvimäki, A. (2007). Experiences of self-determination by older persons living in sheltered housing. *Nursing Ethics*, **14**(3), 413–24.

Hood, B. (2014). *The Domesticated Brain*. London: Penguin Books.

Hopp, F.P. (2000). Preferences for surrogate decision makers, informal communication, and advance directives among community-dwelling elders: Results from a national study. *Gerontologist*, **40**(4), 449–57.

Hwang, H.L., Lin, H.S., Tung, Y.L. and Wu, H.C. (2006). Correlates of perceived autonomy among elders in a senior citizen home: A cross-sectional survey. *International Journal of Nursing Studies*, **43**(4), 429–37.

Iacono, T., West, D., Bloomberg, K. and Johnson, H. (2009). Reliability and validity of the revised Triple C: Checklist of communicative competencies for adults with severe and multiple disabilities. *Journal of Intellectual Disability Research*, **53**(1), 44–53.

Johnson, H., Bigby, C., Iacono, T., Douglas, J. and Katthagen, S. (2014). *Improving Staff Capacity to Form and Facilitate Relationships for People with Severe Intellectual Disability: "It's a Slow Process"*. Melbourne: Living with Disability Research Group, La Trobe University.

Kawachi, I. and Berkman, L. (2001). Social ties and mental health. *Journal of Urban Health: Bulletin of the New York Academy of Medicine*, **78**, 458–67.

Kilduff, M. (1992). The friendship network as a decision-making resource: Dispositional moderators of social influences on organizational choice. *Journal of Personality and Social Psychology*, **62**(1), 168.

Kittay, E. and Carlson, L. (2010). *Cognitive Disability and its Challenge to Moral Philosophy*. Chichester, UK and Malden, MA, USA: Wiley-Blackwell.

Leher, J. (2009). *How we Decide*. New York, NY: Mariner Books.

Lyng, K. (2007). How do you know what I want? Exploring quality of life with people with no functional speech. Paper presented at the National Disability Services: Aging and disability conference, Adelaide, Australia.

Markus, H. and Kitayama, S. (2003). Models of agency: Sociocultural diversity in the construction of action. Paper presented at the Nebraska Symposium on Motivation: Cross cultural differences on the self, Lincoln, Nebraska, USA.

McSherry, B. (2015). Decision-making, legal capacity and neuroscience: Implications for mental health laws. *Laws*, **4**, 125–38.

Mirenda, P., Iacono, T. and Williams, R. (1990). Communication options for persons with severe and profound disabilities: State of the art and future directions. *Journal of the Association for Persons with Severe Handicaps*, **15**(1), 3–21.

Nedelsky, J. (1989). Reconceiving autonomy: Sources, thoughts and possibilities, *Yale Journal of Law & Feminism*, **1**(1).

Ogletree, B. and Pierce, K.H. (2010). AAC for individuals with severe intellectual disabilities: Ideas for nonsymbolic communicators, *Journal of Developmental & Physical Disabilities*, **22**(3), 273–87.

Portes, A. (1998). Social capital: Its origins and applications in modern sociology. *Annual Review of Sociology*, **24**, 1–24.

Putnam, R. (2000). *Bowling Alone: The Collapse and Revival of American Community*. New York, NY: Simon & Schuster.

Quinn, G. (2016). *Keynote Address "From Civil Death to Civil Life: the Decline and Re-birth of Legal Capacity Law Thoughout the World"*. Paper presented at the Australian Guardianship and Administration Council Conference, Sydney, Australia.

Reblin, M. and Uchino, B.N. (2008). Social and emotional support and its implication for health. *Current Opinion in Psychiatry*, **21**(2), 201–5.

Rose, R. (2000). How much does social capital add to individual health? A survey study of Russians. *Social Science & Medicine*, **51**(9), 1421–35.

Schobel, M., Rieskamp, J. and Huber, R. (2016). Social influences in sequential decision making. *PLoS One*, **11**(1), e0146536.

Scocco, P., Rapattoni, M. and Fantoni, G. (2006). Nursing home institutionalization: A source of eustress or distress for the elderly? *International Journal of Geriatric Psychiatry*, **21**(3), 281–7.

UN Convention on the Rights of Persons with Disabilities (2007). G.A. Res. 61/106, U.N. Doc A/RES/61/106, 13 December 2006.

Victor, C., Scrambler, S. and Bond, J. (2008). *The Social World of Older People: Understanding Loneliness and Social Isolation in Later Life*. Maidenhead: McGraw-Hill Education.

Watson, J. (2016). *The Right to Supported Decision Making for People Rarely Heard* (PhD), Deakin University, Melbourne.

Watson, J. (2017). Assumptions of decision making capacity. In A.E. Arstein-Kerslake (ed.), *Disability Human Rights Law*. Basel: MDPI.

Watson, J. and Joseph, R. (2015). *People With Severe to Profound Intellectual Disabilities Leading Lives They Prefer Through Supported Decision Making: Listening to those Rarely Heard. A Guide for Supporters*. Melbourne: Scope Australia.

Watson, J., Wilson, E. and Hagiliassis, N. (2017). Supporting end of life decision making: Case studies of relational closeness in supported decision making for people with severe or profound intellectual disability. *Journal of Applied Research in Intellectual Disability*, **30**(6), 1022–34.

White, A.M., Philogene, G.S., Fine, L. and Sinha, S. (2009). Social support and self-reported health status of older adults in the United States. *American Journal of Public Health*, **99**(10), 1872–78.

World Bank (2015). *World Development Report 2015: Mind, Society, and Behavior*. Washington, DC: World Bank.

World Health Organisation (WHO) (2004). *The World Health Report 2004: Changing History*. Geneva: World Health Organisation.

World Health Organization (WHO) (2007). *Global Age-Friendly Cities: A Guide*. Geneva: World Health Organisation.

PART II

Realities and legal experiences

4. Legal basis of active ageing: European developments

Barbara Mikołajczyk

INTRODUCTION

By 2025 more than 20 per cent of Europeans will be 65 or over, with a particularly rapid increase in the numbers of over-80s. Currently in EU countries there are 36 people over the age of 60 for every 100 persons. In 2025 this number will rise to 56. Simultaneously, old-age dependency ratios are changing extremely quickly (World Health Organization, 2002; 2015; ALCOVE, 2013; European Commission, 2015; OECD, 2016). This demographic situation demands the need to adopt new solutions, both factual and legal, drawing upon the conviction that not only do older generations not constitute a burden, but rather that they can also significantly contribute to society. This depends not least on creating conditions conducive to helping older persons remain active, independent and in good health for as long as possible. Active ageing allows people to use the potential they have and participate in many spheres of social, political and economic life (Zrałek, 2014; Adamczyk, 2015).

The degree of activity in older age in the European Union (EU) States is measured by the Active Ageing Index (AAI) in four domains: employment, participation in society, independent living, and the ability to age actively. Each domain reflects a different aspect of active ageing, and takes into account differences in active ageing for men and women. This tool, created in 2012 by the United Nations Economic Commission for Europe (UNECE) and the European Commission, is used by policy-makers and stakeholders to identify challenges and opportunities and to set targets for improvement, based on international comparisons (UNECE/European Commission, 2015: 44). The AAI shows that European citizens are not particularly active in later life and that there are significant differences among States. Therefore, the European Union and the Council of Europe as two integrational organizations have a wide scope to target this issue.

However, the AAI does not provide a complete picture of the ageing population in Europe; for example it does not contain indicators on age discrimination, intergenerational relationships, acceptance of new technologies, purchasing power of older adults and so on (Klimczuk, 2016). The AAI is criticized for neglecting the differences in individual capacities, resources and preferences, as well as the cultural diversity that exists in the EU (De São José et al., 2017). That is why the European community gathered in these two organizations must be sensitive to many other aspects of ageing such as, for example, the phenomenon of ageism.

Not only is the AAI criticized. The concept and meaning of "active ageing" as such are the subject of fierce debate, mainly among gerontologists (Boudiny and Mortelmans, 2011; Boudiny, 2013; Zaidi and Howse, 2017). It is argued, among other things, that the concept of active ageing devalues older persons' life experiences and it does not take into account their vulnerability as well as specific needs (Biggs, 2004; Calasanti, 2003; Holstein and Minkler, 2003; Minkler and Holstein, 2008; Moody, 2001; Ranzijn, 2010). Moreover, the active ageing policy of States, forcing older citizens to stay in the labour market who at the same time look after other old people and children, only seems to present a solution to social problems (Timonen, 2016).

However, this relatively new issue in international law is not contested. It may arise from the fact that the international instruments take into account various "aspects of being old" to the same degree and old persons' productivity is not the main focus. Second, international law relies on inter-state consensus, which imposes the development of a reasonable and widely acceptable compromise in this area.

As a result of such a compromise, we can identify determinants of active ageing in the *acquis* of the international community achieved at a global forum, namely in the United Nations (UN) Principles for Older Persons of 1991 (United Nations General Assembly, 1991) in the sphere of independence, participation, self-fulfillment, care, and dignity of older persons as well as in the Madrid Political Declaration and the Madrid International Plan of Action on Ageing (MIPAA) adopted in 2002 (United Nations, 2002).

Pursuant to the UN Principles, the independence of this social category should be comprised of a whole social "package", whose fundamental part is addressing basic human needs. Furthermore, older persons should have the opportunity to undertake work or have access to other income-generating opportunities, and should be able to determine when they want to withdraw from the labour market. Old age should not be an obstacle to education and participation in various forms of training programs. They should for as long as possible be able to reside in their own homes and enjoy living in a safe environment that is adaptable to their changing capacities.

As far as participation is concerned, the Principles indicate that older persons should remain integrated in society, joining or creating associations and participating actively in the formulation and implementation of policies referring to them. In the area of self-fulfillment, older persons should be able to pursue opportunities for the full development of their potential through having access to the educational, cultural, spiritual and recreational resources of society.

In 2002 the UN States gathered in Madrid reaffirmed in Article 5 of their Political Declaration the older persons' right to development and recognized that "persons, as they age, should enjoy a life of fulfillment, health, security and active participation in the economic, social, cultural and political life of their societies". Following the Political Declaration, the Madrid Plan of Action for Ageing contains numerous goals and recommendations on independence. They concern human life, including health promotion, financial/income security and living conditions as well as mobility. Special emphasis has been placed in the Plan on measures geared to the eradication of poverty and the creation of an age-friendly environment.

Neither the Principles nor the extensive Madrid output are legally binding documents and all of their objectives and recommendations merely serve as guidelines for States and other actors, including governmental and non-governmental organizations. Nevertheless, the Principles and the Madrid documents create international standards, including in the field of active ageing.

It can be assumed that all of the components of active ageing referred to in the Principles and Madrid documents have been included in the synthetic definitions authored by such international institutions as the World Health Organization (WHO) and the United Nations Economic Commission for Europe (UNECE). Thus, the WHO defines active ageing as "the process of optimizing opportunities for health, participation and security in order to enhance quality of life as people age" (World Health Organization, 2002: 12). Similarly, the UNECE and the European Commission in the Active Ageing Index have postulated that "[a]ctive ageing means growing older in good health and as a full member of society, feeling more fulfilled in our jobs and social engagements, more independent in our daily lives and more engaged as citizens" (UNECE/ European Commission, 2015: 4). This definition, which associates active ageing with full membership in society, will be the starting point for further reflection. Accordingly, legal and policy instruments adopted by the Council of Europe and the European Union will be examined from two different perspectives: (1) the promotion of independence and autonomy; and (2) promoting participation in economic, political, social and cultural life.

THREE PILLARS OF ACTIVE AGEING

Before reflecting on the approach of European organizations towards active ageing, we must assume that promotion and realization of active ageing are only possible if measures undertaken by these organizations are based on three strong pillars: (1) effective legal instruments preventing age discrimination; (2) awareness of threats posed by ageism; (3) adoption of legal and factual solutions based on the idea of inter-generational solidarity. The existence of instruments, including legal ones, intended to prevent age discrimination, fight stereotypes, combat prejudice against older persons, and promote intergenerational solidarity are *sine qua non* conditions for active ageing.

However, it is worth stressing that the position of the prohibition of age discrimination is not particularly strong at the European forum. This holds true with respect to age discrimination in employment as well (Numhauser-Henning and Rönnmar, 2015; Numhauser-Henning, Chapter 5, this volume). Likewise, the concept of ageism does not appear in European hard law at all (Mikołajczyk, 2015).

The 1950 Convention for the Protection of Human Rights and Funda-mental Freedoms (ECHR) does not contain any references to the rights of older persons or even to age discrimination (Council of Europe, 1950). Article 14 of the ECHR and Protocol No. 12 to the Convention (Council of Europe, 2000) prohibiting discrimination in all spheres of life do not list the premise of age among the reasons for non-discrimination. Following the example of the ECHR, neither of the European Social Charters prohibits age discrimination (Council of Europe 1961; 1996). In consequence, although a significant number of authors of complaints to the European Court of Human Rights (ECtHR) are people over 60, the problem of age and age discrimination is invoked relatively seldom before the Court. The notion of ageism does not appear at all. If the ECtHR refers to the question of age, it usually combines this circum-stance with an applicant's state of health and conditions of detention, procedural safeguards or gender discrimination (De Pauw, 2014; Spanier et al., 2013; Mikołajczyk, 2013; Martin et al., 2015). A distinct example of such an approach is the recent judgment of the ECtHR in *Carvalho Pinto de Sousa Morais v. Portugal* (EctHR, 2017), where the premise of age gave way to the premise of gender, although the applicant regarded both premises equally (Mantovani et al., Chapter 6, this volume).

This is not to say, however, that the notion of ageism is unknown to the Council of Europe. It is in fact defined in the Council of Europe Parliamentary Assembly's (2011) Resolution 1793 entitled "Promoting active ageing – capitalizing on older people's working potential". There, ageism is labelled as

> a harmful prejudice that results in widespread lack of respect for older people, whether through the media, which promote stereotypical and degrading images of older people, within society, where they are the victims of physical and financial abuse, in the workplace, where they are subject to unequal treatment, or in the health sector where they do not always receive appropriate medical care and services. (Council of Europe Parliamentary Assembly, 2011).

Similarly, in the Parliamentary Assembly Resolution 1958 (Council of Europe Parliamentary Assembly, 2013) "Combating discrimination against older persons on the labour market", the Assembly states that age discrimination goes hand in hand with ageism and stresses that it is vital to strive to change mentalities in order to eliminate stereotypes as well as build a positive and true image of workers in each age. Therefore, the Assembly invited the Council of Europe member States to, among other things, support information campaigns aimed at changing mentalities regarding ageing, raise public awareness of the substantial experience of older workers, and encourage mentoring programs to facilitate an inter-generational dialogue (Council of Europe Parliamentary Assembly, 2013).

While ageism is entirely absent in the primary law of the European Union, the Treaty on the Functioning of the European Union (TFEU) (European Union, 2007) and the Charter of Fundamental Rights (European Union, 2000) placed age in their anti-discrimination clauses, in Article 19 of the TFEU and Article 21 of the Charter. In the secondary EU law, a ban on age discrimination was introduced through the Council's Directive 2000/78/EC (Council of the European Union, 2000). It establishes a general framework for equal treatment only in employment and occupation, and allows States to introduce exceptions required by the labour market. Given that the extent of the Directive's impact is limited to employment relationships, since 2008 the EU has endeavoured to draw up a so-called "horizontal directive" implementing the principle of equal treatment between persons, irrespective of religion or belief, disability, age or sexual orientation and applying to everybody in the private or public sectors and covering social protection, social security, health care, education, as well as access to and the supply of goods and services, such as housing and transport. Unfortunately, the negotiations have come to a standstill (AGE Platform Europe, 2015).

The situation is different with the third pillar that active ageing should be based on, namely intergenerational solidarity. The notion is described as a desirable value and/or relationship when generations have a positive view of one another and when they understand each other and when there are also mechanisms supporting mutually beneficial exchanges, both monetary and non-monetary, between generations (OECD, 2011). It must be emphasized that the concept of solidarity is incorporated into the essence of the European Union. The European Union Treaty in its Article 3 [3] states that the Union "shall combat social exclusion and discrimination, and shall promote social justice and protection, equality between women and men, solidarity between generations and protection of the rights of the child". Moreover, the preamble of the Charter of Fundamental Rights of the European Union states that "[T]he Union is founded on the indivisible, universal values of human dignity, freedom, equality and solidarity." It is indisputable that the notion of solidarity, as indicated in the Charter, also encompasses intergenerational solidarity.

Justice together with solidarity between the generations as fundamental values of European cooperation appear in various documents adopted by the European Parliament (European Parliament, 2006) and in the Commission's green papers and communications (Commission of the European Union, 2005; 2007). However, the crucial decision of the European Parliament and the Council of the European Union declaring 2012 the "European Year for Active Ageing and Solidarity between Generations" (European Parliament and Council, 2011), established the objectives, measures, and the budget for this initiative. The objectives include, *inter alia*, highlighting the value of active ageing, and organization of debates and exchanges of information as well as mutual learning on how to promote active ageing policies, share good practices, and cooperate in the future (Tymowski, 2015).

A similar approach is presented at the Council of Europe's forum, for example in the New Strategy and Council of Europe Action Plan for Social Cohesion of 2010 (Council of Europe Committee of Ministers, 2010). Some duties of local authorities in the sphere of intergenerational solidarity were set forth in Recommendation 228 (2007) on intergenerational cooperation and participatory democracy, issued by the Congress of Local and Regional Authorities. This Recommendation is accompanied by a Manifesto aimed at combating the exclusion and marginalization of any section of the population and at promoting understanding and reconciliation between the generations (Council of Europe Congress of Local and Regional Authorities, 2007).

Promotion of intergenerational solidarity, prevention of discrimination and awareness of threats posed by ageism constitute a foundation on which active ageing can be built. It is only after favourable legal, social and spatial conditions are provided, combined with an approach free from prejudice, stereotypes and the like, that older persons will be able to enjoy independent living, real participation in the life of society and self-fulfillment.

ESSENCE OF ACTIVE AGEING

Independence and Autonomy

As observed by Robert Butler, one of the main losses that come with ageing is the loss of opportunities for choice (Butler, 1969). Older people are frequently deprived of the possibility of making their own choices and of deciding for themselves in many aspects of life, including making decisions on where to live. The liberty to make one's own independent decisions is the first step towards full participation in society.

What corroborates the assertion that independence goes hand in hand with participation is the wording of Article 25 of the EU Charter of Fundamental Rights, which stipulates that "The Union recognizes and respects the rights of the elderly to lead a life of dignity and independence and to participate in social and cultural life." That said, it must be added that Article 25 does not belong to "strong" provisions, such as provisions that ensure equality between men and women (Article 23) or that protect the rights of the child (Article 24). The weakness of the solution as to respect for independence and participation of older persons can be exemplified by the rejection by the European Commission as manifestly outside the framework of its powers of the European citizens' initiative entitled "Right to Lifelong Care: Leading a life of dignity and independence is a fundamental right!" The initiative was to invite the EU to propose legislation that ensures, among other things, that all citizens, especially older people, enjoy the right to dignity throughout their lives by providing social protection against dependency. The Court of Justice of the European Union (CJEU) shared the Commission's opinion on 19 April 2016 in the *Bruno Costantini* judgment (CJEU, 2016).

In light of the above, it is rather unlikely that any "hard steps", such as adoption of regulations or directives, will be taken by the EU in the area discussed here. However, all aspects related to independence, both physical and financial, have been included in the Guiding Principles for Active Ageing and Solidarity between Generations, which the Council of the European Union annexed to the Council's Declaration on the European Year for Active Ageing and Solidarity between Generations (2012): The Way Forward (Council of the European Union, 2012). The Principles act as a kind of checklist for national authorities and other stakeholders on what needs to be done to promote active ageing. In the area of independent living, the Council called on them to take measures to increase the years of healthy life and reduce the risk of dependency through implementation of health promotion and disease prevention. According to the Principles, health promotion should also cover providing opportunities for physical and mental activity adapted to the capacities of older people. Other postulates refer to the adaptation of housing and services which can allow older persons to live with the highest possible degree of autonomy. The Principles also indicate the need to adapt transport systems to make them accessible, affordable, safe and secure for older people, allowing them to remain autonomous and participate actively in society. Furthermore, they call on the authorities of Member States and other stakeholders (for example local self-governments) to implement the design-for-all approach and to arrange adaptation of local environments as well as goods and services to make them suitable for people of all ages, and also through the use of information technologies (IT), including eHealth. There is no doubt that IT plays a crucial role in fostering active ageing. It can prevent decline, compensate for lost capabilities, support care and enhance existing capabilities (Parra et al., 2013). The role of access to the Internet as well as the ability to enjoy it are emphasized. It is argued that for older people, the Internet gives opportunities for active ageing, optimizes the quality of their life in various aspects, increases communication, and helps to avoid isolation and loneliness (Llorente-Barroso et al., 2015: 34; Casado-Muñoz et al., 2015: 37).

New technologies and digital literacy are given particular prominence in the work of the EU for older people. It goes without saying that, in the contemporary world, digital literacy and inclusion of older people in the information society allow them to have a better quality of life and lead to an independent and fuller, as well as a more participatory life (Abad, 2014). Unfortunately in the area of innovation, European older people lag behind their peers in the USA, Japan and Singapore (Renda, 2016). Therefore, the EU undertakes or finances various initiatives in this respect, for example, information and communication technology for the ageing population is encompassed by the Digital Agenda for Europe

(European Commission, 2010b), and the European Innovation Partnership on Active and Healthy Ageing aims at doubling the average number of healthy years of life by 2020.

In this context, it is worth highlighting the proposal for a directive from the European Parliament and the Council on the accessibility of public sector bodies' websites (European Parliament, 2014). The future directive would set forth the first EU-wide requirements for websites and mobile apps of public sector bodies to make them more accessible for the blind, the deaf and the hearing impaired. However, it must be remembered that in their daily lives, older persons have problems with access to much less advanced products and services, such as household, travel, life and vehicle insurance, as well as borrowing and credits or other banking products.

That said, the most common and fundamental problem is that of spatial barriers. Given that older people are often persons with disabilities, it is important that the European Union is a party to the UN Convention on the Rights of Persons with Disabilities (United Nations, 2006) and has thus committed to adopting measures that are in line with the underlying principles of this treaty. In order to monitor and promote the Convention, the EU has launched the Framework for the UN Convention on the Rights of Persons with Disabilities, which covers areas such as non-discrimination, passenger rights, and access to documents (European Commission, 2012).

The EU has also adopted "The European Disability Strategy 2010–2020: A Renewed Commitment to a Barrier-Free Europe" (European Commission, 2010c). In the strategy, the Commission recognized accessibility as a precondition for participation in society and in the economy, but it also indicated that over a third of people aged over 75 have disabilities restricting them to some extent, and over 20 per cent are considerably restricted. Therefore, the Commission decided to take its own initiatives (using legislative and other instruments) and to support Member States as well as other stakeholders in optimizing accessibility of the built environment, transport, ICT, education, products, services and so on. It will also foster an EU-wide market for assistive technology.

Whereas it is without question that autonomy and accessibility are important components of independence, they cannot be utilized if a given person is not financially independent, that is to say, if they have no income-earning opportunities, or if their pension is insufficient to cover their needs. Pension systems undeniably play a principal role in maintaining the living standards of older people. However, the pension does not always ensure a standard of living comparable to that achieved by a retiree during his/her working life. The newly-retired face a drop in their standard of living and/or severe material deprivation. There is no doubt that lack of financial means directly leads to social exclusion. Moreover, as a general rule, in almost all Member States, single older women bear a much higher risk of poverty compared to single older men, and the risk of poverty is especially high in the 75+ age group (Directorate-General for Employment, Social Affairs and Inclusion & Social Protection Committee, 2012).

Furthermore, the EU has adopted the European Platform against Poverty and Social Exclusion, created as one of the flagship initiatives of the Europe 2020 Strategy for Smart, Sustainable and Inclusive Growth (European Commission, 2010a). One of the key factors that led to the elaboration of the strategy was the ageing of the European population. Indeed, the strategy observed that due to demographic changes, the European workforce is about to shrink and the employment rates of women and older workers are particularly low.

Despite the above, it turns out that work for people who have reached pensionable age is a considerable problem. Reaching pensionable age, which is laid down either in labour codes or in collective agreements, frequently entails forced retirement although it has long been commented that forcing an employee into retirement in spite of their physical and intellectual capacities constitutes a violation of human dignity (McDougal et al., 1976).

Summing up the European Union's approach to the issue of the independence of older persons, it must be emphasized that it is not the EU itself, but rather its respective Member States that are responsible for such matters as employment, social protection, and social inclusion policies. Even so, as observed above, the EU makes an important contribution by supporting States in these areas. This process is known as the Open Method of Coordination (OMC) on social protection and social inclusion, including pensions, healthcare and long-term care. It provides Member States with programmes, strategies, monitoring, a framework for reporting, and benchmarking to compare performance and identify best practice.

The Council of Europe operates in a different way and uses different instruments. The most important treaty adopted by the Council of Europe, namely the ECHR, protects the independence of older persons in a limited way; however, this is not to say that cases pertaining (at least indirectly) to independence and the freedom to make decisions do not appear before the ECtHR. For example, in relation to autonomy, the Court considered cases *H.M. v. Switzerland* (ECtHR, 2002c) and *Watts v. United Kingdom* (ECtHR, 2010b) referring to placement in or transfer to nursing homes. The issue of independence in the context of the legal capacity of individuals was considered in the case *X and Y v. Croatia*. In this case, the Court found a violation of Article 6 (the right to a fair trial) in relation to an applicant born in 1923, bedridden and suspected to be suffering from dementia (ECtHR, 2011b). According to the Court, the same provision was violated in the case *Dewicka v. Poland*. This case referred to the everyday independence of an 89-year-old applicant being exposed to the excessive length of proceedings in relation to the refusal to install a telephone line (ECtHR, 1997).

Financial independence, whose core elements include possessions and enjoyment of one's possessions, is protected by Article 1 of the First Protocol to the ECHR (Council of Europe, 1952). Claims lodged with the ECtHR in this respect predominantly concern reductions in pensions in times of economic crisis, for example in the cases *Klaus and Iouri Kiladze v. Georgia* (ECtHR, 2010a), *Da Conceição Mateus v. Portugal and Santos Januário v. Portugal* (ECtHR, 2013), and *Mauriello v. Italy* (ECtHR, 2016). It is worth mentioning that only in the case *Klaus and Iouri Kiladze*, did the ECtHR decided there was a violation of Article 1 of the Protocol.

The economic situation of claimants was also considered in the cases *Larioshina v. Russia* (ECtHR, 2002a) and *Budina v. Russia* (ECtHR, 2009). Applicants unsuccessfully invoked insufficiency of old-age pensions to maintain an adequate standard of living which is a violation of the prohibition of torture and inhuman or degrading punishment or treatment contained in Article 3 of the Convention.

Finally, there were complaints in the cases of *Stummer v. Austria* (ECtHR, 2011a) and *Meier v. Switzerland* (ECtHR, 2002b) submitted by working prisoners excluded from affiliation to the old-age pension, referring to financial independence in old age. The ECtHR did not find a violation of Art. 4 (prohibition of slavery and forced labour) in these cases.

The cases mentioned above are just a few examples of the "independence issues" considered by the ECtHR. Most of them were recognized as manifestly unfounded or the Court did not find a violation of the conventional provisions. However, all of them show that some aspects of older persons' independence and autonomy are or may be potentially covered by the ECHR's provisions.

Notwithstanding, the protection of social independence is predominantly the domain of the Council of Europe's social law which encompasses the European Social Charter of 1961 and its Additional Protocols of 1988, 1991 and 1995 (Council of Europe, 1988, 1991, 1995) and the revised European Social Charter – RESC (Council of Europe, 1996). Furthermore, the Council of Europe has adopted a significant number of agreements concerning social security, including the European Code of Social Security (Council of Europe, 1964). However, the primary treaty that can have a positive impact on the independence of older persons is definitely the revised European Social Charter. Its Article 23 refers directly to the independence of older persons. Pursuant to this provision, parties are obliged to ensure the effective exercize of this right by the adoption of appropriate measures aimed in general at enabling older persons to remain full members of society for as long as possible. That is why States should take several steps listed in this provision allowing older persons to have adequate resources to lead a decent life and play an active part in public, social and cultural life as well as to choose their lifestyle freely and to lead independent lives in familiar surroundings.

Analyzing the issue of older persons' independence, other provisions of the Charter should also be borne in mind, especially Art. 30 RESC, concerning the right to protection against poverty and social exclusion and Article 31 devoted to the right to housing. It compels States to promote access to housing of an adequate standard, prevent and reduce homelessness with a view to its gradual elimination, and make the price of housing accessible to those who do not have adequate resources.

Unfortunately, pursuant to Article A of the third part of the Charter, State parties are not obliged to undertake obligations arising from those provisions which are of key importance for older citizens. Instead, States can select a specific number of articles and consider themselves bound by their respective provisions. As it turns out, Article 23 and other provisions mentioned are not "popular" in this respect among the Member States of the Council of Europe. However, "independence situations" of older people are considered by the European Committee of Social Rights when monitoring the realization by States of their obligations arising from both Charters (Spanier and Doron, Chapter 7, this volume).

Moreover, situations going beyond States' treaty obligations are very often covered by soft law adopted by international organizations to fill in this loophole. The issue of independence was first addressed by the Council of Europe in the mid-1990s, for example in the Committee of Ministers' Recommendation (94) 14 on coherent and integrated family policies. Its passage no. 10 contains a principle stipulating that "In order for older family members to enjoy a dignified and secure old age, it is particularly necessary to respect their capacity to stay independent, to continue to take their own decisions and to remain a part of the community" (Council of Europe Committee of Ministers, 1994).

Financial independence is the subject of the Parliamentary Assembly Resolution 1752 (2010) with Recommendation 1932 (2010) on decent pensions for women (Council of Europe Parliamentary Assembly, 2010) as well as Resolution 1882 (2012) on decent pensions for all (Council of Europe Parliamentary Assembly, 2012).

Recommendation (2014) 2, adopted by the Committee of Ministers on 19 February 2014, on the promotion of human rights of older persons (Committee of Ministers, 2014) in the field of independence, recommends that Member States take measures allowing older persons to live their lives independently, in a self-determined and autonomous manner. This means the right of an older person to take independent decisions with regard to all issues which may concern him or her, for example, property, income, finances, place of residence, health, medical treatment or care, as well as funeral arrangements. Each person should be treated individually and his or her specific situation ought to be taken into account if any limitations should be implemented. Whenever this is the case, such measures should be proportionate and provided with effective safeguards to prevent abuse and discrimination. Moreover, if necessary, older persons ought to receive appropriate support in taking their decisions. Such support or assistance should be provided in conformity with the will and preferences of a given person.

The Recommendation does not have the value of a treaty, but on the other hand, it may be assumed that it is part of a new generation of soft law acts, as it contains guidelines and good practices and significantly, despite its non-binding nature, it is equipped with a type of follow-up mechanism (verification of its implementation by the Committee of Ministers of the Council of Europe). Thus, despite its non-binding force, it has a quite strong enforcement mechanism.

Participation and Self-fulfillment

Old persons' presence in the labour market may be considered not only as an element of independence and autonomy, but also as a form of self-fulfillment and participation in the life of society. However, European States apparently find it difficult to strike a happy medium between balancing the interests of employers, older employees and young people only just entering the labour market. They ought to be interested in their citizens being professionally active for as long as possible, as this is the best protection against poverty. Nevertheless, in comparison to the USA and Japan, where over 62 per cent of persons aged 55–64 are active on the labour market, in the European Union the corresponding figure is 46 per cent. Simultaneously, forced retirement, age discrimination and ageism are a common practice and a significant legal problem (Schlachter, 2011; Numhauser-Henning and Rönnmar, 2015; Numhauser-Henning, Chapter 5, this volume).

Moreover, it is often the case that reluctance to hire older persons, restricting their access to promotion and preventing their development is a result not only of outdated systemic solutions, but also of stereotypes suggesting that older workers are less motivated in learning new skills, less physically active and mentally prepared, and have a low level of qualifications (Radović-Marković, 2013).

However, European treaties and soft law documents issued by organs of both organizations give a clear response to such ageist attitudes and to States' dilemmas in this sphere. Both Article 15 of the EU Charter on Fundamental Rights and Article 1 of the first part of the revised European Social Charter adopted proclaim the freedom to choose an occupation and the right to engage in work. Article 1 of the revised Charter states that: "Everyone shall have the opportunity to earn his living in an occupation freely entered upon." It is obvious that this right is not subject to restrictions related to age or other circumstances.

The documents which most explicitly draw attention to the unequal treatment of older employees are two Resolutions of the Parliamentary Assembly: Resolution 1793 (2011), entitled "Promoting active ageing – capitalizing on older people's working potential" and Resolution 1958 (2013), "Combating discrimination against older persons on the labour market." They actually invite the Member States to take relevant measures allowing older workers to remain competent and valuable employees. In order to achieve this, access to training could be developed with a view to facilitating re-entry to the labour market (in the case of unemployment) or simply updating knowledge, perfecting skills and helping to adapt to new technologies and technological developments, and so on. The first Resolution also stresses that the higher the number of older employees who are willing to work and are capable of working, the more financial resources governments will be able to assign to improving the quality of life of the unemployed or "inactive" persons, in particular in the 50+ age group (Council of Europe Parliamentary Assembly, 2011).

Similarly, the Recommendation of the Committee of Ministers of the Council of Europe of 2014 on the promotion of human rights of older persons calls on Member States to ensure that older persons do not face discrimination in access to employment (including recruitment conditions), vocational initial and continuous training, working conditions (including dismissal and remuneration), membership of trade unions or retirement, and puts an obligation on States to include older persons' participation in the labour market in their employment policies.

Other determinants of active ageing are participation in the economic, political and cultural life of the community that a given person lives in, and opportunities for self-fulfillment in various areas of life. In regard to political life, it must be said that demographic changes taking place mean that the so-called silver electorate is becoming stronger and stronger. However, a great diversity of organizations, parties, movements, clubs and informal circles gathering older people are rarely interested in taking over political power. Their main aim is to improve their social position and defend their social and economic rights as well as to participate in decision-making processes referring to their daily life (Riekkinen, 2011; Binstock, 2000). The participation in social, economic and cultural life is determined by the possibility of exercising the right of association, freedom of speech and expression, access to the media, education, culture, recreation and so on. It should be remembered that civil and political rights are void if they are not completed by social and cultural rights (Mikołajczyk, 2012).

As far as the protection of political rights in Europe is concerned, provisions protecting electoral rights undoubtedly occupy a central place, although it must be added that Article 3 of the First Protocol to the ECHR has been worded in a specific way. Namely, in said Article 3 of the Protocol, the State-Parties have merely undertaken to hold free elections at reasonable intervals by secret ballot, under conditions which ensure the free expression of the opinion of the people in the choice of the legislature, which is not to say, of course, that a subjective right cannot be derived from this provision (Garlicki, 2010). Other rights which safeguard possibilities for active participation in public and social life laid down in the ECHR are stipulated in Article 10 (freedom of expression, including freedom to hold opinions and to receive and impart information and ideas), Article 9 (freedom of thought, conscience and religion), and Article 11 (freedom of assembly and information).

Interpretation of these provisions with reference to the situation of older persons requires resorting to soft law of the Council of Europe, and in particular to the Parliamentary Assembly's Recommendation 1428 (1999) "Future of senior citizens: protection, participation, promotion", (Council of Europe Parliamentary Assembly, 1999) and the newest Committee of Ministers' Recommendation of 2014. Unfortunately, these documents refer to political rights in very general terms. As a matter of fact, the only Recommendation of 2014 on the promotion of the human rights of older persons states that "older persons should have the possibility to interact with others and to fully participate in social, cultural and education and training activities, as well as in public life". It is also worth adding that the said Recommendation is provided by the British Equality Act of 2010, banning age discrimination in the provision of goods, facilities and services, the exercise of public functions and the running of public clubs and associations, as an example of good practice.

A key aspect of participation and self-fulfillment of older persons is respect for the broadly-defined right to education, as provided for by the First Protocol to the ECHR. It also encompasses supplementation of education at all levels, provision of access to vocational training, and the possibility to develop and participate in courses of various types, including those offered by the so-called Universities of the Third (Golden) Age. The entire network of Universities of the Third Age operating in Poland has been indicated in the compilation of good practice.

Lifelong learning constitutes the fulfillment of postulates put forward by the World Health Organization, which considers older persons' access to different forms of education and the educational process itself to be important factors facilitating participation in social life, which in turn positively influences the quality of life in its final stages (World Health Organization, 2002). Research has confirmed that lifelong learning contributes to good health and life satisfaction and thus to reducing costs related to the treatment of various physical and mental conditions (Boulton-Lewis, 2010). Moreover, education is without doubt a way of combating poverty (Dhillon, 2011).

Similar postulates with respect to political and social inclusion and self-fulfillment have been put forward in the above-mentioned European Union Guiding Principles for Active Ageing and Solidarity between Generations. As for social inclusion, these call for "fight[ing] social exclusion and isolation of older people by offering them equal opportunities to participate in society through cultural, political and social activities" and highlight the importance of senior volunteering and lifelong learning.

Yet another essential element of participation and self-fulfillment is the participation of older persons in a broadly-defined cultural life, understood as access to cultural assets. This encompasses not just culture in the traditional meaning of the term (concerts, performances, publications, and so on) but also *digital culture*, which covers both virtual museums and, for example, access to YouTube (Shaver and Sganga, 2009).

Contrary to the universal system, the ECHR and the European Social Charters and even the European Cultural Convention (Council of Europe, 1953) do not include any provisions on cultural rights either. They must be extracted from the aforesaid freedoms of: expression, thought, religion, association, and also with the right to education, as safeguarded by the Convention. A scarcity of cultural rights protected directly in the most important conventions of the Council of Europe has led to cultural rights being referred to as the "Cinderella" of human rights (McGoldrick, 2007). This is not to say, however, that these rights are entirely absent at the Council of Europe forum. Cultural rights are predominantly the domain of the soft law of the Council of Europe (Laaksonen, 2010). That said, analysis of the soft law of the Council of Europe concerning older persons reveals that even the Recommendation of the Committee of Ministers of 2014 on the promotion of human rights of older persons treats participation of older persons in cultural life in very general terms.

The problem of the scarcity of cultural rights in relation to older citizens also appears at the European Union forum. Even in the framework of the OMC, it is still easy to notice that leading documents such as the European Agenda for Culture (Council of the European Union, 2007) and the Conclusions of the Council and of the Representatives of the Governments of the Member States on a Work Plan for Culture (2015–2018) (Council of the European Union, 2014) do not mention older persons' inclusion in cultural initiatives. Such a situation constitutes a significant flaw in the promotion of active ageing. After all, in daily life, access to culture, especially popular culture, is much more important for older persons than, say, participation in political debates or elections, which are held every few years.

CONCLUSION

The Council of Europe and the European Union, in accordance with their competences laid down in the respective founding treaty, undertake different measures in regard to the promotion of active ageing. Comparing both organizations, it may be stated that the European Union through the Open Method of Coordination has worked out measures of a more practical character, whereas the Council of Europe does it predominantly through resolutions and recommendations belonging to soft law. In fact, we can currently observe the growing effectiveness of documents classified as soft law. If they are equipped with monitoring mechanisms, as Recommendation 2014 (2) is, and are used in grounds for judgments of international courts, their relevance increases significantly (Spanier et al., 2016). That is why, it may be assumed, there is great potential in the soft law of the Council of Europe referring to older persons' well-being.

Soft law documents as well as various programs, platforms and strategies play a major role when hard law contains no explicit provisions on older adults and discrimination against this category of persons. They positively affect the awareness of European governments and societies in the field discussed.

It should be stressed that regardless of the methods and possibilities of each organization, their activities on promoting the concept of active ageing do not ignore the problem of the vulnerability of older persons. Such an approach allows for avoiding contestation of this concept on the grounds of international and European laws. Moreover, an analysis of all the efforts and documents adopted undoubtedly demonstrates that active ageing has not only economic, sociological, psychological and other dimensions but is first and foremost a human rights issue.

On the other hand, it may also be concluded that although significant progress has been made in this respect, there is still a lot of work to do in this area. It is noticeable that the activity of both organizations concerning ageing and older persons' rights intensified significantly in the period 2011–14. Since then there has been a certain stagnation in the promotion of active ageing. For instance, in the Proposal for a Council Decision establishing a Multiannual Framework for the European Union Agency for Fundamental Rights for 2018–2022 of July 2016 (European Commission, 2016), active ageing and older persons' issues are not on the list of issues to be tackled by the Agency in the next few years. Therefore there is real need for a new impulse for acting. Such a stimulus may come from the UN and its Open-Ended Working Group on Ageing that is currently the main forum in which the debate for a new international binding instrument on the rights of older persons is taking place (De Pauw et al., Chapter 8, this volume).

Moreover, evaluating the existing output of both European forums, first it must be stressed that the very foundations of active ageing are still inadequate in that there is no satisfactory protection against age discrimination and there is still not enough awareness of ageism. Second, the huge number of documents dedicated to various issues, only some of which were mentioned in this chapter, makes one suspect that Europe has not worked out a single consolidated strategy for older persons. On the other hand, all these documents seem to be selective in nature, as they fail to address important aspects of the lives of older persons (for example, access to culture).

Therefore, there is a need to work on the consolidated European strategy similar to the Madrid Plan of Action, or the solutions adopted with regard to disabled persons, which would encourage States to adopt an active ageing approach in their internal policies. The overall objective is for active ageing not to become an empty concept or a "theatrical metaphor" (Moulaert and Paris, 2013), used in future Years for Active Ageing and Intergenerational Solidarity.

REFERENCES

Abad, L. (2014). Media literacy for older people facing the digital divide: The e-inclusion programmes design, *Media Education Research Journal, Comunicar*, **XXI** (42): 173–80.

Adamczyk, M.D. (2015). *Aktywnie ku Emeryturze* [Actively towards Retirement], Lublin: TWWP Oddz.

Age Platform (2015). Press release: Equal treatment law should not leave older people behind! Brussels, 17 June. Accessed at http://www.age-platform.eu/age-communication-to-the-media-press-releases-en-gb-6/2705-equal-treatment-law-should-not-leave-older-people-behind.

ALCOVE (2013). *Epidemiological Data on Dementia*. Accessed at http://www.alcove-project.eu/images/synthesis-report/ALCOVE_SYNTHESIS_REPORT_WP4.pdf.

Biggs, S. (2004). New ageism: Age imperialism, personal experience and ageing policy. In S.O. Daatland and S. Biggs (eds), *Ageing and Diversity*. Bristol: Policy Press, pp. 95–106.

Binstock, R.H. (2000). Older people and voting participation: Past and future international legal obligations. *The Gerontologist*, **40** (1): 18–31.

Boudiny, K. (2013). 'Active ageing': From empty rhetoric to effective policy tool. *Ageing & Society*, **33**: 1077–98.

Boudiny, K. and Mortelmans, D. (2011). A critical perspective: Towards a broader understanding of 'active ageing'. *Electronic Journal of Applied Psychology*, 7 (1): 8–14.

Boulton-Lewis, G.M. (2010). Education and learning for the elderly: Why, how, what. *Educational Gerontology*, **36** (3): 213–28.

Butler, R.N. (1969). Age-ism: Another form of bigotry. *The Gerontologist*, **9**: 243–6.

Calasanti, T. (2003). Theorizing age relations. In S. Biggs, A. Lowenstein and J. Hendricks (eds), *The Need For Theory: Critical Approaches to Social Gerontology*. Amityville, NY: Baywood, pp. 199–218.

Casado-Muñoz, R., Lezcano, F. and Rodríguez-Conde, M.J. (2015). Active ageing and access to technology: An evolving empirical study. *Media Education Research Journal*, **XXIII** (45): 37–46.

CJEU (2016). Judgment of the Court of the European Union 19 April 2016, *Bruno Costantini and Others v European Commission*, Case T-44/14, ECLI:EU:T:2016:223m http://curia.europa.eu/juris/liste.jsf?language=en&num=T-44/14.

Commission of the European Union (2005). *The Commission Green Paper on "Confronting demographic change: a new solidarity between the generations"* (COM(2005) 0094).

Commission of the European Union (2007). *The Commission Communication "Towards a Europe for all ages – promoting prosperity and intergenerational solidarity"*, OJ C 232, of 17 August 2001.

Council of Europe (1950). *Convention for the Protection of Human Rights and Fundamental Freedoms of 5 November 1950*. Council of Europe Treaty Series no. 005.

Council of Europe (1952). *Protocol to the Convention for the Protection of Human Rights and Fundamental Freedoms.* Council of Europe Treaty Series no. 9.

Council of Europe (1953). *European Cultural Convention.* Council of Europe Treaty Series no. 18.

Council of Europe (1961). *European Social Charter of 18 October 1961.* Council of Europe Treaty Series no. 035.

Council of Europe (1964). *European Code of Social Security.* Council of Europe Treaty Series no. 48.

Council of Europe (1988). *Additional Protocol to the European Social Charter.* Council of Europe Treaty Series no. 128.

Council of Europe (1991). *Protocol amending the European Social Charter.* Council of Europe Treaty Series no. 142.

Council of Europe (1995). *Additional Protocol to the European Social Charter Providing for a System of Collective Complaints.* Council of Europe Treaty Series no. 158.

Council of Europe (1996). *European Social Charter (revised) of 3 May 1996.* Council of Europe Treaty Series no. 163.

Council of Europe (2000). *Protocol No. 12 to the Convention for the Protection of Human Rights and Fundamental Freedoms of 4 November 2000.* Council of Europe Treaty Series no.177.

Council of Europe Committee of Ministers (1994). *Recommendation (94) 14 on Coherent and Integrated Family Policies.*

Council of Europe Committee of Ministers (2010). *New Strategy and Council of Europe Action Plan for Social Cohesion approved by the Committee of Ministers of the Council of Europe on 7 July 2010.*

Council of Europe Committee of Ministers Recommendation (2014). *CM/Rec(2014)2 to Member States on the Promotion of Human Rights of Older Persons of 19 February 2014.*

Council of Europe Congress of Local and Regional Authorities (2007). *Recommendation 209 (2007) Intergenerational Co-operation and Participatory Democracy.*

Council of Europe Parliamentary Assembly (1999). *Recommendation 1428 (1999) Future of Senior Citizens: Protection, Participation, Promotion.*

Council of Europe Parliamentary Assembly (2010). *Parliamentary Assembly Resolution 1752 (2010) and Recommendation 1932 (2010), Decent Pensions for Women.*

Council of Europe Parliamentary Assembly (2011). *Resolution 1793 (2011) Promoting Active Ageing – Capitalising on Older People's Working Potential.*

Council of Europe Parliamentary Assembly (2012). *Parliamentary Assembly Resolution 1882 (2012) Decent Pensions for All.*

Council of Europe Parliamentary Assembly (2013). *Resolution 1958 (2013) Combating Discrimination Against Older Persons on the Labour Market.*

Council of the European Union (2000). *Council Directive 2000/78/EC of 27 November 2000 Establishing a General Framework for Equal Treatment in Employment and Occupation. Official Journal L 303 of 2 December 2000.*

Council of the European Union (2007). *Resolution of the Council of 16 November 2007 on a European Agenda for Culture. Official Journal* C 287 of 29 November 2007.

Council of the European Union (2012). *Council Declaration on the European Year for Active Ageing and Solidarity between Generations (2012): The Way Forward in 2012.* Brussels, 7 December, no. 16592/12 SOC 948 SAN 289.

Council of the European Union (2014). *Conclusions of the Council and of the Representatives of the Governments of the Member States, meeting within the Council, on a Work Plan for Culture (2015–2018) Official Journal* C 463 of 23 December 2014.

De Pauw, M. (2014). Interpreting the European Convention on Human Rights in light of emerging human rights issues: An older person's perspective. *Human Rights and International Legal Discourse*, **1** (8): 235–57.

De São José, J.M., Timonen, V., Filipe Amado, C.A. and Pereira Santos, S. (2017). A Critique of the Active Ageing Index, *Journal of Aging Studies*, **40**: 49–56.

Dhillon, P. (2011). The role of education in freedom from poverty as a human right. &*Educational Philosophy Theory*, **43** (3): 249–59.

Directorate-General for Employment, Social Affairs and Inclusion & Social Protection Committee (2012). *Pension Adequacy in the European Union 2010–2050.* Report prepared jointly by the Directorate-General for Employment, Social Affairs and Inclusion of the European Commission and the Social Protection Committee. Luxembourg: Publications Office of the European Union.

ECtHR (1997). *Dewicka v. Poland.* Application no. 38670/97, judgment of 4 April 2000.

ECtHR (2002a). *Larioshina v. Russia.* Application no. 56869/00, decision on inadmissibility of 23 April 2002.

ECtHR (2002b). *Meier v. Switzerland.* Application no. 10109/14, judgment of 9 February 2016.

ECtHR (2002c). *H.M. v. Switzerland*, Application no. 39187/98, judgment of 26 February 2002.

ECtHR (2009). *Budina v. Russia.* Application no. 45603/05, decision on inadmissibility of 18 June 2009.

ECtHR (2010a). *Klaus and Iouri Kiladze v. Georgia.* Application no. 7975/06, judgment of 2 February 2010.

ECtHR (2010b). *Watts v. United Kingdom.* Application no. 53586/09, decision on inadmissibility of 4 May 2010.

ECtHR (2011a). *Stummer v. Austria.* Application no. 37452/02, judgment of 7 July 2011.

ECtHR (2011b). *X and Y v. Croatia.* Application no. 5193/09, judgment of 3 November 2011.

ECtHR (2013). *Da Conceição Mateus v. Portugal* and *Santos Januário v. Portugal.* Applications no. 62235/12 and no. 57725/12, decision on inadmissibility of 8 October 2013.

ECtHR (2016). *Mauriello v. Italy.* Application no. 14862/07, decision on inadmissibility of 13 October 2016.

ECtHR (2017). *Carvalho Pinto de Sousa Morais v. Portugal.* Application no. 17484/15, judgment of 25 July 2017.

European Commission (2016). *Proposal for a Council Decision establishing a Multiannual Framework for the European Union Agency for Fundamental Rights for 2018–2022 of July 2016.* COM(2016) 442 final.

European Commission (2010a). *Communication from the Commission to the European Parliament, the Council, the European Economic and Social Committee and the Committee of the Regions: European Disability Strategy 2010–2020: A strategy for smart, sustainable and inclusive growth.* COM(2010) 2020 final.

European Commission (2010b). *Communication from the Commission to the European Parliament, the Council, the European Economic and Social Committee and the Committee of the Regions: A Digital Agenda for Europe.* COM/2010/0245 f/2.

European Commission (2010c). *Communication from the Commission to the European Parliament, the Council, the European Economic and Social Committee and the Committee of the Regions: European Disability Strategy 2010–2020: A Renewed Commitment to a Barrier-Free Europe Brussels.* COM(2010) 636 final.

European Commission (2012). *Commission non Paper on the Setting-Up at EU Level of the Framework Required by Art. 33.2 of the UN Convention on the Rights of Persons with Disabilities.* Accessed at http://ec.europa.eu/social/main.jsp?catId=1189&langId=en.

European Commission (2015). *Public Health Ageing Policy.* Accessed at http://ec.europa.eu/health/ageing/policy/index_en.htm.

European Parliament (2006). *Resolution of 23 March 2006 on demographic challenges and solidarity between the generations. Official Journal* C 292 E, of 1 December 2006.

European Parliament (2014). *European Parliament legislative resolution of 26 February 2014 on the proposal for a directive of the European Parliament and of the Council on the accessibility of public sector bodies' websites* (COM(2012)0721 – C7-0394/2012 – 2012/0340(COD)). Accessed at http://www.europarl.europa.eu/sides/getDoc.do?pubRef=-//EP//TEXT+TA+P7-TA-2014-0158+0+DOC+XML+V0//EN.

European Parliament & Council (2011). *Decision No. 940/2011/EU of the European Parliament and of the Council of 14 September 2011 on the European Year for Active Ageing and Solidarity between Generations (2012). Official Journal* L 246/5 of 23 September 2011.

European Union (2000). *Charter of Fundamental Rights of the European Union of 7 December 2000 with amendments adopted on 12 December 2007. Official Journal of the European Union* C 326/ 391 of 26 October 2012.

European Union (2007). *Treaty on the Functioning of the European Union of 13 December 2007. The Consolidated version of the Treaty on the Functioning of the European Union. Official Journal* L 326/of 26 October 2012.

Garlicki, L. (2010). *Konwencja o Ochronie Praw Człowieka i Podstawowych Wolności. Komentarz.* Tom II. [Convention on the Protection of Human Rights and Fundamental Freedoms. Commentary, Vol. II]. Warsaw: C.H. Beck.

Holstein, M.B. and Minkler, M. (2003). Self, society and the 'new gerontology'. *The Gerontologist*, **43** (6): 787–96.

Klimczuk, A. (2016). Comparative analysis of national and regional models of the silver economy in the European Union. *International Journal of Ageing and Later Life*, **10** (2): 31–59.

Laaksonen, A. (2010). *Making Culture Accessible: Access, Participation and Cultural Provision in the Context of Cultural Rights in Europe*. Strasbourg: Council of Europe Publishing.

Llorente-Barroso, C., Viñarás-Abad, M. and Sánchez-Valle, M. (2015). Internet and the elderly: Enhancing active ageing. *Media Education Research Journal*, **XXIII** (45): 29–36. Accessed at http://eprints.rclis.org/25443/1/c4503en.pdf.

Martin, C., Rodríguez-Pinzón, D. and Brown, B. (2015). *Human Rights of Older People: Universal and Regional Legal Perspectives*. London, UK, Dordrecht, the Netherlands and New York, NY, USA: Springer.

McDougal, M.S., Lasswell, H.D. and Chen, L. (1976). The human rights of the aged: An application of the general norm of nondiscrimination. *University of Florida Law Review*, **XXVIII** (5): 639–54.

McGoldrick, D. (2007). Culture, cultures, and cultural rights. In M.A. Baderin and R. McCorquodale (eds), *Economic, Social and Cultural Rights in Action*. Oxford: Oxford University Press, pp. 447–73.

Mikołajczyk, B. (2012). Older persons' right to participate in social and economic life: New challenges for Europe. Paper presented at the 5th Warsaw Seminar on Human Rights: Warsaw, 29 September–1 October 2011. Warsaw: Kontrast, pp. 158–67.

Mikołajczyk, B. (2013). Is the ECHR ready for global ageing? *International Journal of Human Rights*, **17** (4): 511–29.

Mikołajczyk, B. (2015). International law and ageism, *Polish Yearbook of International Law*, **XXXV** (1): 83–107.

Minkler, M. and Holstein, M. (2008). From civil rights to … civic engagement? Concerns of two older critical gerontologists about a "newsocialmovement" and what it portends. *Journal of Aging Studies*, **22** (2): 196–204.

Moody, H.R. (2001). Productive aging and the ideology of old age. In N. Morrow-Howell, J. Hinterlong and M. Sherraden (eds), *Productive Aging. Concepts and Challenges*. Baltimore, MD, USA and London, UK: The Johns Hopkins University Press, pp. 175–96.

Moulaert, T. and Paris, M. (2013). Social policy on ageing: The case of "active ageing" as a theatrical metaphor. *International Journal of Social Science Studies*, **1** (2): 113–23.

Numhauser-Henning, A. and Rönnmar, M. (2015). *Age Discrimination and Labour Law. Comparative and Conceptual Perspectives in the EU and Beyond*. Lund: Lund University.

OECD (2011). *Paying for the Past, Providing for the Future: Intergenerational Solidarity*. Background Document. OECD Ministerial Meeting on Social Policy. Paris, 2–3 May 2011. Accessed at http://www.oecd.org/els/public-pensions/47712019.pdf.

OECD (2016). Elderly population (indicator). Accessed at https://data.oecd.org/pop/population.htm.

Parra, C., Silveira, P., Far, I.K., Daniel, F., De Bruin, E.D., Cernuzzi, L., D'Andrea, V. et al. (2014). Information technology for active ageing: A review of theory and practice. *Foundations and Trends® in Human–Computer Interaction*, **7** (4): 351–447.

Radović-Marković, M. (2013). An aging workforce: Employment opportunities and obstacles. *Cadmus*, **1** (6): 142–55.

Ranzijn, R. (2010). Active ageing – another way to oppress marginalized and disadvantaged elders? Aboriginal elders as a case study. *Journal of Health Psychology*, **15** (5): 716–72.

Renda, A. (2016). *Regulation and R&I Policies: Comparing Europe and the USA*. CEPS and Duke University. European Commission. Accessed at https://ec.europa.eu/research/innovation-union/pdf/expert-groups/rise/renda_innovation_report.pdf.

Riekkinen, M. (2011). Assisting the elderly in remaining politically active: A focus on Russia and its international legal obligations, *Review of Central and East European Law*, **36** (2): 157–95.

Schlachter, M. (2011). Mandatory retirement and age discrimination under EU law. *International Journal of Comparative Labour Law and Industrial Relations*, **27** (3): 287–99.

Shaver, L. and Sganga, C. (2009). The right to take part in cultural life: On copyright and human rights. *Wisconsin International Law Journal*, **27** (4): 637–62.

Spanier, B., Doron, I. and Milman-Sivan, F. (2013). Older persons' use of the European Court of Human Rights. *Journal of Cross-Cultural Gerontology*, **28** (4): 407–20.

Spanier, B., Doron, I. and Milman-Sivan, F. (2016). In course of change? Soft law, elder rights, and the European Court of Human Rights. *Law and Inequality*, **34** (1): 55–86.

Timonen, V. (2016). *Beyond Successful and Active Ageing: A Theory of Model Ageing*. Bristol: Policy Press.

Tymowski, J. (2015). *European Year for Active Ageing and Solidarity between Generations: European Implementation Assessment. In-Depth Analysis*. European Parliamentary Research Service. Accessed at http://www.europarl.europa.eu/RegData/etudes/IDAN/2015/536344/EPRS_IDA(2015)536344_EN.pdf.

UNECE/ European Commission (2015). *Active Ageing Index 2014: Analytical Report*, Report prepared by Asghar Zaidi of Centre for Research on Ageing, University of Southampton and David Stanton.

United Nations (2002). *Political Declaration and the Madrid International Plan of Action on Ageing.* Second World Assembly on Ageing, Madrid, Spain, 8–12 April. New York, NY: United Nations. Accessed at http://social.un.org/ageing-working-group/documents/mipaa-en.pdf.

United Nations (2006). *UN Convention on the Rights of Persons with Disabilities*, Treaty Series, vol. 2515.

United Nations General Assembly (1991). United Nations Principles for Older Persons. The General Assembly Resolution A/RES/46/91 adopted 16 December 1991. Accessed at http://www.un.org/documents/ga/res/46/a46r091.htm.

World Health Organization (2002). *Active Ageing: A Policy Framework*. WHO 2002, p. 16. Accessed at: http://whqlibdoc.who.int/hq/2002/WHO_NMH_NPH_02.8.pdf.
World Health Organization (2015). *Fact Sheet No. 362*, March. Accessed at http://www.who.int/mediacentre/factsheets/fs362/en/.
Zaidi, A. and Howse, K. (2017). The policy discourse of active ageing: Some reflections. *Journal of Population and Ageing*, **10** (1): 1–10.
Zrałek, M. (2014). *Tworzenie warunków sprzyjających aktywności ludzi starszych* [Creation of conditions fostering activity of older persons]. In: *Osoby starsze w przestrzeni życia społecznego* [Older persons in the area of social life]. Katowice: ROPS, pp. 27–40.

5. Ageism, age discrimination and employment law in the EU

Ann Numhauser-Henning

1. INTRODUCTION

Ageism in working life is a central concern when it comes to active ageing. This chapter aims at discussing the relation between the EU ban on age discrimination, European employment law and active ageing strategies. In doing this it draws heavily on some earlier works of this author (see especially Numhauser-Henning 2015 and 2017, chapters 4, 7 and 9, with further references).

There is a special and close connection between ageism – the overall theme of this book – and non-discrimination regulation on the grounds of age. Discrimination, or discriminatory behaviour, is thus an integral part of most definitions of ageism (Iversen et al., 2009).[1]

The EU ban on age discrimination was introduced into secondary law through the 2000/78/EC Directive – The Employment Equality Directive. It was preceded by the new competences bestowed on the European Council by the Amsterdam Treaty and its Article 13 (now Art. 19 of the Treaty on the Functioning of the European Union, TFEU) and later on confirmed in the EU Charter of Fundamental Rights (CFR) 2000 – since the Lisbon Treaty part of primary law. The CFR in its Article 21 contains a non-discrimination clause listing age among other grounds in an open list.

The Employment Equality Directive bans direct and indirect discrimination as well as harassment and instructions to discriminate on the grounds of age (among other grounds) in a working life context. The ban is neutral in the sense that it covers all ages – in contrast to the regulation in place in the US, acting as a model in introducing this discrimination ground.[2] A special characteristic of the age discrimination ban as compared to those of other grounds is its weak format – it opens up for the justification of direct age discrimination. According to Article 6.1 in the Employment Equality Directive:

differences of treatment on the grounds of age shall not constitute discrimination, if, in the context of national law, they are objectively and reasonably justified by a legitimate aim, including legitimate employment policy, labour market, and vocational training objectives, and if the means of achieving that aim are appropriate and necessary.

The scope for justification is ultimately decided by the European Union Court of Justice (CJEU) in its case law and – as compared to other grounds – the Court has been flooded by age discrimination cases since the Directive's entering into force.

What is then European employment law? EU labour law, like equality law, is regulated by a complex mix of treaty provisions, fundamental rights and general principles of EU law, secondary law, collective agreements at EU level, case law from the CJEU and soft law measures only to be complemented by regulation at national level. Despite growing competences for the EU institutions over time, there is still a great variety between the Member States' labour law and industrial relations systems. EU labour law, so far, only aims for a partial harmonization of these systems and labour law being an area of shared competences, the principles of subsidiarity and proportionality are important. Some – also central – issues of labour law and industrial relations, such as pay, the right of association, the right to strike and right to impose lock-outs, are even principally excluded from the EU's competences to adopt Directives. Notwithstanding, there is now a considerable number of secondary law directives in place – among them the many equality directives as well as directives on restructuring of enterprises, information, consultation and worker participation, collective redundancies, flexible work and working conditions, including working time and health and safety. This is not the place to describe these existing rules in any detail. The lens here is rather the age discrimination ban and what can be deducted in relation to labour law regulations from the case law of the CJEU in this area. A central concern is age differentials in relation to working conditions including employment protection, redundancy benefits, wages, and so on. In an overall perspective, fundamental rights such as those set out in CFR are of course important when forming an idea not only of EU labour law but also of Member States' labour law traditions. Treaty regulation has long since made references to the European Convention of Human Rights (ECHR) as well as the European Social Charter, acting as common denominators of Member States' legal traditions. Another common denominator for many EU Member States is central ILO conventions.

2. EMPLOYMENT LAW

From the case law of the CJEU it becomes clear that employment protection law is of special concern when it comes to age discrimination. According to Article 30 in th CFR, "[e]very worker has the right to protection against unjustified dismissal, in accordance with Union law and national laws and practices". Despite a partly harmonized EU law framework and a "constitutionalization" of employment protection through Article 30 of the CFR, employment protection regulation in the Member States – and the strength of the protection it offers not only to older workers, but to employees generally – still differs considerably.

The Charter applies only within the scope of Union law and there is thus as yet no harmonization proper concerning employment protection. Secondary law does exist partially, however, on issues such as collective redundancies (Dir. 1998/59/EC) and the transfer of undertakings (Dir. 2001/23/EC) – with a common emphasis on information and consultation rather than substantive employment protection – and, on discriminatory dismissals. There are also directives concerning so-called flexible work: that is Dir. 97/81/EC on Part-time Work, Dir. 99/70/EC on Fixed-term Work and Dir. 2008/104/EC on Temporary Agency Work.

2.1 Employment Law and the Standard Employment Contract

In lack of harmonization, employment protection regulation can be said to differ quite a lot between the EU Member States. Notwithstanding, the common background – both with regard to history, legal culture and welfare society – is reflected in Article 30 of the CFR and its declaration that workers are protected against unjustified dismissal. The centre of concern is arbitrary dismissal, whereas the employee protection in dismissal for redundancy relies mainly upon economic compensation and/or seniority rules. The right to protection from arbitrary dismissals can ultimately be related to "the right to work" in welfare society and property rights, with its "spillover" effects of claims to non-discriminatory employment practices and ultimately decent working conditions (Zekic, 2017). The idea of an open-ended contract that insures a degree of job stability as the pursued goal of EU law can also be said to be indirectly reflected by the very existence of the flexible work directives.

This view on employment is ultimately a reflection of what has been labelled the standard employment contract, developed during the main part of the twentieth century and implying a long-term trade-off in wage society. Wage work became the dominant "distributive" order in early industrial society and according to the logic of the market, pay equals work. At the same time, it was obvious that the individual is not always conditioned for work, whether on the grounds of illness or due to young or old age, which led to complementary social security systems evolving. Freedland's understanding of the standard employment contract is thus one entailing continuous full-time employment with a single employer, with accompanying expected levels of remuneration and benefits (Freedland, 2013). In their book *Rethinking Workplace Regulation*, Stone and Arthurs illustrate the standard employment contract – labelled one of the pillars of the post-war economic system – in the following way: "For four or five decades after 1945, in most industrialized countries large numbers of workers enjoyed an array of job rights that included decent wages, protections against unfair treatment at work, social insurance provided by the state or the employer and, notably, some degree of job security" (Stone and Arthurs, 2013, p. 2). The standard employment contract was never a one-dimensional and altogether standardized concept or pattern of employment. It took on somewhat different legal forms in different national contexts (Freedland, 2013, p. 86). Bearing in mind that "to speak of a standard employment contract is a way of conceptualizing a body of practice and regulation that at a certain period and in a certain set of locations produced a strong convergence on rather stable or secure worker-protective patterns of employment" (Freedland, 2013, p. 91), the concept is used here as an overall starting point in order to understand the interrelations between employment law and age discrimination regulation as interpreted by the CJEU.

The standard employment contract was intrinsically related not only to employment protection devices but also to seniority rules and retirement practices. The influential American economist Edward Lazear launched his lifecycle theory of mandatory retirement as building on an implicit contract model inherent to the standard employment contract. Employers pay employees a wage premium towards the end of their careers on the assumption that the employment relationship will come to an end at a predictable, fixed point in time (Lazear, 1979). Wage thus does not fluctuate throughout a worker's career in response to actual productivity; it tends to rise consistently until retirement. This wage arrangement is desirable for the employer because employees are less likely to shirk in mid-career, and more likely to increase their productivity to a level above wages, so they may receive deferred compensation when they are older. It is also – at least *ex ante* – desirable for the employee receiving higher wages than deserved at a higher age. In short, according to Lazear, mandatory retirement is "the necessary consequence of an optimal wage scheme which makes both workers and firms better off" (Lazear, 1979, p. 1274).

The implicit contract, as described by Lazear, is dependent on employment protection devices to maintain the inherent promise of a wage premium. The promise of the implicit contract is just as reliable as the employment protection provided, Indeed, the fact that wage rates, in relation to older workers according to the standard employment contract, exceed their marginal products is evidenced by the fact that employers are often willing to buy out employees with higher pensions if they retire early. This also means that the implicit contract, as described, in itself implies a drift towards early retirement (Lazear, 1982)!

Throughout large parts of the twentieth century it is this logic of the standard employment contract – with its related standard pension contract solutions (Strauss, 2013) – that has typically informed labour law in European countries. No doubt, the standard employment contract was influential also in other industrialized countries. Whereas the implicit contract was taken to its extreme in Japan in the "life-long employment" system with its elaborate seniority wage-setting and internal labour market practices (Araki, 2015), it never really got to characterize US labour law, though. Instead, the dismissal-at-will doctrine has dominated legal developments (Fineman, 2013), which is of great importance for discrimination law developments.

2.2   The Flexibilization of Work

The flexibilization of work relates to labour market segmentation and the legal tension between standard employment contracts – associated with employment protection – and precarious and "flexible" employment. Basically there is broad agreement that we now live in an era of work flexibilization. Flexibilization has thus been pictured as a new trade-off between market flexibility needs and traditional standard employment and pension contracts. Much has been written about the flexibilization of work, including EU developments, within the flexicurity discourse (Fudge, 2013). This is not the place to go into any detail with regard to this line of research. Assessing the extent and significance of the decline of the standard employment contract and exploring changing legal conceptions of employment contracts, Stone and Arthurs state that "fewer and fewer workers in the advanced economies are covered by standard employment contracts", and continue, "we believe it unlikely that the standard employment contract can be revived or that the regulatory regimes once intertwined with it can be resuscitated" (Stone and Arthurs, 2013, p. 3). Employers simply "no longer hire for life with the expectation that their workers will gain experience and receive training during the course of a lengthy tenure within the firm's internal labour market".

Fudge describes this process of "labour law decline" as provoked by neoclassical economic labour-market policies and anti-welfare state politics in the late 1970s and continues: "in official accounts labour law, redistribution and protection have given way to competition and flexibility. Forms of work outside of the standard employment relationship have proliferated and the scope of collective bargaining has contracted in most developed economies" (Fudge, 2011, pp. 122 and 124f).

An area where a certain harmonization of labour law at EU level exists is thus flexible work, that is, part-time, fixed-term and temporary agency work. These regulations are in themselves a reflection of European employment law standards as described above, offering a certain employment protection in "regular" employment. There is thus a close relationship between especially fixed-term work regulation and employment protection in that the *raison d'être* of such regulation is to prevent circumvention of employment protection linked to permanent employment contracts. The more developed the employment protection regulation is, the more important a restricted use of fixed-term employment becomes.

Developments have thus led to the use of new "flexible" contract forms such as fixed-term and part-time employment, but also "outsourcing" and temporary agency work, typically implying less protection in terms of labour law. As far as the EU is concerned, the answer has been the development of the flexicurity strategy and secondary law regulation in the form of the Part-Time Work, Fixed-Term Work and Temporary Agency Work Directives. These directives aim to increase quality in these new forms of flexible work – mainly by introducing the non-discrimination principle (as compared to more traditional forms of work) together with a few, fairly weak legal restraints – but also work to "normalize" them. And, they come with the EU Flexicurity Strategy, a dominant strategy within EU employment policies since the beginning of this century. The Council has adopted Common Principles of Flexicurity, which are handled within the context of the European Employment Strategy and the Europe 2020 Strategy (Communication "Towards common principles of flexicurity: more and better jobs through flexibility and security", COM(2007) 359 final). The aim of flexicurity is to reduce labour-market segmentation, but also to increase economic growth and Europe's competitiveness in a global perspective. Flexicurity at EU level includes flexible and reliable contractual arrangements, effective, active labour-market policies, reliable and adaptable systems for lifelong learning, and modern social security systems.

Countouris and Freedland have described flexibilization as "the de-mutualization of personal work relations – a process of transforming the individual worker into the sole bearer of risks formerly mutualized as between workers and employing enterprises and, in a different sense, between workers themselves" (Countouris and Freedland, 2013) and Fudge points to a shift towards individualization in terms of contract of employment, human rights and anti-discrimination law (Fudge, 2011, p. 5).

3. AGE DISCRIMINATION AND EMPLOYMENT LAW AS REFLECTED IN THE CASE LAW OF THE CJEU

There is thus a special relation between anti-discrimination law and labour law and, especially, employment protection devices. Non-discrimination law developed early in the US, where it is widely recognized that it became an important substitute for poorly developed employment protection, dominated by the dismissal-at-will doctrine (Fineman, 2013). In Europe, on the other hand, with its generally speaking more developed regulation of employment protection, non-discrimination can instead be seen as a replacement mechanism in times of weakening employment protection and flexibilization of work. Anti-discrimination law can thus – with Fudge, compare above – be seen as an expression of the general trend towards individualization going hand in hand with the flexibilization of work and a parallel deregulation of traditional employment protection. With Somek, anti-discrimination regulation can even be seen as a forerunner of flexibilization (Somek, 2011).

Non-discrimination regulation is in itself very flexible in times of change. This regulation supplies only a relative protection in terms of equal treatment, according to the circumstances at hand, and does not really question the reference norms in working life themselves. Non-discrimination regulation thus does not imply a certain quality of treatment and, generally speaking, has no distributional functions. It is only to be expected that non-discrimination law in general has been growing in importance as the standard employment contract has had to give way to more flexible and individualized work arrangements.

Where in this context do we situate the age discrimination ban? The ban on age discrimination and employment protection intersect, as reflected in case law, in fixed-term employment contracts for older workers, seniority rules in redundancy situations and compulsory retirement practices. One reason for this, as already indicated, is that age has traditionally been influential in the organization of labour markets and labour law regulation. This, in its turn, is, however, also a crucial reason for the weaker template of EU age discrimination law as compared to other grounds of non-discrimination regulation: implying that direct age discrimination still to a considerable extent can be justified. Article 6.1 of the Employment Equality Directive reflects this "double bind" of age discrimination law (Hendrickx, 2012; Numhauser-Henning, 2015; 2017). Whereas the ban on direct age discrimination fulfils the "classical" purpose of being a basis for individual claims of non-discrimination – to uphold individual dignity – the opening for justification makes room for collective interests at a more societal level, in terms of age as a traditional stratifier but also (competing) active ageing strategies of a more instrumental nature.

An important bulk of the case law of the CJEU is the many cases concerning compulsory retirement. Compulsory retirement practices are maybe what best reflect the important links between labour law, employment protection, standard employment contracts and pension systems, referred to above. Whereas retirement age as such is outside the scope of the Employment Equality Directive (preamble 14), the termination of employment in terms of retirement is not. A compulsory retirement age can be set by legislation, collective agreements or personal employment contracts. Compulsory retirement rules may provide for the automatic termination of the employment relationship when the employee reaches a certain age (for example the pensionable age) or imply a possibility for the employer to terminate the employment relationship at a specific age. Compulsory retirement is thus an important part of the "implicit contract" in standard employment (Lazear, 1979).

Despite the fact that compulsory retirement is far from a general norm in EU Member States (O'Dempsey and Beale, 2011), the substantial amount of case law from the CJEU in this area reveals that such schemes still prevail in a number of EU Member States. In many cases the CJEU has accepted compulsory retirement rules and found them justifiable.

A first case was *Palacios de la Villa*, concerning a Spanish worker forced to terminate his employment at the age of 65 in accordance with the collective agreement in place (CJEU, C-411/05). The Court found the "interests of promoting employment" to be an aim of public interest not "unduly prejudicing the legitimate claims of workers" as "the relevant legislation is not based only on a specific age, but also takes account of the fact that the persons concerned are entitled to financial compensation by way of a retirement pension … the level of which cannot be regarded as unreasonable" (the judgment, p. 73). The Court has confirmed this judgment in a number of following cases (C-388/07, C-45/09, C-141/11), referring to legitimate aims such as intergenerational fairness in terms of access to employment, prevention of humiliating forms of termination of employment, and a reasonable balance between labour market and budgetary concerns. In these cases, the CJEU has given much consideration to Member States' traditions because "the automatic termination of the employment contracts for employees who meet the conditions as regards age and contributions paid for the liquidation of their pension rights has, for a long time, been a feature of employment law in many Member States and is widely used in employment relationships" (C-141/11, p. 28). The Member States and the social partners have also been given a broad margin of appreciation. From the *Hörnfeldt* case (C-141/11) it also became clear that compulsory retirement at a set age of about 65 years is compatible with the Employment Equality Directive's requirements, provided there is a reasonable *system* of pensions in place (C-411/05, C-45/09) regardless of the pension *in casu* being quite low.

The CJEU has also decided a number of cases on compulsory retirement of specific professional groups (such as C-447/09 and C-341/08). The latter case, *Commission v Hungary*, concerned reduced rights for judges, prosecutors and notaries to keep on working, lowering the age of compulsory retirement from 70 to 62 years of age. Whereas the Hungarian aim of "standardization" as regards compulsory retirement age was acknowledged as legitimate, the regulation was deemed not to meet the requirements to be appropriate and necessary since it did not meet the "well-founded expectations" on behalf of the employees concerned to be able to stay on until the age of 70.

Another set of cases has concerned redundancy payments and other working conditions in lay-off situations, relating them to eligibility to pension rights (C-499/08, C-152/11, C-546/11). Whereas the CJEU in the *Andersen* case (C-499/08) regarded the denial of redundancy payment to a worker eligible for employer pension at the age of 63 neither appropriate nor necessary as it neglected the individual's wish not to opt for the pension but to continue working, in *Odar* (C-152/11) reduced redundancy payments in view of pension rights was indeed accepted. Later cases such as *Toftgaard* (C-546/11) and *Tekniq* (C-515/13) reveal an equally careful scrutiny of the consequences in the individual case, also regarding workers 65+, in relation to denied availability pay and reduced severance allowances, respectively.

For a long time the cases hitherto referred to and other case law of the CJEU related to retirement were discussed in terms of the proportionality test applied: a "leaner" test for compulsory retirement systems in general and a stricter one in relation to specific occupational groups, retirement reforms and redundancy conditions related to pre-pension rights (Schlachter, 2011; Kilpatrick, 2011; Dewhurst, 2013). Recent case law developments point to a more nuanced test than discussed so far (C-515/13, C-546/11). Now, we have to conclude that in regard to working conditions such as redundancy and availability pay, the CJEU also applies a stricter proportionality test in relation to workers 65 years or older – or beyond the applicable default retirement age – and scrutinizes the effects for the individual employee (though occasionally accepting differential treatment of workers with reference to the right to a state pension when these effects are limited).

The CJEU's acceptance of rules on compulsory retirement harmonizes poorly with the promotion of active ageing and efforts to prolong working lives for older workers. It also contrasts with economic research on the "lump of labour fallacy" (Dewhurst, 2013). However, the abolition of compulsory retirement practices requires alternative ways of ending the employment relationship, such as voluntary retirement (encouraged with financial incentives) or performance management (followed by a possible dismissal on grounds of lack of performance). This entails a risk of weakening employment protection before actual retirement age (Numhauser-Henning, 2015). The continued acceptance of compulsory retirement can thus be seen as a defence of the standard employment contract and traditional European employment protection. Upholding the ban would weaken employment protection further since it would lead to an increased emphasis on "capability" as an employment requirement, and the undermining not only of active ageing strategies but also employment protection well before retirement age.

Accepting compulsory retirement (in defence of the standard employment contract) can be said to challenge the "general" flexibilization functions of non-discrimination law. There are thus good reasons to believe that to uphold instead the ban on age discrimination in these cases would increase flexible employment in higher ages. The dismissal of an elderly worker from a permanent employment can be expected to be a difficult process, making a fixed-term contract even more attractive. However, also the acceptance of compulsory retirement paradoxically seems to purport fixed-term employment: a rule on compulsory retirement does not necessarily mean definite withdrawal from the labour market. Working life can continue, and now often in the form of fixed-term employment (compare C-250/09). It is worth noticing that otherwise restricted use of fixed-term employment is often more generous beyond "normal" pensionable age, that is, following compulsory retirement, a practice which in itself needs to be justified in accordance with article 6.1 in the Employment Equality Directive (and also the Fixed-term Work Directive!).

Seniority principles – relating to age and length of service – have traditionally been influential in European labour law and remain so in many EU Member States when it comes to wage-setting and working conditions, such as periods of notice, length of annual leave, severance pay and specific bonuses. A reference to age and length of service in this context gives rise to directly or indirectly age-related differential treatment and thus needs to be justified in terms of Article 6.1 in the Employment Equality Directive. Legitimate aims put forward in this context include the value of experience on the job and rewarding loyalty as well as the need for extra protection of older workers. Finally, a few words about age-related wage-setting. Seniority wage-setting is thus seen as a constituent of the standard employment contract. At the same time, seniority wage-setting practices tend to work to the detriment of active ageing: they become very expensive when employees grow older. Still, these practices are common and the question is to what extent they – as compulsory retirement – are still found to be compatible with a ban on age discrimination. It is already evident from the CJEU's case law in sex discrimination cases that experience in terms of length of service – and thus with an indirect connection to age – is a justified criterion as far as wage-setting is concerned, without the employer having to establish the bearing this experience has on the performance of specific tasks entrusted to the employee at stake (C-109/88 and C-17/05). This does not mean that a more "automatic" age-related wage-setting system is acceptable though, as demonstrated by the *Hennigs* case (C-297 and 298/10). A collective agreement, providing that the basic pay determined on appointment of the employee was based directly on the employee's age, was found impermissible under Article 6.1 of the Employment Equality Directive, whereas there was a broad scope for the social partners providing a transitional way out of these practices also in somewhat discriminatory terms (Numhauser-Henning and Rönnmar, 2016).

4. MANAGERIAL AGEISM

Case law before the CJEU has thus in the main dealt with Article 6.1 and how to balance the ban on age discrimination with the scope for justification of differential treatment on the grounds of age in view of "the double bind". As issues of proof are for domestic courts to settle, these cases have dealt with the acceptance or rejection of directly age-related norms.

When it comes to "ageism" at the individual employer level, alleged claims of discrimination are mainly handled by national courts and/or supervisory bodies – or not at all!

Stereotyping is a central concern when we are talking about employer ageism as played out in managerial decisions. Stereotypes have been described as beliefs about groups of people which are then attributed to all individual members of the group in question. Like ageism itself, stereotypes may be positive, negative or ambivalent in content and they have been suggested to come in four forms: role-typing, false, statistical and prescriptive stereotypes (Timmer, 2016). Role-typing stereotypes may be about the role of elderly employees in a work organization as compared to younger ones. False stereotypes are also about the typical role or behaviour of an older worker, whereas statistical stereotypes reflect a statistical truth about a group as a whole, but are not necessarily true at individual level. Prescriptive stereotypes expect a certain behaviour/characteristic of certain people – older workers are not interested/trained in new technologies, and so on. No doubt, many stereotypes can be classified under multiple forms simultaneously.

Whereas ageist behaviour is well known to exist in working life, there are relatively few cases brought to court. Empirical studies of employer behaviour and/or attitudes at workplace level thus frequently reveal ageist practices (Glover and Branine, 2001; Munnell et al., 2006). Country reports on age discrimination do give examples of cases of age discrimination brought to domestic courts (Numhauser-Henning and Rönnmar, 2015; see also Dewhurst, 2016). A Swedish example is the 62-year-old woman – applying for a job as a job-coach with the Swedish Employment Office – who was not even called for an interview, nor employed, despite being better qualified than other male and younger female applicants (Swedish Labour Court case AD 2010:91). The Swedish Labour Court found that she had been discriminated against both on the grounds of sex and age regarding not being called for an interview and on the grounds of age regarding not being employed. There are good reasons to believe that many people 70+ are simply being neglected when applying for a job! In the UK – after the abolition of compulsory retirement in 2011 – a number of cases can be expected to surface as individual applications of "Employer Justified Retirement Ages", a "loophole" in the new regulations, are looked into (Barnard and Deakin, 2015; Dewhurst, 2016). The same is true for the "performance management" regarding dismissal practices in relation to older workers following this abolition (Barnard and Deakin, 2015).

Still, it is fair to say that case law in this area is still rather scarce. One reason for this is the typical design of non-discrimination legislation as complaints-led individual claims in the liberal tradition. In a world where the "wrongness" of precisely differential treatment on the grounds of age is still disputed as compared to other grounds – much in the wake of its weaker format and age as a traditional stratifier – the hurdles to climb for an individual claiming age discrimination are higher than regarding other grounds of discrimination and the difficulties to prove discrimination are as harsh as ever. Add to this the "elitist" design of non-discrimination bans in general. The right to equal treatment does not imply the right to a certain quality of treatment as such; the normal "reference norms" in working life apply and these are known to be basically meritocratic in character. Therefore, the non-hiring of an older applicant may well be defended by arguments about the more "up-to-date" education of a younger candidate, while a dismissal may be defended by arguments about the older worker's ability to work and availability in terms of working time. Some of these problems could possibly be avoided by requiring "proactive" measures (compare reasonable accommodation) in relation to age as well, but such a development has basically yet to be seen. "Senior Performance Management" is, however, a developing topic within labour law (Ilmarinen, 2001).

5. CONCLUDING REMARKS

Ageism per se – according to its definition – may work both to the detriment and the advantage of old people. This is thus also true with regard to the application of the EU ban on age discrimination as it is portrayed in the case law of the CJEU. And, it is not entirely easy to decide once and for all which interpretation of the rules of the Employment Equality Directive, and especially so Article 6.1 therein, is to the benefit and which is to the detriment of ageing workers. It simply depends on the circumstances.

Age discrimination regulation may well be considered an anti-ageist measure. On the other hand, it has been argued – just as well as in relation to elder law as such – that the conception of ageing as a profound social challenge as the bottom line of the discrimination ban, is per se ageist. The "neutral" design of the EU ban on age discrimination, covering all ages, is of course an argument against this perception. On the other hand, the weak format of the age discrimination ban provides plenty of room for precisely – at least formally – ageist applications.

The ban against age discrimination is in principle designed to counteract ageism at the individual level, as the general rationale of such bans is "overcoming disadvantages related to ascribed otherness" covering the right to individuation (or to enable persons to choose beyond stereotypes imposed on them) and the aim to preserve diversity (Schiek, 2015). Taking compulsory retirement as the example, at individual level, older workers typically push for legislation to make these practices illegal. The elimination of compulsory retirement – which in itself implies immediate cessation of employment – would promote not only active ageing in terms of work beyond retirement age, but also employment protection *in casu* for the ageing individual.

Still, compulsory retirement practices are thus allowed under Article 6.1 of the Employment Equality Directive. The opposite would be to the detriment of the younger generations in the sense that older workers thus do not abstain from their developed employment protection and other "senior" working conditions which, by tradition, is part of the implicit contract within standard employment. And, older workers themselves have typically benefited from this implicit contract throughout their working lives in the form of wage premiums and employment protection devices. Not to allow compulsory retirement would thus also imply a threat of weakening employment protection at earlier ages as well as humiliating dismissals as the "norm" and also further the flexibilization and thus precariousness of working life – and even pensions – especially for ageing workers. Older workers may be better off upholding decent, although collective, retirement orders than striving on their own to maintain a reasonable standard in their old age.

However, many ageing workers have not historically followed the normative employment pattern inherent in the standard employment contract and life course on which the prevalent notion of inter-generational solidarity is based; therefore, policy rules that seek to uphold that solidarity tend to disadvantage these workers in ways that are not only unfair but also inherently systematic. For example, age or service-related requirements or cut-offs typically fail to account for the fact that disabled workers or women are likely to have work histories that do not reflect the norm, as they are more prone to have career interruptions or atypical jobs – by reason of either their disability in the first case or their engagement in provision of unpaid care work within the home in the latter case. Such workers may be unable to accrue pension entitlements that are equal to those of other workers, or even sufficient to live on, or be entitled to wage increments or other employment-related benefits that are tied to seniority and years of service. For these workers, to permit compulsory retirement may seem utterly unfair.

Worth contemplating is also the experience of countries that have already eliminated compulsory retirement: there is a continued need of age distinctions in employee benefits (also indicated by the very excep-tion in Article 6.2 of the Employment Equality Directive). For instance, Canadian legislation and case law recognize "the principle that even in the absence of compulsory retirement employers, employees and govern-ment policymakers cannot simply disregard the inevitable consequences of ageing when establishing employment benefits" such as long-term disability plans, and "the need to balance the competing interests that bargaining unit members have at different times in their lives is an inherent part of the collective bargaining process. Moreover, younger employees generally want higher wages, while older employees may prefer such benefits as life insurance, pensions or retirement allowances" (Charney and Horner, 2013).

The immediate conclusion is that there does not seem to be one solution that fits all. To uphold the ban on age discrimination in terms of dignity and respect at the individual level may well answer to a quest for formal "anti-ageism". In practice it is more complicated: true well-being for the ageing individual may well also imply certain clearly more paternalistic solutions articulated at the collective interest side of the double bind in age discrimination regulation. Differential treatment on the grounds of age cannot be fought successfully only at individual level and in terms of dignity if we want to come to terms with substantive inequalities in today's societies.

NOTES

1. Ageism is there defined as covering "negative or positive stereotypes, prejudices and/or discrimination against (or to the advantage of) elderly people on the basis of their chronological age or on the basis of a perception of them as being "old" or "elderly". Ageism can be implicit or explicit and can be expressed on a micro-, meso- or macro-level."
2. The US Age Discrimination in Employment Act (ADEA) of 1967 – modelled on title VII of the 1964 Civil Rights Act – contains an asymmetric ban that protects only older persons, now 40+.

BIBLIOGRAPHY

Araki, Tadashi (2015), "Age Discrimination and Labor Law in Japan: An Alternative Approach to Age Discrimination Law in Most Rapidly Aging Country" in A. Numhauser-Henning and M. Rönnmar (eds), *Age Discrimination and Labour Law: Comparative and Conceptual Perspectives in the EU and Beyond*, Alphen aan den Rijn: Kluwer Law International.

Barnard, Catherine and Deakin, Simon (2015), "Age Discrimination and Labour Law in the UK: Managing Ageing", in A. Numhauser-Henning and M. Rönnmar (eds), *Age Discrimination and Labour Law: Comparative and Conceptual Perspectives in the EU and Beyond*, Alphen aan den Rijn: Kluwer Law International.

Charney, Robert and Horner, Matthew (2013), "Defending Age Distinctions in Employee Benefits after the Elimination of Mandatory Retirement", *Canadian Labour & Employment Law Journal*, **17**, 255–79.

Countouris, Nicola and Freedland, Mark (eds) (2013), *Resocialising Europe in a Time of Crisis*, Cambridge: Cambridge University Press.

Dewhurst, Elaine (2013), "Intergenerational Balance, Mandatory Retirement and Age Discrimination in Europe: How can the ECJ Better Support National Courts in Finding a Balance Between the Generations?", *Common Market Law Review*, **50**(5), 1333–62.

Dewhurst, Elaine (2016), "Proportionality Assessments of Mandatory Retirement Measures: Uncovering Guidance for National Courts in Age Discrimination Cases, *Industrial Law Journal*, **45**(1), 60–88.

European Council Directive 97/81/EC on Part-time Work.

European Council Directive 98/59/EC on Collective Redundancies.

European Council Directive 99/70/EC on Fixed-term Work.

European Council Directive 2000/78/EC establishing a general framework for equal treatment in employment and occupation.

European Council Directive 2001/23/EC on the transfer of undertakings.

European Council Directive 2008/104/EC on Temporary Agency Work.

European Union Court of Justice, case C-109/88, *Danfoss*, EU:C:1989:383.

European Union Court of Justice, case C-17/05, *Cadman*, EU:C:2006:633.

European Union Court of Justice, case C-411/05, *Palacios de la Villa v Cortefiel Servicios Union SA*, EU:C:2007:604.

European Union Court of Justice, case C-388/07, *Age Concern England v Secretary of State for Business, Enterprise and Regulatory Reform*, EU:C:2009:128

European Union Court of Justice, case C-499/08, *Ole Andersen v Region Syddanmark*, EU:C:2010:600.

European Union Court of Justice, case C-45/09, *Rosenbladt v Oellerking Gebäudereinigungsges mbH*, EU:C:2010:601.

European Union Court of Justice, cases 250/09 and C-268/09, *Georgiev v Technisheski Universitet, Sofia*, EU:C:2010:699.

European Union Court of Justice, case C-297 and 298/10, *Hennigs v Eisenban-Bundesamt and Land Berlin v Alexander Mai*, EU:C:2011:560.

European Union Court of Justice, case C-447/09, *Prigge v Deutsche Lufthansa AB*, EU:C:2011:573.

European Union Court of Justice, case C-141/11, *Hörnfeldt v Posten Meddelande AB*, EU:C:2012:421.

European Union Court of Justice, case C-341/08, *Commission v Hungary*, EU:C:2012:687.

European Union Court of Justice, case C-152/11, *Odar v Baxter Deutschland GmbH*, EU:C:2012:772.

European Union Court of Justice, case C-546/11, *Toftgaard v Indenrigs- og Sundhedsministeriet*, EU:C:2013:603.

European Union Court of Justice, case C-515/13, *Ingeniörforeningen I Danmark v Tekniq*, EU:C:2015:776.

Fineman, Jonathan (2013), "The Vulnerable Subject at Work: A New Perspective on the Employment-At-Will Debate", *Southwestern Law Review*, **43**, 275–317.

Freedland, Mark (2013), "Burying Caesar: What Was the Standard Employment Contract?", in K. Stone and H. Arthurs (eds), *Rethinking Workplace Regulation: Beyond the Standard Contract of Employment*, New York, NY: Russell Sage Foundation.

Fudge, Judy (2011), "Labour as a 'Fictive Commodity': Radically Reconceptualizing Labour Law", in G. Davidov and B. Langille (eds), *The Idea of Labour Law*, Oxford: Oxford University Press.

Fudge, Judy (2013), "Flexicurity and Labour Law: Labour Market Segmentation, Precarious Work and Just Distribution", in A. Numhauser-Henning and M. Rönnmar (eds), *Normative Patterns and Legal Developments in the Social Dimension of the EU*, Oxford: Hart Publishing.

Glover, I. and Branine, M. (2001), *Ageism and Employment*, Burlington, VT: Ashgate Publishing Ltd.

Hendrickx, Frank (2012), "Age and European Employment Discrimination Law", in F. Hendrickx (ed.), *Active Ageing and Labour Law, Contributions in Honour of Professor Roger Blanpain*, Cambridge: Intersentia

Ilmarinen, Juhani (2001), *Ageing Workers in the European Union: Status and Promotion of Workability, Employability and Employment*, Finnish Institute of Occupational Health, Ministry of Social Affairs and Health, Ministry of Labour.

Iversen, Thomas Nicolaj, Larsen, Lars and Solem, Per Erik (2009), "A Conceptual Analysis of Ageism", *Nordic Psychology*, **61**(3), 4–22.

Kilpatrick, Claire (2011), "The Court of Justice and Labour Law in 2010: a New EU Discrimination Law Architecture, *Industrial Law Journal*, **40**(3), 280–301.

Lazear, Edward (1979), "Why is there Mandatory Retirement?", *Journal of Political Economy*, **87**(6), 1261–84.

Lazear, Edward (1982), "Severance Pay, Pensions, and Efficient Mobility", Working Paper no. 854, National Bureau of Economic Research, Cambridge MA, February.

Munnell, A.H., Sass, S.A. and Soto, M. (2006), "Employer Attitudes Towards Older Workers: Survey Results. Work Opportunities for Older Americans". An Issue in Brief: Series 3, Boston Center for Retirement Research at Boston College.

Numhauser-Henning, Ann (2015), "Labour Law, Pension Norms and the EU Ban on Age Discrimination: Towards Ultimate Flexibilisation?", in A. Numhauser-Henning and M. Rönnmar (eds), *Age Discrimination and Labour Law: Comparative and Conceptual Perspectives in the EU and Beyond*, Alphen aan den Rijn: Kluwer Law International.

Numhauser-Henning, Ann (ed.) (2017), *Elder Law: Evolving European Perspectives*, Cheltenham, UK and Northampton, MA, USA: Edward Elgar Publishing.

Numhauser-Henning, Ann and Rönnmar, Mia (eds) (2015), *Age Discrimination and Labour Law: Comparative and Conceptual Perspectives in the EU and Beyond*, Alphen aan den Rijn: Kluwer Law International.

Numhauser-Henning, Ann and Rönnmar, Mia (2016), "Age Discrimination Law and Social Partners and Collective Bargaining", in B.J. Mulder, M.J. Hotvedt, M. Nesvik and T. Løkken Sundet (eds), *Sui Generis: Festskrift til Stein Evju*, Oslo: Universitetsforlaget.

O'Dempsey, Declan and Beale, Anna (2011), *Age and Employment*, Report from the Network of Legal Experts in the non-discrimination field to the European Commission. Brussels: European Commission.

Schiek, Dagmar (2015), "Proportionality in Age Discrimination Cases: Towards a Model Suitable for Socially Embedded Rights", in A. Numhauser-Henning and M. Rönnmar (eds), *Age Discrimination and Labour Law: Comparative and Conceptual Perspectives in the EU and Beyond*, Alphen aan den Rijn: Kluwer Law International.

Schlachter, Monika (2011), "Mandatory Retirement and Age Discrimination under EU Law", *International Journal of Comparative Labour Law and Industrial Relations*, **27**.

Somek, Alexander (2011), *Engineering Equality*, Oxford: Oxford University Press.

Stone, Katherine and Arthurs, Harry (eds) (2013), *Rethinking Workplace Regulation: Beyond the Standard Contract of Employment*, New York, NY: Russell Sage Foundation.

Strauss, Kendra (2013), "Equality, Fair-mutualisation and the Socialisation of Risk and Reward in European Pensions", in N. Countouris and M. Freedland (eds), *Resocialising Europe in a Time of Crisis*, Cambridge: Cambridge University Press.

Swedish Labour Court, case AD 2010:91.

Timmer, Alexandra (2016), "Gender Stereotyping in the Case Law of the EU Court of Justice", in *European Equality Law Review*, No. 1, 37–46.

Zekic, Nuna (2017), "Job Security or Employment Security: What's in a Name?", unpublished manuscript.

6. Stereotyping and other "forms of discrimination" in the Chicago Declaration on the Rights of Older Persons and in the case law of the European Court of Human Rights

Eugenio Mantovani, Paul Quinn and Paul de Hert

INTRODUCTION

This chapter begins with a quote from the non-binding draft of the "Chicago Declaration of the Human Rights of Older Persons", one of the most recent contributions to the ongoing debate on the human rights status of older persons. The authors of this chapter note that a paragraph in the preamble of that Declaration conflates discrimination on the grounds of (old) age, on the one hand, and other "forms of discrimination", namely *bias, stereotypes, prejudices*, and *stigma of older persons*, on the other. Observing that, in recent years, the European Court of Human Rights has acknowledged in its case law that stereotyping and other forms of discrimination can affect human rights, this chapter asks how the European Convention of Human Rights (ECHR) and the Court of Human Rights (ECtHR) deal with such cases.[1] The purpose of our research is to highlight both the potential and the limitations of human rights law to stem the manifestations of ageism, as the proponents of the Chicago Declaration recommend.

The chapter is structured as follows. In section 1, the authors introduce the preambular consideration C and familiarize the reader with the terminology mobilized by the drafters of the Declaration, that is, "discrimination" and other "forms of discrimination", pausing, in particular, on stereotyping and stigma, their modes of activation and the coping mechanisms that individuals put in place. Section 2 points out how, in the perspective of the social gerontology literature, discrimination *and* "other forms of discrimination" (stereotypes and stigma in particular) are seen as mutually reinforcing manifestations of a complex diffuse social phenomenon: ageism. Section 3 disengages from the perspective of social gerontology to annotate the difference between these "forms of discrimination" and "discrimination", from a legal point of view. In order to shed light on how courts of law grasp or seize stereotyping and stigma, section 4 invites the reader to discuss a series of cases from the European Court of Human Rights (ECtHR). For this case law review, attention is drawn to cases involving the alleged use of stereotyping and stigma, in the areas of race and gender equality. For our research purpose, we have been interested in bringing into relief the reasoning of the Court about the underlying justifications of differences in treatment (Article 14, the prohibition of discrimination) in relation to an individual right, notably the right to private and family life (Article 8), protected by the Convention. As section 5 discusses, instances in which the Court has censored "treatment" have occurred where they were motivated by stereotyping considered invidious to human rights. In section 6, the authors focus on the case law on stigma and stigmatizing expressions. Stigmatizing expressions do not constitute treatment itself in the terms of Article 14; stigmatizing expressions mobilize another fundamental freedom, namely, the freedom of expression (Article 10). For our research purpose, we have asked under which circumstances the Court may consider speech that is merely stigmatizing (that is, not considered as hate speech) to be serious enough to warrant an infringement upon freedom of speech.

1. THE TERMINOLOGY OF THE PREAMBLE CONSIDERATION C OF THE CHICAGO DECLARATION ON THE RIGHTS OF OLDER PERSONS: DISCRIMINATION AND OTHER "FORMS OF DISCRIMINATION"

Adopted on 11 July 2014 at the John Marshall Law School in Chicago, Illinois, USA,[2] the *Chicago Declaration on the Rights of Older Persons* is one of the most recent, non-binding, efforts to determine the human rights status of older persons in law.[3] An interesting statement is contained in the third preamble (consideration C), where, as is customary, the authors outline the qua situation and the objectives the hypothetical contracting parties would have in executing the charter. Preamble consideration C states:

> Recognizing that discrimination against any person on the basis of age is a
> violation of the inherent dignity and worth of the human person, and ageism
> and the social construction of old age, including bias, stereotypes, prejudices,
> and stigma of older persons are forms of discrimination that hinder the full
> realization of their human rights and participation of older persons as equal
> members of society;

This consideration includes both discrimination based on age *and* other
"forms of discrimination": bias, stereotypes, prejudices and stigma. At
first glance, discrimination seemingly attracts a more powerful label ("is
a violation of the inherent dignity and worth of the human person"),
whilst ageism, social construction of old age, bias, stereotypes and
stigma are more generally defined as "forms of discrimination that
hinder" the realization of human rights and the participation of older
persons in society. Reading this consideration in the light of other
provisions of the Chicago Declaration, however, one has the clear
impression that the drafters actually wanted to put "age discrimination"
and other "forms of discrimination" in the same boat, at the same level.
More explicitly, what they arguably suggest is that a human rights law
genuinely concerned with the rights of older persons should tackle both.
As section 2 discusses, this resolute position reflects an important view in
the field of social gerontology, the branch of gerontology with close ties
with social sciences and humanities that study the social context of
ageing and the impact of population ageing upon society.[4] This scholarly
vein, supported by a growing empirical research, claims that ageism, the
process of systematic stereotyping and discrimination against people
because they are old, is pervasive in our society, affecting older persons
at different levels and in various sectors of social life.[5]

The Chicago Declaration is a non-binding document. It does not
produce legal effects. Nonetheless it does contain traits that make it
recognizable as a legal text: the language is unmistakably legalistic, it
presents the structure of a human rights convention, the articles contain
"written performatives" that create or specify rights and obligations of
individuals and signatory states.[6] Granted the declaration can be considered as a legal text, the aforementioned preamble consideration C can,
and will be, in this chapter, assessed against legal bounds, factors and
considerations (sections 5 and 6). Before doing that, however, it is
sensible to consider the expressions employed by the drafters of the
Chicago Declaration, starting from the mentioned other "forms of
discrimination".

Bias and prejudice are unproblematic notions. Bias refers to the point
of view one has when looking at the world. The etymological dictionary

casts the noun's origin in the ancient Greek for "obliquous", conveying the idea of an inclination, a perspective whence one looks at a certain event, person or group. Accordingly, bias is popularly associated with partiality, preference, leaning: as its antonyms stand impartiality, fairness, justness, evidence. Prejudice originates in the Latin word *praeiudicium*, from "pre-", before, and "iudicium", a court's decision. In Ancient Rome, *praeiudicium* consisted of a legal procedure organized to ascertain a fact, in order to prepare or avoid a future judgment.[7] Today prejudice refers to an opinion concerning facts, persons or things, that is pre-formed and strongly conditions the evaluation of facts, persons or groups. In the eyes of the beholder, prejudice is correct for no other reason than it appears reasonable in his or her mind, often without a direct knowledge (of facts, persons or things). Thence, prejudices on the professional skills of women, caste prejudices, moral, racial, religious, social, political prejudices and so on.

Stereotyping and stigma are well-studied phenomena in the social sciences and deserve more attention. The origin of the noun "stigma" is in the Ancient Greek verb *stizein*, meaning to mark and to stick: the noun accordingly evokes something sticking to an individual, like a tattoo or a piercing. Unlike a modern tattoo or piercing, designed for attracting attention or prestige, stigmata or stigmas are marks that educe blemish and negative connotations on its bearer, instead.[8] Famously, Ervin Goffman describes the process of stigmatization in his seminal work *Stigma: Notes on the Management of Spoiled Identity*.[9] Historically, he shows how cuts, bruises, amputations, tattoos and so on were made precisely to stick and to advertise that "the bearer is a blemished person, ritually polluted, to be avoided, especially in public places".[10] Stigmatization, Goffman explains, is a process whereby "normal individuals" discern or might be able to discern that the stigmatized individual possesses traits that make him or her different from "normal individuals". Goffman distinguishes between two groups, the *discredited* and the *discreditable*[11] by the way they experience stigma. For the discredited, the external signs of his or her stigma are strong and unavoidable. They have a trait that "can obtrude itself upon the attention and turn those of us whom he meets away from him, breaking the claim that his other attributes have upon him".[12] Thus, an intelligent individual with a bodily disfigurement will be regarded by others as a disfigured individual, and not an intelligent individual. Other stigmas are not so obvious. *Discreditable* are those who may reveal themselves as stigmatized individuals, after certain information is uncovered. Individuals with HIV or diabetes, for instance.[13] Such an individual is discreditable as long as something or someone reveals his or her stigma, the administration of a certain medicament by injection in a public place, for example. Once this occurs, the individual concerned moves from being a *discreditable* individual to a *discredited* one.

Stereotypes can be defined as attributions of specific characteristics of a group. According to psychologist Charles Stangor, they are "traits that we view as characteristic of social groups, or of individual members of those groups, and particularly those that differentiate groups from each other". In short, they are "the traits that come to mind quickly when we think about the groups".[14] Unlike stigma, they are not necessarily negative. For Thomas Cole, stereotypes reflect larger models, categories, or types, ideals, or even myths that societies and individuals use, he writes, "to infuse experience with shared meaning and coherence".[15] For psychologists John Turner and Katherine Reynolds, "self-stereotyping" is the way through which people define themselves and others as members of the same category.[16] Psychologists Fiske, Cuddy, Glick and Xu propose a Stereotype Content Model or theory (SCM)[17], which seeks to assess the content of stereotypes along two dimensions, which they call the "warmth dimension" and the "competence dimension". The first indicates how much a person is perceived in terms of being good or ill-intentioned: the second, whether the person or the group are capable, intelligent or not, confident or less confident and so on.

Another interesting insight comes from gender studies, where, based on empirical research, Michael North and Susan Fiske introduce an interesting distinction between descriptive and prescriptive stereotypes.[18] *Descriptive age stereotypes* describe beliefs about a social group, for example, what women, children or adults are typically like. *Prescriptive age stereotypes* focus on expected or normative behaviours by group members, for example, how women, children, adults or older adults should behave.

The existence of prescriptive stereotypes and, more in general, the definition of stereotyping as knowledge frames suggests that the latter can be a vehicle of power and social pressure. Stereotypes, more or less subtly, can influence what is expected or accepted behaviour and, by doing so, entrench existing hierarchies and social roles, and reinforce inequality.[19] As the case law of the European Court of Human Rights discussed in section 4 shows, assumptions that "women are responsible for childcare" underlie the Russian law denying parental leave to male parents (*Konstantin Martin v. Russia*): "people with a mental disability are incapable of forming political opinions", underlies the legal ban from voting in elections (*Alajos Kiss v. Hungary*); "sex is less important in later life" justifies lower compensation for non-pecuniary damage for older women in cases of medical malpractice (*Carvalho v. Portugal*), and so forth. More subtly, a gender stereotype such as "women are gentler than men" may appear positive, but it entails a generalized view about attributes or characteristics of women, that *ought to be* possessed by women and about roles that *should* be performed by women.[20]

The last notion inscribed in the preamble consideration C of the Chicago Declaration on the rights of older persons is discrimination. The notion evokes distinction, diversification or differentiation made between people, things, cases or situations. Historically, the idea of negative discrimination ('to discriminate against') enters popular usage towards the end of the nineteenth century, especially with regard to race equality.[21] The principle of equality, rooted in the French Revolution (1789), is today enshrined in the bill of rights and constitutions of many constitutional democratic states. In essence, the principle prohibits different treatment of groups or persons who are substantially in the same situation. Historically, it has been implemented, and is being implemented, slowly, progressively, and not without conflict. It is primarily implemented as prohibition to discriminate, without a reasonable justification, on certain "forbidden" or "suspect" grounds: sex, race, colour, language, religion, political or other opinions, national or social origin, association with a national minority, property, birth or other status. Today, age is considered a new suspect ground, included under the category "other status".[22] Starting from the year 2000, under the impulse of the European Union, some European countries have adopted age discrimination legislation in specific sectors, notably employment and occupation.[23] Discrimination law and courts of law can thus be evoked by an individual who complains that a practice, act, regulation or measure produces differential, negative effects on him or her because of his or her age. Before turning in section 3 to analyze the limits of discrimination law to seize forms of discrimination such as stereotyping, the next section advances the perspective of social gerontology. As was mentioned earlier, it is in this branch of gerontology studies that one finds the strong conviction that bias, prejudice, stereotyping and stigma are strictly related and mutually reinforcing (as reflected in the preamble declaration C of the Chicago Charter).

2. THE POINT OF VIEW OF SOCIAL GERONTOLOGY: DISCRIMINATION AND "OTHER FORMS OF DISCRIMINATION" AS MUTUALLY REINFORCING ACTORS IN AN AGEIST ENVIRONMENT

Established in the United States since the 1960s, in England, and only recently gaining foothold in continental Europe, social gerontology research on ageing, ageism and its manifestations departs from a common point: the distinction between biological ageing and social ageing. Pioneering social gerontologist Bernice Neugarten illustrates the distinction well:

> Age is one of the bases for the ascription of status and one of the underlying dimensions by which social interaction is regulated [...]. In all societies, rights, rewards and responsibilities are differentially distributed by age, all societies rationalise the passage of life time, divide life time into socially relevant units, and thus transform biological time into social time.[24]

This quotation highlights that age categories and age roles exist in "all societies" and are part of social arrangements which reflect a given, for example, Western, Asian, culture and way to "rationalize the passage of life time". Since the late 1960s, social gerontology scholars in the United States and later in Europe started observing how the rapid ageing of American and European societies was accompanied by a cultural and societal predisposition towards devaluing ageing and its manifestations: ageism.

The social phenomenon of "ageism" refers to the categorizing of persons solely based on their old age.[25] Similar to other "isms", such as sexism or racism, ageism leverages on group identity and fear for the other, ushering in daily practices which can humiliate and harm older persons solely based on their age.[26] Writing in the early 1990s, Eric Midwinter saw ageism as endemic in all social relations: there is, he argued, a bias against older people as consumers in fashion and design, in marketing strategies (which constantly perpetuate "negative" images of ageing), in civic life (via age barriers to jury service, for example) and in politics and the media.[27] Indeed, since then, empirical research has detected ageism in different areas: in the access to health care and medical treatments,[28] in matters of guardianship,[29] participation in civic services,[30] in employment and occupation,[31] and in economic life,[32] in language and media,[33] and so on. More recent research has started to study how ageism is conveyed through prejudices, stereotypes and stigmas woven into everyday life.[34]

The Stereotype Content Model mentioned earlier, contains two dimensions, warmth and competence, which are used to define a stereotype's content. According to these parameters, older persons score high in the "warmth" dimension, that is, they are nice and inoffensive, and low in the "competence" dimension, that is, they do not know how to do things properly.[35] A person wishing to counter an age stereotype will accordingly want to show that he or she is competent, not just "warm". Empirical research has observed the effects of exposing older persons to negative age stereotypes concerning their competence.[36] Others have underlined that older individuals who try to counter age stereotypes can be penalised.[37] In this connection, Michael North and Susan Fiske, also mentioned earlier, flag an alarm concerning the impact of *prescriptive* age stereotypes, which expect, in fact prescribe, older persons to behave in a certain way.[38] They observe that older adults are pressured into releasing their hold on shared resources such as income, employment, and allocation of government spending. They claim that older persons wishing to counter this prescriptive narrative and, for example, to keep working, may face hostile prejudice. Older persons who relinquish their hold on personal resources may find themselves in the position of Shakespeare's King Lear, if the environment around them is unsupportive.[39]

According to another line of research, influenced by Foucauldian thinking, a key element to understanding ageism is society's "glorification" of youth. For Robert Butler, who coined the term "ageism", "at [other] times ageism serves a highly personal objective, protecting younger (usually middle-aged) individuals – often at high emotional cost – from thinking about things they fear (aging, illness and death.)"[40] According to Jason Powell, ageism reflects a broader societal mindset that attaches value to anti-ageing, that is, to the *non-conformity* to natural discourses of senescence, lowliness and deterioration, morbidity, or dependency.[41] For John Hendricks and Davis Hendricks we tend to see the old as "somehow different from our present and future selves and therefore not subject to the same desires, concerns or fears".[42] The glorification of youth is undeniably well assimilated in contemporary society. The label "anti-ageing" features on goods such as Botox, Viagra, facelifts, potions, and a veritable industry claims to postpone the insurgence of the signs of ageing. "There is much pressure on people to 'age well,'" write Simon Biggs and Jason Powell, "and that is understood to mean that they should maintain as youthful an appearance as possible."[43] Jonathan Herring notes that "we are constantly encouraged to transcend our real age and void the appearance of the lifestyle of the old. That is a costly and painful procedure for many."[44]

When being or appearing old becomes tantamount to a deviant act, being or appearing old could be stigmatizing in itself. Sociologist Toni Calasanti has provided a glimpse of the personal and social cost of trying to look and feel younger than one's age. In an article tellingly titled "How successful is successful ageing,"[45] she relays the results of in-depth interviews with middle-aged men and women around the notion of "successful aging", a well-known theory in gerontology.[46] Calasanti's conclusions are trenchant:

> The unintended consequence of the successful aging paradigm may be both intensified ageism and greater burden on individuals to avoid being marked as old. Focusing on individual lifestyles and personal choices leaves age relations intact. […] Difference, or distance from normative, middle-aged standards is not challenged. Instead, the goal is to show that old people (the stigmatized group) are really 'not that different' from younger groups and thus are worthy. This successful aging framework saddles individuals with responsibility for fixing a problem – ageism – that is social in origin.[47]

Calasanti's statements on the "mark" of being old and of being part of "the stigmatized group", echo with the notion of stigmatization described earlier. In Goffman's description of stigma, older persons can be considered as falling within both *the discredited* and *discreditable* individuals. A person who feels *discreditable* on account of her age will seek to avoid her age being revealed and thus becoming a *discredited* individual. In this imaginary situation, a person feeling discreditable on account of her age can choose between two options. The first, she is open about her age, she refrains from trying to appear of a different age, and she is freed. This option, however, presupposes that she feels that such actions would be well received in her environment. If she is not so confident of a good reception, she would do what Goffman terms as "passing". Passing involves attempting to pass oneself off as a "normal, middle aged individual". As Calasanti writes, hiding evidence of old-age stigma has a cost; it can cause anxiety and stress to the individual who feels lessened in the capacity to act herself.

The last consideration of this section concerns age discrimination, seen from the perspective of social gerontology. As anticipated earlier, age discrimination refers to the use of age categories in the employment and occupation sector, of age as a proxy for decisions relating to hiring, firing, promotion, retraining and retirement. According to a critical view in social gerontology that emerges in the text of the Chicago Declaration, in modern industrial societies and capitalistic economies, age categories have been particularly invidious to those who have less time and who are diminishing in autonomy: older persons. According to this narrative, the transition to modernity has brought about a degradation in the status of old age. For Macnicol, roughly since the late nineteenth century, "capitalism appeared to be entering a new phase, which was dispensing with the labour of older males.[48] [...] It began to be noticed that significant new developments were rendering the older worker obsolete, surplus to requirements and 'worn out' at an earlier stage."[49] Another social gerontologist, Christopher Phillipson, in his *Capitalism and the Construction of Old Age*, maintains that once they are removed from the labour market, older workers are redefined in terms of income as "old age pensioners" and in terms of social policy as "the old and needy".[50] For Peter Townsend, the social protection of older persons has "colonised" the representation of old age, reducing it to a period of unproductivity and of need:[51] thus, the perception of older persons as a burden dependent on the state.[52] The increasing use of age discrimination, while pursuing the welfare of older persons reinforces, in the socio-economic contexts of modern societies of industrialized countries, the structural dependency of older persons. Against this backdrop, stereotypes about older persons are both descriptive and prescriptive.

3. THE POINT OF VIEW OF THE LAW: THE NOTION OF TREATMENT AND THE DIFFERENCE BETWEEN OTHER "FORMS OF DISCRIMINATION" AND "DISCRIMINATION"

From the previous section, the reader must have come under the impression that bias, prejudice, and in particular stereotyping and stigma, "forms of discrimination", on one hand, and "discrimination", on the other, are intertwined. According to the viewpoint of social gerontology, which echoes in the preamble consideration C of the Chicago Declaration, more often than not, the presence of an environment filled with ageist prejudices makes the other forms of discrimination more likely. Conversely, the use of the ground "age", less problematic than class, race or gender, and likely to be accepted as normal,[53] further entrenches ageist social norms and attitudes. From a factual point of view, prejudices or stigmatizing environments may embolden or even provide justification to those who wish to discriminate. The negative prejudices of employers struggling with their own sense of ageing may influence personnel policies towards their older employees, for instance. In many contexts, it is not possible to separate the intent to discriminate and the implicit ageism that influence personal feelings towards old people, which "exist and operate without conscious awareness, intention or control".[54]

While this may be factually correct, there is however an important conceptual difference that needs to be elaborated, as it influences the reach of the law to stem other "forms of discrimination" against older persons. Whilst, from the points of view of social gerontology the concepts of "stereotype", "stigmatization" and "discrimination" are closely related, from a legal viewpoint they differ. The conceptual difference matters, and it is worth clarifying it since it has an effect on the expectations that human rights advocates, such as the drafters of the Chicago Declaration, can lay on discrimination law to tackle ageism.

As Paul Quinn explains, the "induction of psychological effects" is the hallmark of stigmatization. As discussed earlier, stigmatization brings about a situation where the person, individual or group concerned, is or becomes aware of negative views concerning them.[55] As a consequence, the stigmatized individual will activate, consciously or subconsciously, various coping mechanisms to moderate the stimulus of being the object of a prejudice.[56] For instance, imagine a job-seeker in his or her fifties who comes under the clear impression that the employer has a preference for younger applicants. Where this happens, he or she "may" activate coping mechanisms: one such coping mechanism includes avoidance of the stigmatizing stimulus in questions (for example, the 50+-year-old applicant will avoid applying for certain positions, or may develop feelings of anxiety that will influence his or her performance in the interview process). It is important to emphasize the great variability of coping mechanisms. Individuals may employ different coping mechanisms, depending on a range of factors including individual background, personal experience, personality, and so on. Importantly, some individuals may be able to ignore the stigmatizing stimulus and act as if no stigmas were stuck to them. This point, the possibility to ignore the stigmatizing stimulus, is key to understanding the difference between stereotyping/stigmatization and discrimination.

As the case law review carried out in the next section exposes, stigmatizing or stereotyping behaviours or expressions, however offensive, are activities that are purely expressive in nature. Activity that is purely expressive does not compel individuals; individuals remain, at least in theory, able to ignore the negative stimulus. In the example above, the job applicant can ignore the impression of being prejudiced against and may perform well or apply for similar positions within that or another company. In theory, in the absence of other forms of binding "treatment", the induction of psychological effect alone "may" steer the individual, but it does not compel nor does it preclude a person from pursuing his or her preferred course of action. Accordingly, the employer who uses stigmatizing expressions can bring about the harms associated with negative expressions but will not be classified as having committed a discriminatory act under most anti-discrimination approaches (that is, those that require "treatment").

Here lies the conceptual difference. If the hallmark of stigmatization (and negative stereotyping, in some cases) is the "induction of psychological effects", the hallmark of discrimination is the compulsion of a "treatment". As shown below in the case law review, the mark of most legal definitions of discriminatory treatments is that they are capable of bringing about binding changes upon individuals. This entails a "treatment", in the sense that it entails a concrete action (or inaction) that, directly or indirectly, intentionally or unintentionally, "compels" an individual into a certain course of action. In the example above, the job-seeker finds out that the position is open to applicants aged between 25 and 40. The 50+ are precluded from applying to that position, even if they wish to do so.

This legal distinction, as was pointed out earlier, wrestles with the de facto reality. As suggested in sections 1 ad 2 of this chapter, these two phenomena are more often than not found together and the presence of one makes the other more likely. It is unsurprising, therefore, that the drafters of the Chicago Declaration have decided to lump together discrimination, negative stereotypes, and stigma of older persons. However, the possibility for stigmatizing expressions or stereotypes to exist and to procure harmful effects, despite a legal prohibition to discriminate, demonstrates that the two concepts are not the same. The following section shows how the law deals with negative stereotypes or stigmatizing expressions in concrete cases debated in front of the ECtHR.

4. THE CASE LAW OF THE EUROPEAN COURT OF HUMAN RIGHTS ON STEREOTYPES AND STIGMATIZATION

This section analyses a string of cases from the court of Strasbourg's case law with a view to clarify how this human rights court grasps these "forms of discrimination", in particular stereotyping and stigmatization. The next sections 5 and 6 will discuss the circumstances in which the court has deemed these "forms of discrimination" invidious, and the implications for ageist stereotyping and stigma.

Most of the relevant case law of the ECtHR emerges from the jurisprudence on Article 14, the prohibition of discrimination,[57] and Article 8, the right to private and family life.[58] Another relevant string of cases concern freedom of expression (Article 10) and the possibility to infringe upon freedom of speech to stem stigmatization expressions, for instance through hate speech laws (see below section 5).

As a preliminary remark, the prohibition of discrimination has no independent existence but is applicable only in relation to the rights set forth in the Convention,[59] notably Article 8, the right to private and family life, but also other provisions, such as Article 3 protocol 1 on the right to participate in free elections. Most cases, as we will see, relate to race and gender equality issues, as these are the areas where stereotyping, stigma and prejudice have emerged more frequently.

In general, the Court defines discrimination as a difference in treatment between persons in analogous or relevantly similar situations, without an objective and reasonable justification.[60] While States enjoy a certain margin of appreciation in assessing the justification of a different treatment, it is for the Court to give the final ruling.[61] The anti-stereotyping or anti-stigmatization reasoning of the Court thus appears at the stage when the justifications of the defendant state (to implement a difference in treatment) are exposed, weighted and assessed against other rights, competing interests and the Court's own standards.

4.1   Case no.1: *Alajos Kiss v. Hungary* (2010)

The applicant in the case *Alajos Kiss v. Hungary* of 20 May 2010 was a man suffering from manic depression, a condition known as "bipolar disorder", who was placed under partial guardianship. As the country's 2006 political national elections drew near, Mr Kiss realized that a (constitutional) law provision disenfranchised him and all persons under partial or complete guardianship from the right to vote. Mr Kiss complained that this law violated his right to vote, protected in Article 3, Protocol 1 to the European Convention. In front of the Court, the Hungarian government argued that the exclusion of persons affected by Mr Kiss' condition pursued a legitimate aim and it was proportional to the aim: persons are placed under guardianship after a court's decisions; they are excluded from the right to vote because they are deemed incapable of assessing the consequences of their decisions or of making conscious or judicious decisions (paragraph 26); the ban is proportional because the applicant, as any other person, would see his right to vote statutorily restored if his guardianship were rescinded at one of the regular judicial reviews (paragraph 27). In its assessment, the Court accepted that national legislatures have a legitimate interest and a wide "margin of appreciation" in regulating the right to vote (paragraph 41). However, the Court could not accept the argument that the measure was proportionate. The Court explained that it "questions certain classifications per se".[62] Some grounds are suspect because they define groups, such as persons with disabilities, which have been "historically subject to prejudice with lasting consequences, resulting in their social exclusion".[63] The Court could not accept, more specifically, "that an absolute bar on voting by any person under partial guardianship, irrespective of his or her actual faculties, falls within an acceptable margin of appreciation [...]" (paragraph 42). The restriction on a fundamental right of a "particularly vulnerable group in society who have suffered considerable discrimination in the past" must be justified on "very weighty reasons" (paragraph 42). As part of its reasoning, the Court drew the attention to international human rights law, notably the Convention on the Rights of People with Disabilities (CRPD), which protects participation in political and public life (Article 29).[64] A general measure excluding the mentally disabled from voting in elections without consideration of individual cases, "may entail legislative stereotyping which prohibits the individualized evaluation of their capacities and needs" (paragraph 42).

4.2 Case no. 2: *Konstantin Martin v. Russia* (2016)

The second case is *Konstantin Martin v. Russia* of 2016. The case arose after Mr Markin, an employee in the Russian army, who was divorced and the principal tutor to three children, requested and was refused by his employer, the Russian army, three years' parental leave, on the grounds that such a long period of leave could be accorded to female military personnel only. Mr Markin complained to the ECtHR that the refusal constituted discrimination on the basis of sex (Article 14) in conjunction with Article 8, the right to private and family life.[65]

The Russian state offered two justifications in defence of the difference in treatment: first, by granting the right to parental leave to servicewomen only, the legislature had considered the special social role of women associated with motherhood (paragraph 34) and the socially accepted division of tasks between men (breadwinners) and women (carers of children). The government additionally argued that the differential treatment was a positive discrimination measure aimed at "correcting the disadvantaged position of women in society". The Court of Strasbourg turned down both justifications. First, it explained that "references to traditions, general assumptions or prevailing social attitudes in a particular country are insufficient justification for a difference in treatment on grounds of sex. For example, States are prevented from imposing traditions that derive from the man's primordial role and the woman's secondary role in the family." (paragraph 127). The Court asserted that a difference in treatment on the ground of sex requires "very weighty reasons". As in *Kiss*, the Court referred to the general, well established, trends in international human rights law, such as the Convention on the Elimination of all Forms of Discrimination Against Women (CEDAW) and in particular the obligation of signatory states to address harmful gender stereotypes (Art. 5(a)). As for the second justification, the Court did not accept the Russian government's reference to positive discrimination, finding it "misconceived". The different treatment of men and women with regard to entitlement to parental leave, explained the Court, "is clearly not intended to correct the disadvantaged position of women in society or 'factual inequalities' between men and women [...]". The Court retorted that, "instead of protecting a vulnerable group in society" as the government claims, the allegedly preferential measure "has the effect of perpetuating gender stereotypes and is disadvantageous both to women's careers and to men's family life" (paragraph 141). Gender stereotypes based on a traditional distribution of roles are thus negative in general, not only for the father who is denied parental leave, for example, but also for the mother, and for a democratic pluralistic society, because it entrenches existing inequalities. And states shall not impose traditional gender roles and gender stereotypes.[66]

4.3   Case no. 3: *Aksu v. Turkey* (2012)

The case *Aksu v. Turkey* brings to the fore stigmatizing expressions and the impact on the private life of the stigmatized person. Mr Aksu, a Turkish citizen of Roma origin, complained about a book and a dictionary sponsored by the Turkish state that included negative descriptions of Roma people, suggesting they were grudging, dishonest and aggressive. Mr Aksu, who in vain brought civil action asking for non-pecuniary damages and the banning of the publications, filed a complaint to the ECtHR for discrimination on the basis of ethnic origin in conjunction with Art. 8, arguing that these publications harmed his feelings of self-worth and cultural identity.

The Court's jurisprudence on Article 8 is rich and includes within its ambit the protection of personal autonomy.[67] The Court's case law, more specifically, has recognized that cultural identity is an important part of one's autonomy. According to this jurisprudence, it is incumbent on states to take appropriate measures to protect the individual against acts that inhibit the expression and the exercise of one's identity in public. In

Aksu, the question was whether the Turkish government had complied with the positive obligation under Article 8 to protect the applicant's private life from alleged interference by a third party, namely the author of the book (paragraph 61).

Unlike the previous cases, in *Aksu* the Court was not asked to assess the justification of a differential treatment; in this case, the complaint concerned an alleged breach of Article 8 as a consequence of others' exercise of freedom of expression. The Court was asked to balance the conflict between Article 8, which protects private and family life, and Article 10 of the Convention, which protects freedom of expression (paragraph 63).

On one hand, the Court recognized that negative stereotyping can be construed as an interference in the right to private and family life. "Any negative stereotyping of a group," stated the Court, "when it reaches a certain level, is capable of impacting on the group's sense of identity and the feelings of self-worth and self-confidence of members of the group. It is in this sense that it can be seen as affecting the private life of members of the group." (paragraph 58).

On the other hand, the Court pointed out that the private life interests protected by Article 8, must be balanced against the public interest in freedom of expression, "one of the essential foundations of a democratic society" (paragraph 64). In this connection, the Court recalled its well-established position, expressed in the case *Handyside v. the United Kingdom* of 7 December 1976, which is worth quoting:

> Freedom of information is applicable not only to "information" or "ideas" that are favourably received or regarded as inoffensive or as a matter of indifference, but also to those that offend, shock or disturb. Such are the demands of pluralism, tolerance and broadmindedness without which there is no democratic society.[68]

Given the high-pitched demands of pluralism, tolerance and broadmindedness "without which there is no 'democratic society'",[69] it is only in limited contexts, where it is both necessary and proportional, that speech may be restricted. As section 6 discusses in more detail, in *Aksu*, the large majority of the Court did not find a violation of Article 8, because they deemed that the requirements of Article 10, including respect for the rights of others, were respected. All of the jury agreed, save for one judge who strongly disagreed. In the opinion of the dissenting judge, the protection of the right to private life of the applicant did not conflict with the public interest protected by Article 10. The dissenting judge asserted that, according to Article 10.2, the exercise of freedom of expression carries with it duties and responsibilities, including the protection of the reputation or rights of others. "It cannot therefore be interpreted as allowing the promotion or dissemination of the ideas of ethnic hatred and the superiority of one nation vis-à-vis other ethnic groups." (paragraph 10, Dissenting opinion Judge Gyulumyan.)

4.4   Case no. 4: *R.B. v. Hungary* (2016)

This case originated when R.B., a woman of Roma origin, filed a complaint with the ECtHR against Hungarian authorities for failing to adequately investigate harassment and violence against her by demonstrators during an anti-Roma rally, in a village where out of 2800 inhabitants, 400 were of Roma origin. The complaint alleged violations of Article 3 (prohibition on torture), Article 14 (prohibition on discrimination), and Article 8 (right to respect for private and family life).

As far as Article 3 was concerned, the Court held that discrimination based on race could amount to ill-treatment, and therefore fall within the ambit of Article 3. Anti-Roma protestors openly cried discriminatory remarks against R.B. and other members of the Roma community in her village over a period of several days. However, the Court found that the continuous police presence and lack of confrontation prevented "fear, anguish or feelings of inferiority necessary for Article 3 to come into play" (paragraph 51).

As for the alleged violation of the right to private and family life of the defendant, the Court argued that "treatment which does not reach a level of severity sufficient to bring it within the ambit of Article 3 may nonetheless breach the private-life aspect of Article 8". (paragraph 79.) In assessing the alleged violation of Article 8, the Court recalled the principle expressed in *Aksu* (above), according to which "any negative stereotyping of a group, when it reaches a certain level, is capable of impacting on the group's sense of identity and the feelings of self-worth and self-confidence of members of the group". (paragraph 78.) The Court then reiterated that, under Article 8, the state must not only abstain from discriminatory practices, but also take positive obligations to adopt "measures designed to secure respect for private life even in the sphere of the relations of individuals between themselves". (paragraph 81.) In this regard, the Court highlighted that "making verbal threats may require the States to adopt adequate positive measures in the sphere of criminal-law protection" (paragraph 83). In this case, despite R.B.'s reiterated complaints that she suffered violence and harassment on the basis of her ethnicity, the state's police refused to consider the racial or ethnic motives, treating the verbal attacks as a general crime. But, as the Court stressed, R.B. was insulted and threatened in the context of anti-Roma rallies, and law-enforcement authorities needed to consider this context. The court found that Hungarian law provided no appropriate legal avenue for the applicant to seek remedy for the alleged racially motivated insult. In this connection, the Court found a violation of article 8 (paragraph 90). However, it is important to note, the Court did not accept the argument of the plaintiff R.B. that the state did not try to mitigate the impact of large demonstrations led by anti-Roma groups. Although the Court accepted that the demonstration might have caused stress to R.B., the decision suggests that the law also protects the right to hold public assemblies even if these may be insulting in content and purpose (paragraph 101).

4.5 Case no. 5: *Carvalho Pinto de Sousa Morais v. Portugal* (2017)

In 1995, when she was 50, Ms Carvalho was the victim of a medical error during a surgery procedure that caused her incontinence and pain and left her seriously impaired in her personal and sexual life in particular. Ms Carvalho brought a civil claim against the hospital and was awarded a sum of money as pecuniary and non-pecuniary compensation. Upon appeal, the national Supreme Administrative Court, however, sensibly reduced the amount due for non-pecuniary damage. Ms Carvalho filed a complaint with the ECtHR arguing that the decision of the Supreme Administrative to reduce the said compensation had been taken on the postulation that sexuality was not as important for a 50-year-old woman. She complained of a violation of Article 14 in conjunction with Article 8.

In the impugned judgment, the Supreme Administrative Court justified its decision on the grounds that the medical condition of the plaintiff was old (a), and that surgery had aggravated an already difficult situation (b). In addition, (c), as a partial justification for reducing the compensation, the supreme national court had pointed out, – what was later termed by the defendant government an "unfortunate turn of phrase", namely, "that at the time of the operation the plaintiff was already 50 years old and had two children, that is, *an age when sex is not as important as in younger years, its significance diminishing with age*".[70]

In short, the Court did not accept the explanation that the wording (point c) used by the Supreme Administrative Court's judgment could be regarded as an "unfortunate turn of phrase".[71] Rather, in the Court's view, "the applicant's age and sex appear to have been decisive factors in the final decision, introducing a difference of treatment based on those grounds".[72] The Court laid its ruling after recalling and quoting from two reports from the UN Human Rights Council's Special Rapporteur on the Independence of Judges and Lawyers, and UN Committee on the Elimination of Discrimination against Women (CEDAW), highlighting the existence of sexist prejudices in the Portuguese judiciary. As a decisive factor in the decision, the Court pointed out the blatant contrast between the treatment received by the applicant, on one hand, and the treatment reserved to two male victims of malpractice in other judgments, mentioned by the plaintiff; in those cases, the Supreme Court of Justice awarded a higher compensation amount for non-pecuniary damage, without any reference to their age, their gender, or to whether they had children or not.[73] The majority of the Court concluded that outdated gender stereotypes had influenced a judicial decision and this amounted to a violation of the applicant's Convention rights.

It must be pointed out, however, that the decision on discrimination proved highly divisive, with two judges of the seven judges-strong Court joining in a forceful dissenting opinion. According to the dissenters, the Court failed to recognize that the discrimination of the applicant's sexual life was made dependent on, and based on her age, not on her gender. The minority judges concluded that the majority plainly did not get the facts right; the impugned judgment did not state that "women's sexual life is less important than that of men" but laid its decision on another, evident, and most relevant discriminating factor and stereotype: the age of the applicant and that sex is not important in later life.[74]

5. THE INSTANCES IN WHICH STEREOTYPING MAY INFRINGE ON THE CONVENTION'S RIGHTS

This section elicits some considerations about the legal factors and bonds that the Court needs to take into account to decide on treatments allegedly underlined by stereotyping and discusses some implications for ageist stereotyping.

The first consideration stems from the conceptual difference highlighted in section 3. In all cases engaging Article 14, the Court censors prejudices and stereotypes when they underline differences in treatment. For instance, the idea that "women are responsible for childcare", underlying the Russian law recognizing three years' parental leave to women only (*Konstantin Martin v. Russia*); that "people with a mental disability are incapable of forming political opinions", underlying the constitutional ban from participating in public elections (*Alajos Kiss v. Hungary*); that "sex is less important in later life", underlying the national Court's decision to reduce non-pecuniary damage compensation to older women (*Carvalho v. Portugal*). In contrast, expressions, slogans, and an environment filled with prejudices, as in *Aksu v. Turkey* and in *R.B v. Hungary*, do not necessarily represent acts of discriminatory "treatment".

Second, in cases involving the alleged use of stereotyping, the Court performs an analysis of the justification of the difference in treatment. The Court's point of departure for this analysis is the deference to national legislatures and the recognition of states' "margin of appreciation". In some cases, the width of the margin is narrow and the scrutiny of proportionality strict. It is stricter in cases, such as *Alajos Kiss v Hungary*, where the Court acknowledges "a history of discrimination".[75] As it stated in that case, the Court "questions certain classifications per se".[76] Some grounds are suspect because they define groups that have been historically subject to prejudice with lasting consequences, resulting in their social exclusion. Arguably age classifications do not attract such a strong label because older persons, unlike ethic groups, women, and persons with disabilities, are not associated with such a historical discrimination.[77] Accordingly, the recognition of age stereotyping seems to be less forthcoming than other stereotypes. As pointed out by social gerontologists, age is accepted as a "normal" or "inevitable" discriminatory ground in most contexts; unlike gender, race and disability, age discrimination law applies only to some sectors, notably employment, and it is a more recently established "suspect" ground in state parties' jurisdictions.

Third, not all stereotypes or forms of discrimination are invidious to the rights protected by the Convention. They are invidious when they are based on prejudice and on irrational motives (*Konstantin Martin v. Russia*), because they make it impossible for individuals to be evaluated according to their capacities and needs (*Alajos Kiss v. Hungary*), or because they are downright untrue (*Carvalho v. Portugal*). Research from Alexandra Timmer indicates that, when dealing with cases involving positive measures to correct factual inequalities, the ECtHR is prone to accept the use of stereotypes, for instance in the case of allocation of social benefits awarded to older female widows (but not to men).[78] Age stereotypes which describe older persons in paternalistic terms may thus be accepted.[79]

Fourth, in order to prove that the stereotype is a negative stereotype, the Court often looks at, and takes into account, the reporting from human rights treaty bodies: the reports by United Nations Treaty bodies of the CEDAW and of the CRPD are mobilized in the cases of *Alajos v. Hungary*, *Konstantin Martin v. Russia* and *Carvalho v. Portugal*. It is known that there is no such reporting mechanism concerning the human rights of older persons.[80] This lacuna may be the reflection of a more general lack of awareness about ageism. In the Carvalho case, two judges disagreed about whether the case had to be heard under the rubric of age or sex discrimination. The majority went well beyond the formal legalistic literature and brought in references to gender studies, books and human history, in order to justify their decision regarding the discrimination of women based on gender.[81] Nothing similar was done with reference to the social construction of old age and ageism.[82]

Fifth, *Konstantin Martin v. Russia* may be a landmark decision, because the Court, in this case, censored a stereotype (on the role of women as carers of children) which did not adversely affect that group specifically (women). According to Alexandra Timmer, the case shows the commitment of the human rights court law to implement the principle of "equality among sexes". As the Court stressed, gender-role stereotyping is "disadvantageous both to women's careers and to men's family life".[83] If *Konstantin Martin v. Russia*, according to Timmer, shows the commitment of the human rights court to embrace "equality among sexes", for the reasons explained above concerning the status of age as grounds for discrimination, it seems to us unlikely that a similar term, "equality among ages", may be ascribed to the Court in the future.

6. THE POTENTIAL AND THE LIMITS OF THE LAW ON HATE SPEECH TO TACKLE AGEIST STIGMATIZING EXPRESSIONS

As mentioned in section 3, stigmatizing expressions are a good example of activities that can bring about harm but that will not be classified as discriminatory acts under most anti-discrimination approaches (that is, those that require "treatment"), especially where it reaches a level that would not be considered hate speech. Expressive activity may have evidential value in the presence of treatment, for example in indicating the motives of the party carrying out the "treatment" in question; however, it is alone unable to constitute an act or treatment itself in terms of Article 14. The Court has long accepted (from the case *Handyside v. UK* of 1976 mentioned earlier in the analysis of *Aksu v. Turkey*) that stigmatizing expressions mobilize another fundamental freedom, namely, the freedom of expression (Article 10). As mentioned earlier in the analysis of *Aksu*, the protection offered by Article 10 to expressive activity is ample. It is so ample that the Court has recognized an individual's right to make remarks that "shock, offend or disturb".[84] It might therefore be considered unlikely that a Court would be willing to consider speech that is merely stigmatizing (that is, that at least in theory could be ignored by those whom it might concern) to be serious enough to warrant an infringement upon freedom of speech.

A common example, in Europe, of a situation in which courts may be willing to infringe upon free speech is in the case of hate speech. It is important to nuance this discussion, especially if one is to take a considered position over what exactly hate speech is and what its relationship to stigmatizing remarks might be. First, as just mentioned, matters relating to hate speech are usually considered under Article 10:[85] second, most hate speech cases come before the ECHR as appeals against the imposition of national laws on hate speech. The applicants in such cases are not thus demanding that an act of expression be curtailed, but that the application of a national law be ruled invalid in a particular context.[86] The Court has never directly imposed a positive duty on signatory states of the ECHR to prohibit hate speech, though it has, in *Aksu v. Turkey* and *R.B. v. Hungary*, for example, invoked the existence of such a duty indirectly in its reasoning.[87] Third, in the system of the Convention, the obligations, both positive and negative, of states are defined on a case-by-case basis, balancing, in each concrete instance, the competing interests of the individual and of the community as a whole.

In the light of the foregoing, the question can be raised as to whether, or under which circumstances, a duty to adopt measures designated to prevent hate speech against older persons could materialize. To answer this question, one must ask when remarks against older people can be categorized as hate speech.

An important point concerns the intensity of hate speech. Such intensity is reflected in many ways by the exceptional nature of hate speech crimes, which represent an exception to the generally very high level of freedom of expression expected in democratic societies. Exceptions are usually made for particular groups that have been historical victims of violence or that are in a position of systematic socio-economic disadvantage in many of the most important contexts in society. Members of such groups are usually characterized by conditions that are immutable and that define the status of being member of a certain group in public. An infringement regarding freedom of speech can be justified by the protection of public order. Negative expressive activities against certain groups may be linked with or be conducive to an increase in violent attacks against these groups.

Where such exceptions could or should be made about derogatory remarks concerning older people is at the very least more open to debate, especially in comparison with when remarks are made about particular ethnic groups. This is because older persons are not perceived as being historical victims of violence or as being in a position of systematic socio-economic disadvantage in many of the most important contexts in society. Whilst the elderly face discrimination in the job market, they are in many countries and contexts in an advantageous position (for example relating to property ownership or general level of wealth) with respect to other age groups.

As for the exception of "public order", whilst there may be sporadic examples of attacks on older persons, there is no history of them being systematic victims of violence because of their age.

As for the immutability of the condition, unlike ethnicity, birth, gender and sexual orientation, age is a unique ground for discrimination. Age is constantly changing: we are young, then we grow old, moving through stages of life and age groups. Age is constantly changing and yet no one has any control over it. Accordingly, the applicability of the concept of immutability to a category such as "older people" is less straightforward than it is for other classic, vulnerable groups that commonly receive protection under hate speech laws.[88]

In the hypothesis that ageist remarks were considered, for instance by a plaintiff in a case similar to R.B., as hate speech, what, according to the Court, would be the duty of the state to prevent them? As discussed earlier, the relatively high threshold set by Article 10 ECHR only allows infringement of freedom of expressions in certain limited circumstances. If the Court were to be asked whether there is a positive duty to prevent hate speech against the elderly, it would likely take into consideration the historical, concrete and present conditions in which older people live. It would assess, following *R.B. v. Hungary*, whether such expressions are so serious as to constitute an infringement on Article 8, the right to private life.

In practice, the existence of a positive duty on states that are members of the Council of Europe to implement hate speech laws would have to take into account the great variability across Europe in the substance of hate speech laws and of the form they take. Whilst most states protect a familiar core of categories (for example ethnicity, religious belief, sexual orientation, disability and so on), outside of this there exists great variation on what further categories enjoy protection. In some states "age" may find itself as protected, in many others it is not.[89] In terms of form, the way laws are formulated may also make an important difference. Where, for example, laws exist in the form of "*incitement of hatred*" laws, the threshold of application may be extremely high. Incitement of hatred is often linked to potential threats of violence or expressions that are likely to be conducive to an atmosphere that is harmful for public order. The threshold for such an offensive to be met may thus be high and may not include ambivalent, impolite or politically incorrect language that, although stigmatizing, is unlikely to be seen as intentionally inciting hatred. In some states however, laws may exist that can be categorized under the concept of "incitement to discrimination". Such offences may be thought of as having a lower threshold, given that they simply require calls for differential treatment, that is, that the legal rights and duties of older people be formulated differently from other categories in society. Expressions of such a nature concerning older groups are more common and easier to envisage than expressions of hatred against such groups. One can imagine, for instance, expressions suggesting that certain jobs or financial benefits should not be available to older people. Finally, it must be remembered that two important points will limit the importance of "incitement to discrimination" provisions across Europe in general. The first is that even though the threshold may be relatively lower than that for "incitement to hatred" type offences, the specifics of the offence in question must nonetheless still be met. Where there is no call for differential treatment of older people (that is, in cases where remarks are simply derogatory), such offences will not apply. The second is that such offences do not exist in many jurisdictions across Europe. Where this is the case, such calls for differential treatment of older groups will attract no penalty.

7. CONCLUSION

This chapter began with a quote from the non-binding Chicago Declaration on the Rights of Older Persons:

> Recognizing that discrimination against any person on the basis of age is a violation of the inherent dignity and worth of the human person, and ageism and the social construction of old age, including bias, stereotypes, prejudices, and stigma of older persons are forms of discrimination that hinder the full realization of their human rights and participation of older persons as equal members of society;

As discussed in this chapter, this preamble resonates with the considerations of a vein of social gerontology research and scholarship, which contend that age discrimination and other (non-legal) ageist forms of discrimination are intimately tied manifestations of a social phenomenon: ageism. This chapter has subjected this preambular declaration to the consideration of the law. More specifically, the authors, drawing from case law of the European Court of Human Rights, have tried to bring into relief the legal factors and the bonds that this court of law must reckon with when deciding on, a. discriminatory treatments allegedly underlined by stereotyping notions, and on, b. stigmatizing expressions. The conclusion is that there are inherent limits in terms of using the law, especially general anti-discrimination approaches, to stem ageist stereotypes and stigmatizing expressions. One issue relates to the legal consideration developed in section 3: anti-discrimination law requires "treatment", that is, the existence of a concrete act. The court has chastised stereotypical ideas of social roles only when such ideas were inscribed or underlined legislative measures or administrative decisions. This has not been the case where they were not accompanied by some form of "treatment". Similarly, stigmatizing expressions will not be classified as discriminatory acts under anti-discrimination approaches, which require "treatment".

Another important factor concerns the ground of "age". The Court of Human Rights is particularly sensitive to classifications that define groups, such as persons with disabilities, women, and ethnic groups which have been "historically subject to prejudice with lasting consequences, resulting in their social exclusion".[90]

For a court to detect a negative duty to refrain from using, in a treatment, stereotypical ideas about old age, it would have to take into consideration the historical, concrete and present conditions in which older people live. It would equally have to consider whether a history of social exclusion exists if the court were to detect a positive duty to prevent hate speech against the elderly. One must arguably reckon with the fact that, while the social gerontology literature is large and growing, the social demand and the activism to stem ageism has not reached dimensions comparable to, for example, the feminist, anti-racist or working-class movements, and therefore is unlikely to be considered as requiring a limitation to the liberty of expression.

NOTES

1. Eva Brems and Alexandra Timmer. 2016. *Stereotypes and human rights law*. London: Intersentia; Alexandra Timmer. 2011. "Toward an anti-stereotyping approach for the European Court of Human Rights". *Human Rights Law Review*, 11(4), 707–38. Alexandra Timmer. 2015. "Judging stereotypes: what the European Court of Human Rights can borrow from American and Canadian equal protection law". *The American Journal of Comparative Law*, 63(1), 239–84.
2. The Declaration was drafted at the conclusion of the 2014 International Elder Law and Policy Conference organized by The John Marshall Law School, Roosevelt University of Chicago, College of Arts and Sciences, and the East China University of Political Science and Law (Shanghai, China). The Declaration is the outcome of coordinated efforts of

academics and NGOs. The charter is, of course, not a binding piece of international law. It is work in progress.

3. On the human rights status of older persons see Paul de Hert and Eugenio Mantovani. 2011. "Specific human rights for older persons?" *European Human Rights Law Review*, **4**, 398–418. See also Israel Doron and Apter Itai. 2010. "The debate around the need for an international convention on the rights of older persons". *The Gerontologist*, **50**(5), 586–93.
4. Jill S. Quadagno. 1999. *Aging and the Life Course: An Introduction to Social Gerontology*. Boston, MA: McGraw-Hill College.
5. Robert Butler. 1969. "Age-ism: another form of bigotry". *The Gerontologist*, **9**, 243–6; William Bytheway. 1995. *Ageism*. Buckingham: Open University Press; Jack Levin and William Levin. 1980. *Ageism: Prejudice and Discrimination against the Elderly*. Belmont, CA: Wadsworth Publishing Company. Erdman B. Palmore. 1999. *Ageism: Negative and Positive*. New York, NY: Springer.
6. Peter Tiersma. 2010. *Parchment, Paper, Pixels: Law and the Technologies of Communication*. Chicago, IL: University Press.
7. Vincenzo Arangio-Ruiz. 1935. "Pregiudizio". In *Treccani Enciclopedia Italiana*. Accessed 11 February 2018 at http://www.treccani.it/enciclopedia/pregiudizio_%28Enciclopedia-Italiana%29/.
8. With the exception of Christianity, which imbues *stigma* with a positive meaning related to the virtuous wounds of Christ.
9. L.H. Yang, A. Kleinman, B.G. Link, J.C. Phelan, S. Lee and B. Good 2007. "Culture and stigma: adding moral experience to stigma theory". *Social Science & Medicine*, **64**(7), 1524–35.
10. Erving Goffman. 1963. *Stigma: Notes on the Management of Spoiled Identity*. New York, NY: Simon and Schuster, p. 1.
11. Goffman, 1963, op. cit., p. 14.
12. Goffman, 1963, op. cit., pp. 4–5.
13. Gloria Joachim and Sonia Acorn. 2000. "Stigma of visible and invisible chronic conditions". *Journal of Advanced Nursing*, **32**(1), 243–8.
14. Charles Stangor. 2004. "The study of stereotyping, prejudice, and discrimination within social psychology: a quick history of theory and research". In Todd D. Nelson (ed.). *Handbook of Prejudice, Stereotyping and Discrimination*. New York, NY: Taylor & Francis Group, p. 3. "We desire as much as possible," he writes, "to differentiate individuals from different categories from each other, and to view individuals within categories as maximally similar."
15. Thomas R. Cole. 1992. *The Journey of Life: a Cultural History of Aging in America*. Cambridge: Cambridge University Press, p. 228.
16. John Turner and Katherine Reynolds. 2011. "Self-categorization theory". In Paul A.M. Van Lange, Arie W. Kruglanski and E. Tory Higgins (eds). *Handbook of Theories in Social Psychology*. London: Sage Publications, pp. 399–417. Individuals would "self-stereotype" in relation to the category, called the salient category, and tend to see themselves as more alike in terms of the defining attributes of the category". (p. 403). For example, if a person's salient self-category becomes "lawyer" then that person is likely to act in terms of the norms associated with that category (e.g. to wear a suit and a tie) and to accentuate the similarities between him or herself and other members of the "lawyer" category.
17. Susan Fiske, A. Cuddy, P. Glick and J. Xu. 2002. "A model of (often mixed) stereotype content: competence and warmth respectively follow perceived status and competition." *Journal of Personality and Social Psychology*, **82**, 878–902.
18. Michael North and Susan Fiske. 2013. "Act your (old) age: prescriptive, ageist biases over succession, consumption, and identity." *Personality and Social Psychology Bulletin*, **39**, 720–34.
19. Alexandra Timmer. 2015, op. cit., p. 241.
20. Rebecca J. Cook and Simone Cusack. 2010. *Gender Stereotyping: Transnational Legal Perspectives*. Pennsylvania: University of Pennsylvania Press, p. 9.

21. John Macnicol. 2006. *Age Discrimination: An Historical and Contemporary Analysis*, Cambridge: Cambridge University Press, p. 7.
22. See Helen Meenan. 2007. "Reflecting on age discrimination and rights of the elderly in the European Union and the Council of Europe". *Maastricht Journal of European and Comparative Law*, **14**(1), 39–82.
23. Helen Meenan. 2007, op. cit.
24. Bernice L. Neugarten. 1996. "Age distinctions and their social functions", in Dail A. Neugarten (ed.), *The Meanings of Age: Selected Papers of Bernice L. Neugarten*, Chicago, IL: University of Chicago Press, pp. 59–60.
25. Robert Butler. 1971. *Why Survive? Being Old in America*. Baltimore, MD: Johns Hopkins University Press; Todd D. Nelson. 2004. (ed.). *Ageism: Stereotyping and Prejudice Against Older Persons*. Cambridge, MA: MIT Press; Todd D. Nelson. 2005. "Ageism: prejudice against our feared future self", *Journal of Social Issues*, **61**(2), 207–21. Erdman B. Palmore. 1999. *Ageism: Negative and Positive*. New York, NY: Springer; Thomas N. Iversen, Laris Larsen and Per Erik Solem. 2009. "A conceptual analysis of ageism", *Nordic Psychology*, **61**(3), 4–22. For a European perspective, see the recent book by Liat Ayalon and Clemens Tesch-Römer (eds). 2018. *Contemporary Perspectives on Ageism*. Cham: Springer International Publishing, the result of a European collaboration (COST action).
26. Eugenio Mantovani, Benny Spanier and Israel (Issi) Doron. 2018. "Ageism, human rights, and the European Court of Human Rights: a critical analysis of the Carvalho v. Portugal case". *DePaul Journal for Social Justice*, **11**(2), art. 2.
27. Eric Midwinter. 1992. *Citizenship: from Ageism to Participation*. Carnegie United Kingdom Trust for Carnegie Inquiry into the Third Age, quoted in John Macnicol. 2006, p. 9.
28. Aya Ben-Harush, S. Shiovitz-Ezra, I. Doron, S. Alon, A. Leibovitz, H. Golander, Y. Haron and L. Ayalon. 2017. "Ageism among physicians, nurses, and social workers: findings from a qualitative study". *European Journal of Ageing*, **14**(1), 39–48.
29. Monisha Pasupathi and Corinna Löckenhoff. 2004. "Ageist behavior". In Todd D. Nelson (ed.). *Ageism: Stereotyping and Prejudice Against Older Persons*. Cambridge, MA: MIT Press, pp. 215–16.
30. Shamena Anwar, Patrick Bayer and Randi Hjalmarsson. 2014. "The role of age in jury selection and trial outcomes". *The Journal of Law and Economics*, **57**(4), 1001–30.
31. Dominic Abrams, Hannah Swift and Lisbeth Drury. 2016. "Old and unemployable? How age-based stereotypes affect willingness to hire job candidates". *Journal of Social Issues*, **72**(1), 105–21.
32. Martin Kohli. 2007. "The institutionalization of the life course: looking back to look ahead". *Research in Human Development*, **4**(3–4), 253–71.
33. Tracey Gendron, E. Welleford, J. Inker and J. White. 2016. "The language of ageism: Why we need to use words carefully". *The Gerontologist*, **56**(6), 997–1006.
34. Alison Chasteen and Lindsey A. Cary. 2015. "Age stereotypes and age stigma: connections to research on subjective aging". *Annual Review of Gerontology and Geriatrics*, **35**(1), 99–119; Michael North and Susan Fiske. 2013, op. cit.. Susan Fiske et al. 2002, op. cit.
35. Susan Fiske et al.. 2002, op. cit.
36. Imagine three people of different ages in an office, sitting in front of a PC, with the oldest at the keyboard. During a stereotype-relevant situation like this, the person at the keyboard is concerned about confirming a negative group stereotype, namely: older people have poor IT skills. This concern influences the older person's performance so that he or she may end up confirming the stereotype. Alison Chasteen and Lindsey A. Cary. 2015, op. cit., p. 107, referring to a study by Claude Steele and Joshua Aronson. 1995. "Stereotype threat and the intellectual test performance of African Americans" *Journal of Personality and Social Psychology*, **69,** 797–811.
37. Alison Chasteen and Lindsey A. Cary. 2015. op. cit., pp. 103 and 114.
38. Michael North and Susan Fiske. 2013, op. cit.
39. Emilio Mordini and Eugenio Mantovani. 2010. "Ageing in the information society" In E. Mordini and P. de Hert, *Ageing and Invisibility*, the Netherlands: IOS Press, pp. 59–61.

40. Robert Butler. 1995. "Ageism". In George L. Maddox (ed.) *The Encyclopedia of Aging.* Berlin and Heidelberg: Springer-Verlag, p. 35.
41. Jason Powell. 2004. "Rethinking gerontology: Foucault, surveillance and the positioning of old age", in *Sincronía.* Accessed 11 February 2018 at http://sincronia.cucsh.udg.mx/powell04.htm.
42. John Hendricks and C. Davis Hendricks. 1978. "Ageism and Common Stereotypes". In Vida Carver and Penny Liddiard (eds). *An Ageing Population. A Reader and Sourcebook.* New York, NY: Holmes & Meier Publishers, p. 60.
43. Simon Biggs and Jason L. Powell. 2001. "A Foucauldian analysis of old age and the power of social welfare". *Journal of Aging & Social Policy,* **12**(2), 93–112, p. 101.
44. Jonathan Herring. 2009. *Older People in Law and Society.* Oxford: Oxford University Press, p. 18.
45. Toni Calasanti. 2015. "Combating ageism: How successful is successful aging?" *The Gerontologist,* **56**(6), 1093–101.
46. John Rowe and Robert Kahn. 1997. "Successful aging". *The Gerontologist,* **37**(4), 433–40. Successful ageing is based on three points: (a) the avoidance of disease and disability; (b) maintaining high levels of mental and physical function; and (c) active engagement with life, which revolves around relationships with other people, and behaviour that is productive.
47. Toni Calasanti. 2015, op. cit., p. 1100.
48. John Macnicol. 2006, op. cit., p. 41.
49. John Macnicol. 2006, op. cit., p. 21.
50. Christopher Phillipson. 1982. *Capitalism and the Construction of Old Age.* London: Macmillan, p. 6. For a book review see Phil Slater. 1999. Book Reviews, *The British Journal of Social Work,* **29**(4), 639–41.
51. In industrial society, old age is primarily seen as an age of non-production and non-activity: "The old man in the rural-agriculture society is the wise man; in the industrial society is a relict," writes historian Carlo Maria Cipolla (Carlo Maria Cipolla. 1980. *Storia Economica dell'Europa Pre-industriale.* Bologna: Il Mulino, p. 303).
52. Peter Townsend. 1981. "The structured dependency of the elderly: a creation of social policy in the twentieth century". *Ageing and Society,* **1**(1), 5–28.
53. John Macnicol. 2006, op. cit., p. 6.
54. Todd D. Nelson. 2004, op. cit., p. 51.
55. Paul Quinn. 2017. "The problem of stigmatizing expressions: the limits of anti-discrimination approaches". *International Journal of Discrimination and the Law,* **17**(1), p. 5.
56. Paul Quinn. 2017, op. cit.
57. Article 14 states: "The enjoyment of the rights and freedoms set forth in this Convention shall be secured without discrimination on any ground such as sex, race, colour, language, religion, political or other opinion, national or social origin, association with a national minority, property, birth or other status."
58. Article 8 states: "1. Everyone has the right to respect for his private and family life, his home and his correspondence. 2. There shall be no interference by a public authority with the exercise of this right except such as is in accordance with the law and is necessary in a democratic society in the interests of national security, public safety or the economic well-being of the country, for the prevention of disorder or crime, for the protection of health or morals, or for the protection of the rights and freedoms of others."
59. Janneke Gerards. 2013. "The discrimination grounds of Article 14 of the European Convention on Human Rights". *Human Rights Law Review,* **13**(1), 99–124.
60. ECtHR, Case "relating to certain aspects of the laws on the use of languages in education in Belgium", no. 2126/64, judgment of 23 July 1968.
61. See ECtHR, *Rasmussen v. Denmark,* no. 8777/79, judgment of 28 November 1984, paragraph 40.
62. *Alajos Kiss v. Hungary.* European Court of Human Rights (ECtHR), May 2010, Application no. 38832/06, paragraph 42.

63. *Alajos Kiss v. Hungary*, op. cit.
64. UN General Assembly, Convention on the Rights of Persons with Disabilities: resolution adopted by the General Assembly, 24 January 2007, A/RES/61/106, accessed 10 July 2018 at http://www.refworld.org/docid/45f973632.html.
65. ECtHR, *Konstantin Martin v. Russia*, Application no. 30078/06, of 22 March 2012.
66. ECtHR, *Konstantin Martin v. Russia*, Application no. 30078/06, of 22 March 2012, paragraph 142.
67. See the cases of *Evans v. UK* of 7 March 2006, paragraph 71 and *Pretty v. UK* of 28 April 2002, paragraph 61. In these cases, the Court stated that the notion of private life includes aspects of an individual's physical and social identity, including "the right to personal autonomy".
68. ECtHR, *Handyside v. the United Kingdom*, Application no. 5493/72, of 7 December 1976.
69. ECtHR, *Handyside v. the United Kingdom*, op. cit.
70. ECtHR, *Carvalho Pinto de Sousa Morais v. Portugal*, Application no. 17484/15, of 25 July 2017, para. 16 (our emphasis).
71. ECtHR, *Carvalho Pinto de Sousa Morais v. Portugal*, op. cit., para. 53.
72. ECtHR, *Carvalho Pinto de Sousa Morais v. Portugal*, op. cit.
73. ECtHR, *Carvalho Pinto de Sousa Morais v. Portugal*, op. cit., para. 55.
74. Eugenio Mantovani, Benny Spanier, Israel (Issi) Doron. 2018, op. cit.
75. ECtHR, *Alajos Kiss v. Hungary*, Application no. 38832/06, judgment of 20 May 2010, paras 11–17. The Court refers to Article 12 (equal recognition before the law) and Article 29 (Participation in political and public life) of the 2006 United Nations Convention on the Rights of Persons with Disabilities (CRPD), to Council of Europe Recommendation (99)4 on incapable adults (Article 1.1 Universal suffrage), and Recommendation (2006)5 on persons with disabilities (Action Line no.1).
76. ECtHR, *Alajos Kiss v. Hungary*, Application no. 38832/06, judgment of 20 May 2010, paragraph 42.
77. Mégret states that "there is no doubt that the Holocaust was preceded by, among other things, a campaign of 'euthanasia' that was specifically directed at the old". Fredric Mégret. 2011. "The human rights of older persons: a growing challenge", *Human Rights Law Review*, **111**, 37–66, p. 46.
78. Alexandra Timmer. 2015, op. cit., p. 250. Timmer refers to the case *Runkee and White v. United Kingdom*, of 10 May 2007.
79. For instance, in cases of mandatory retirement. In a case in front of the European Court of Justice (ECJ) of the European Union, concerning the prohibition of discrimination on the ground of age and termination of employment for age limits (Art. 6 Directive 2000/78/EC) the Court accepted the argument of the defendant state that the law on mandatory retirement, the result of social mediations, also sought to avoid the humiliation of workers who, reaching a certain age, have, in order to sustain their needs, to work and compete for work with younger age groups. European Court of Justice, Case C-141/11, *Torsten Hörnfeldt v. Posten Meddelande* AB, published in the electronic Reports of Cases (Court Reports – general), paragraphs 26 and 27 in particular. In this case, the age stereotype is both descriptive and prescriptive, because it describes and prescribes a vision of life span development and the attendant age roles, where active and working life is for the young, slow and retired life for the old. For a detailed overview and a discussion on age discrimination law in the EU and older persons see A. Numhauser-Henning and M. Rönnmar (eds). 2015. *Age Discrimination and Labour Law, Comparative and Conceptual Perspectives in the EU and Beyond*. Alphen aan den Rijn: Wolters Kluwer.
80. Israel Doron and Apter Itai. 2010, op. cit.
81. "For centuries a woman's entire life was confined to the production of children and to their care. 'Kinder, Küche, Kirche' as the only permissible areas for female activity. A woman was not respected as a human being. Her desires were ignored." ECtHR, *Carvalho Pinto de Sousa Morais v. Portugal*, Application no. 17484/15, of 25 July 2017, Concurring opinion of Judge Yudkivska, p. 21.

82. For a critical analysis see Eugenio Mantovani, Benny Spanier, Israel (Issi) Doron, 2018, forthcoming, op. cit.
83. Alexandra Timmer. 2015, op. cit., p. 246.
84. ECtHR, *Handyside v. the United Kingdom* of 7 December 1976, paragraph 49.
85. ECtHR, *Aksu v. Turkey*, Application nos 4149/04 and 41029/04, judgment of 15 March 2012, paragraph 59.
86. The vast majority of cases represent appeals against the application of national laws on hate speech to particular acts of expression (for example notable cases include *Leroy v. France* (application no. 36109/03), *Jerslid v. Denmark* (application no. 15890/89), *Vejdeland and Others v. Sweden* (application no. 1813/07) and *Feret v. Belgium* (application no. 15615/07)).
87. *Aksu v. Turkey*, paragraph 62 and *R.B. v. Hungary*, Application no. 64602/12, judgment of 12 April 2016, paragraph 78.
88. The example of religious or philosophical belief is, however, another commonly protected category that does not sit well with the concept of immutability.
89. Helen Meenan. 2012. "Age discrimination and the future development of elder rights in the European Union: walking side by side or hand in hand?", in I. Doron and A.M. Soden (eds), *Beyond Elder Law*. Berlin and Heidelberg: Springer, pp. 57–97.
90. See above, *Alajos Kiss v. Hungary*.

7. The European Social Charter and the rights of older persons

Benny Spanier and Israel (Issi) Doron

INTRODUCTION

The human rights of older persons in Europe are protected in many different ways. On the regional level, at least two key legal frameworks exist, which are not only well-known, but have their own courts, which rule and set legal precedents in the field. The first framework is the European Convention on Human Rights (ECHR) and its unique court, the European Court of Human Rights (ECtHR). Although no specific reference is made to rights of older persons as such within the ECHR, throughout the years the ECtHR has made decisions on some key cases regarding the rights of older persons (Mikołajczyk, 2013; Spanier et al., 2013). The second framework is that of the European Union (EU); it is the Charter of Fundamental Rights, which has its own unique court, the Court of Justice of the European Union (CJEU). Although specific reference to the human rights of older persons was added only within the proclamation of the Charter of Fundamental Rights (Article 25), here again, through the years the CJEU has built a body of case law regarding the rights of older persons (Doron, 2013; Oliveira, 2016).

However, alongside the ECHR and its ECtHR, and alongside the Charter of Fundamental Rights and its CJEU, other important European human rights frameworks exist, which are much less known and discussed within the context of the human rights of older persons: the European Social Charter (Revised) (hereinafter, ESC or Charter) and its supervisory body, the European Committee of Social Rights (hereinafter, Committee or ECSR). No systematic study of the Committee has been conducted to date, either in regard to its work on the rights of older persons, or about the social construction of old age, in other words, ageism. In this chapter, we therefore present some preliminary findings from both quantitative and qualitative analysis of the decisions and evaluations of the Committee regarding the social rights of older persons.

The chapter consists of three sections: the first section is devoted to describing the ESC, including the background that led to its formation, and its development over the years. Then we describe the Committee and its *modus operandi*: an organization of the Council of Europe that is designed to supervize and examine conformity with the ESC. At this point, we briefly describe the existing procedures for fulfilling its role, namely, the reporting system imposed on the signatory States. At the end of this section, we present article 23 of the ESC (Rights of Older Persons), the article that we monitored in our research. Section 2 presents the empirical findings emerging from the work of the Committee regarding older persons' rights. This section is based on the periodical reports provided by the States who undertook to report under Article 23 and complaints received regarding the violation of older persons' rights, as part of the collective complaints system of the ESC. In the third and final section, we discuss future implications in relation to the ESC and the work of the Committee, with reference to ageism and the rights of older persons.

1. THE EUROPEAN SOCIAL CHARTER

1.1 In General

The ESC is a Council of Europe treaty, adopted in 1961 and revised in 1996, which safeguards social and economic rights, that is, human rights affecting people's everyday lives (De Schutter, 2016). These rights are in addition to the civil and political rights enshrined in the ECHR of 1950. The rights of the Charter have their origin in the Universal Declaration of Human Rights. The ESC sets out to establish binding international legal guarantees without going so far as to set up a dedicated court. The Revised Charter updates and adds to the rights enshrined in the 1961 instrument. One of its sources of inspiration was EU law.

A wide range of fundamental rights, mainly relating to working conditions, freedom to organize, health, housing, and social protection are guaranteed by the Charter. Specific emphasis is laid on the protection of vulnerable persons such as elderly people, children, people with disabilities and migrants. The Charter requires that enjoyment of the rights it lays down should be guaranteed without discrimination.

As is broadly described within the Council of Europe's portal (ESC, 2018), the Charter is based on what is termed an *à la carte* ratification system. This enables the different states, under certain circumstances, to choose the provisions that they are willing to accept as binding inter-national legal obligations. This means that while signatory states are encouraged to make progress in accepting the Charter's provisions, they are also allowed to adapt the commitments they enter into at the time of ratification to the level of legal protection of social rights attained by their own systems (ESC, 2018).

1.2 Monitoring and Compliance

The ESC adopted a different monitoring and compliance system than that established under the ECHR. As described on the Council of Europe's Portal (ESC, 2018), the Committee monitors compliance with the Charter under two complementary mechanisms: through national reports drawn up by Contracting Parties (*Reporting System*) and through collective complaints lodged by the social partners and other NGOs (*Collective Complaints Procedure*). Once again, and for the purposes of this chapter, we will rely heavily and directly on the summary presented by the Committee's website itself in describing its monitoring mechanisms (ESC Reporting, 2018).

The Reporting System is set out in Part IV of the 1961 Charter as amended by the 1991 Turin Protocol (ETS No. 142), which is applied on the basis of a decision taken by the Committee of Ministers. In the framework of the reporting system, States Parties regularly submit a report on the implementation of the Charter in law and in prac-tice. National reports are examined by the Committee, which decides whether the national situations they describe comply with the Charter or not. In the framework of the Reporting System, the Committee adopts Conclusions, which are published every year.

The *Collective Complaints Procedure* (ESC Complaints, 2018), intro-duced by the Additional Protocol, provided for a system of collective complaints, which was adopted in 1995 and entered into force in 1998 (Cullen, 2009). The introduction of the procedure aimed to increase the effectiveness, speed and impact of the implementation of the ESC. The Collective Complaints Procedure has strengthened the role of the social partners and NGOs by enabling them to apply directly to the Committee for rulings on possible non-implementation of the Charter in the coun-tries concerned, namely those States that have accepted its provisions and the complaints procedure. However, only certain NGOs are entitled to lodge collective complaints under the Charter; individuals are not entitled to do so.

Due to their collective nature, complaints may only raise questions concerning non-compliance of a State's law or practice with one of the provisions of the Charter. Individual situations may not be submitted. In light of this, complaints may be lodged without domestic remedies having been exhausted and without the claimant organization necessarily being a victim of the relevant violation.

If a complaint is considered admissible by the Committee, it adopts a decision on the merit of the complaint. This decision establishes whether a State's law and/or practice is in compliance with one or more provisions of the Charter. The decision is forwarded by the Committee to the parties and, in view of its follow-up, to the Committee of Ministers of the Council of Europe.

Insofar as they refer to binding legal provisions and are adopted by a monitoring body established by the Charter and the relevant protocols, decisions and conclusions of the Committee must be respected by the States concerned; even if they are not directly enforceable in the domestic legal systems, they set out the law and can provide the basis for positive developments in social rights through legislation and case law at the national level.

The follow-up of the decisions and conclusions of the Committee is ensured by the Committee of Ministers of the Council of Europe, which intervenes in the last stage of the Reporting and Collective Complaints System. Its work is prepared by the Governmental Committee of the European Social Charter and European Code of Social Security, comprising representatives of the States party to the Charter ESC and assisted by observers representing European trade unions and employers' organizations.

Having regarded the proposals made by the Governmental Committee, the Committee of Ministers adopts a Resolution by a majority of two-thirds of those voting. The Resolution closes each supervizion cycle and may contain individual recommendations to the States Parties concerned. If a State takes no action, the Committee of Ministers, on a proposal from the Governmental Committee, may address a Recommendation to that State, asking it to change the situation in law and/or in practice. In view of the importance of this decision, a two-thirds majority of those voting is required here. In the case of both *Resolutions* and *Recommendations*, only States Parties to the Charter may take part in the vote.

Throughout the years, many important questions have been raised about the role and the success of the ESC in achieving its goals and in serving as an effective legal and social instrument to ensure and promote social and economic rights around Europe (Churchill and Khaliq, 2004; 2007; Gomien et al., 1996). It is beyond the scope of this chapter to provide a full description of these important and significant debates.

However, some references will be made in the discussion section relating to the empirical findings of the study presented hereinafter.

1.3 Rights of Older Persons Specifically

The rights of older persons, as such, are protected and anchored under Article 23 of the Charter (which is identical to Article 4 of the Additional Protocol). The language of the article is as follows:

Article 23 – The right of elderly persons to social protection

With a view to ensuring the effective exercise of the right of elderly persons to social protection, the Parties undertake to adopt or encourage, either directly or in co-operation with public or private organisations, appropriate measures designed in particular:

– to enable elderly persons to remain full members of society for as long as possible, by means of:

   a. adequate resources enabling them to lead a decent life and play an active part in public, social and cultural life;

   b. provision of information about services and facilities available for elderly persons and their opportunities to make use of them;

– to enable elderly persons to choose their life-style freely and to lead independent lives in their familiar surroundings for as long as they wish and are able, by means of:

   a. provision of housing suited to their needs and their state of health or of adequate support for adapting their housing;

   b. the health care and the services necessitated by their state;

– to guarantee elderly persons living in institutions appropriate support, while respecting their privacy, and participation in decisions concerning living conditions in the institution.

In general, as summarized in the official Digest of the Charter (Digest, 2008), the significance of Article 23 is as follows:

Article 23 of the Charter is the first human rights treaty provision to specifically protect the rights of the elderly. The measures envisaged by this provision, by their objectives as much as by the means of implementing them, point towards a new and progressive notion of what life should be for elderly persons, obliging the Parties to devise and carry out coherent actions in the different areas covered. It is a dynamic provision in the sense that 'the appropriate measures it calls for may change over time in line with a new and progressive notion of what life should be for elderly persons'.

Article 23 overlaps with other provisions of the Charter that protect elderly persons as members of the general population, such as Article 11 (Right to protection of health), Article 13 (Right to social and medical assistance), and Article 12 (Right to social security). Article 23 requires states to make focused and planned provision in accordance with the specific needs of elderly persons.

One of the primary objectives of Article 23 is to enable older persons to remain full members of society. The expression "full members" means that elderly[1] persons must suffer no ostracism on account of their age. The right to take part in society's various fields of activity should be granted to everyone active or retired, living in an institution or not. The effects of restrictions on the legal capacity should be limited to the purpose of the measure.

Other than the analysis provided by the Digest, several authors and scholars, while analyzing or studying the rights of older persons within the European context, have referred to Article 23 and have mentioned some of the decisions made or conclusions reached with reference to this article (for example, Rodriguez-Pinzon and Martin, 2003; Seatzu, 2015). However, these references were usually part of a general or broad analysis of the rights of older persons in the European context and were not based on a systematic empirical review of the ECSR decisions and conclusions. Hence, the goal of the present study was to fill this gap by empirically and quantitatively analyzing the Committee's work in the field of the rights of older persons.

2. AN EMPIRICAL STUDY OF THE COMMITTEE'S WORK

2.1 Methodology

In order to empirically examine the Committee's work, we used a mixed quantitative and qualitative analysis method. The database that served as our source was the Committee's website (http://www.coe.int/en/web/turin-european-social-charter/national-reports). The website contains full texts of the conclusions of all of the Committees regarding the information contained in the reports submitted by the States along with a well-developed search engine, which enables a search to be carried out for the texts of all the Committees via different search categories (for example, keywords, articles of the Charter, name of country, and more). For the purposes of this study, we narrowed our search and based it solely on conclusions and complaints made under Article 23, but without any other limitations. This web-based textual search resulted in 70 conclusions from 1995 until 2015. This collection of conclusions was used as the sample for the quantitative part of this study. All these decisions and conclusions were coded and analyzed for their different characteristics (for example, country, date, outcome, and more). All data was entered into a computerized database and was descriptively analyzed, as will be provided below.

It should be noted that in line with similar legal studies that are based solely on the textual analysis of legal decisions and recommendations, this study has some significant limitations that should be taken into account. First, the analysis ignores the reality in the sense that it relies exclusively on the textual image of the reality – but not on any attempt to actually examine the "reality" in real life. This gap between the "law on the books" and "law in reality" is well-known in legal research and exists in this study as well. Second, the analysis is based solely on the published and written documents, and hence ignores potentially relevant aspects presented as part of the internal discussions and interactions.

2.2   Findings: the Overall Picture

The Committee began to deliver its conclusions in 1995, and in that year it delivered two conclusions regarding the rights of the elderly (Finland and Sweden).[2] Since then, the number has gradually increased to 21 in 2013.[3] To date (2015), overall 70 conclusions have been delivered by the Committee. Since the signing of the Charter and over the years, the work of the Committee has increased, and fixed patterns have been formed. The growth in the number of conclusions can be seen in Figure 7.1.

The growing number of conclusions is derived mostly from the States' gradual acceptance of the ESC in general and of Article 23 in particular.[4] As can be seen from the graph in Figure 7.1, growth peaked in 2013, the year that saw the Committee deliver its conclusions for all 21 signatory States to Article 23.[5]

The Committee's summarizing report means literally that after a long and detailed discussion, the conclusions can be summarized as what can be viewed as a "bottom line", which can be one of the following three possibilities: (1) conformity of the State with the requirements of Article 23 of the Charter; (2) non-conformity; or (3) a deferral of the decision. A deferral is usually the result of the absence of information conveyed by the States. Figure 7.2 presents the distribution of the different types of decisions made over the years by the Committee.

An examination of the Committee's three possible types of conclusions over the years produced the picture presented in Figure 7.2.

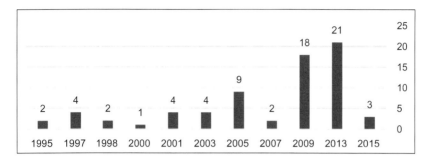

Notes:
1995: Finland, Sweden; 1997: Finland, Sweden, Norway, Italy; 2000: Denmark; 2001: Finland, Norway, Italy, Sweden; 2003: Italy, France, Slovenia, Sweden; 2005 : Czech Republic, Denmark, Finland, France, Greece, Norway, Slovenia, Spain, Sweden; 2007: Italy, Finland; 2009: Finland, Norway, Sweden, Ireland, France, Greece, Italy, Malta, Netherlands, Slovak Republic, Portugal, Slovenia, Turkey, Ukraine, Andorra, Czech Republic, Spain, Denmark; 2013: Finland, Norway, Sweden, Ireland, France, Greece, Italy, Malta, Netherlands, Slovak Republic, Portugal, Slovenia,Turkey, Ukraine, Andorra, Czech Republic, Spain, Denmark, Montenegro, Bosnia and Herzegovina, Serbia; 2015: Finland,Turkey, Italy.

Figure 7.1   Growth of conclusions by year

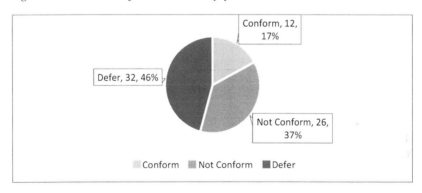

Figure 7.2   Overall distribution of the types of decisions over 1995–2015

Figure 7.2 shows that deferrals have over the years made up the largest number of conclusions under Article 23, followed by non-conformity with the demands of Article 23, and only a minority of conclusions authorize the States' conformity with the requirements of the Charter.

Regarding the types of conclusions, Figure 7.3 shows an overall clear direction by the Committee as well as a change in the conclusions

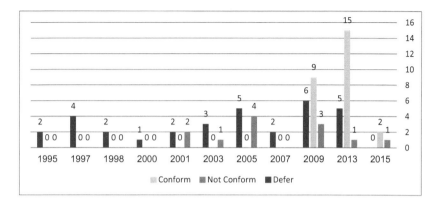

Figure 7.3   Distribution of the Committee's decisions over the years

delivered over the years. In the early years, the large majority of
decisions were deferred because of a lack of data in the States' reports.[6]
This stage can be interpreted as involving years of construction and
creation of a system of clear norms, in relation to the reporting
requirements of the Committee and in relation to the States and the
reports that they were requested to deliver. It is noteworthy, as mentioned
above, that relatively few reports were submitted during those years.

A change in the trend was seen in 2005, when the number of
conclusions delivered by the Committee more than doubled (from four to
nine), but cases of deferral and conformity to the Article's requirements
were still evenly distributed. In 2009, the Committee changed its mode of
delivering conclusions. In that year, half of the conclusions (nine)
declared that the States were not in conformity with the requirements,
whereas six conclusions were deferred, and only three conformed.

In 2013, consolidated, stringent norms were apparent in everything to
do with the rights of older persons. All 21 signatory States to Article 23
submitted reports. An overwhelming majority, 71 per cent (15 states), did
not conform to the required norm set by the Committee. The Committee
deferred its conclusions regarding issues of five States, and only one
State (5 per cent) was in conformity with the Article.

Even if it is possible to examine the changes in norms over the years,
the appropriate way to understand the Committee's policy today, while
looking toward the future, seems to be by examining the norms set down
by the Committee in its current conclusions. This will enable understanding and coordination of expectations in everything regarding the rights of
older persons as required by the Charter.

2.3 Findings: a Separate Analysis of the Different Categories under Article 23

With regard to Article 23, the Committee currently examines seven categories derived from what is written in the Charter. Six of them were only finalized after 2008.[7] The following categories are currently being examined by the Committee, according to the order in which they appear in the conclusions: (1) Legislative Frameworks; (2) Adequate Resources; (3) Elder Abuse; (4) Services and Facilities; (5) Housing; (6) Health Care; and (7) Institutional Care. We will hereby elaborate on each category separately.

2.3.1 Legislative frameworks
In this category, the Committee seeks legislation that ensures the prevention of age discrimination. The legislation must encompass more than the field of work, including areas such as services, housing and so on. A State whose legislation does not ensure the prevention of ageism in all areas will be considered as not conforming to the requirements of the Article (see below). In all the reports in this category, the Committee demands information about legislation on assisted decision-making for older persons (ESC, 2013, Ireland).

2.3.2 Adequate resources
The Committee defines the aim of this category as follows: "… Committee takes into account all the social protection measures guaranteed to elderly persons and aimed at maintaining an income level allowing them to lead a decent life, as well as to participate actively in public, social and cultural life" (ESC, 2013, Sweden, p. 1).

For this purpose, the Committee examines the existing income for older persons within the framework of the laws of the State. It examines all possible sources, including contributory or non-contributory pensions. The Committee then compares this income to the median equivalized income and to the indicators relating to at-risk poverty rates. In addition, the Committee examines reports by other authorities such as the World Bank to obtain precise information about the State's economic situation.

At the end of the process, the Committee examines the amounts, and if these do not meet the required standard, in other words, the older persons' sources of income from the State do not place them above the poverty line, the State will be considered as not conforming to the requirements of Article 23 of the Charter. Furthermore, the Committee draws the State's attention to older persons whose income is conspicuously below the poverty line. For example, the Committee's 2013 report notes that in Sweden in 2011, 2.1 per cent of the over-65 age group had an income 40 per cent below the median income. The Committee asks Sweden to explain why the income of these older persons does not meet the required standard and what can be done to rectify the situation (ESC, 2013, Sweden).

2.3.3 Elder abuse

The Committee included this category for the first time in its 2009 conclusions and recognizes it as a phenomenon. Leading international organizations (the World Health Organization and the International Network for the Prevention of Elder Abuse) warn of an increase in elder abuse (ESC, 2013, Serbia). Therefore, within the framework of the Committee's conclusions, any States that do not currently provide a legal response to elder abuse are referred by the Committee to the required standard for States, noting the Toronto Declaration on the Global Prevention of Elder Abuse (2002) as a source for legislation (ESC, 2013, Serbia).

The Committee, in its conclusions, mentions States that already have legislation for the prevention of elder abuse, such as Finland (ESC, 2013), where local authorities are given government recommendations for creating a system of locating and preventing the possibility of elder abuse within the welfare services. The Committee is also assisted by additional, internal resources in the States to learn about older persons' status. Ireland (ESC, 2013), for example, used the National Centre for the Protection of Older People report, from which it learned that in 2010, 2.2 per cent of older persons in Ireland (approximately 10 000 people) had suffered from some form of abuse in the previous 12 months.

At this stage, the Committee's conclusions wish only to create a unified norm that can be promoted. On the one hand, in some of the States, the Committee publicizes the data on elder abuse and examines the human resources allocated to deal with the issue. In its conclusions, the Committee asks the States to continue to provide information and does not declare that they are not in conformity with the requirements of Article 23 (ESC, 2013, Ireland; Denmark; Spain). On the other hand, it refers to international sources, which, from now on, will be the norm according to which the State's compliance with the ESC requirements will be determined (ESC, 2013, Spain).

2.3.4 Services and facilities

In accordance with the Charter, the Committee emphasizes the services provided to older persons as well as their accessibility to information on these services. *Inter alia*, the Committee requests information about the type of social aid provided to needy older persons. Who is responsible for the services provided (ESC, 2013, Serbia), the State or the local authorities? How many people are being cared for (ESC, 2013, Denmark)? Is assistance given to families caring for older persons with emphasis on care for people with dementia? Do organizations providing assistance in this area exist (ESC, 2013, Denmark; Serbia)?

In Spain (ESC, 2013), for example, the Committee notes new legislation mentioned in the 2013 report. According to this legislation, most care for older persons in Spain is undertaken by the family. The new law proposes a wide variety of assistance for older persons and their families, including financial aid, help with living arrangements, as well as round-the-clock nursing assistance, and so on. The Committee states that in 2013, such assistance was provided to 752 400 older persons. The Committee requests details of the payment demanded for these services.

Another example is the Netherlands, where the local authorities are required by law to ensure that people can continue to live independent lives for as long as possible and to enable their participation in social life (ESC, 2013, Netherlands). Local authorities provide social services, such as household help, or other forms of support, for instance, for volunteers and informal carers. Various services tailored to needs and personal circumstances are offered. For example, different options for providing meals are possible, such as home-delivered hot meals or meals in a local home for the elderly. Depending on the individual's financial situation, a personal contribution may be required. Older persons who do not receive the required assistance are entitled to sue the local authority. Within the framework of its conclusions, the Committee wishes to know whether help, and which kind of help, is given to families caring for older persons, especially those requiring nursing 24/7.

In its conclusions, the Committee reviews alternative provision of services. For example, it explains that in Italy emphasis is placed on caring for the older person within the family. In a 2009 ruling, Italy's Constitutional Court extended to two years the right to paid leave from work to care for parents, including for children living with parents, if no other solution could be found. However, the Committee requested more information as to whether the service provided met the requirements and whether a mechanism existed for examining the quality of care of older persons provided by family members (ESC, 2013, Italy).

It can be seen that States differ greatly in the services provided to older persons and the means at their disposal. These differences are due to a wide range of financial, cultural and other reasons. The Committee's conclusions seem to touch mainly on the need to ensure that the services reach all older persons in need and that, even if the services are not under State control, the standard of the service must be supervized.

2.3.5 Housing

The Committee examines the housing solutions allocated to older persons in the different States and appreciates that this is a challenging area. On the one hand, the Charter is committed to ensuring housing that meets their needs and state of health. If necessary, the States are obliged to adapt older persons' housing to their situations[8] and are, therefore, required to build housing tailored to older persons in need of assistance and protection. (This does not refer to nursing institutions, which are discussed in a separate section below.) On the other hand, it is clear to the Committee that this requirement demands significant financial investment by the State. The Committee summarizes its demands in this area in its conclusions for Montenegro (ESC, 2013, p. 4):

> The Committee recalls that appropriate housing conditions are very important for an old person's well-being. However, it is also aware that the improvement of housing conditions of senior citizens is not an easy task. First, it requires considerable public funding, as the average elderly person usually cannot afford the costs of modernisation of his apartment or purchasing a new apartment of a higher standard. Second, improvement of housing conditions by moving elsewhere is often not a viable option in that it uproots the elderly person from his/her "natural" environment. Bearing in mind these constraints, the Committee wishes to be kept informed of any public policies providing financial assistance for the adaptation of housing.

Indeed, it can be seen that the Committee examines the financial means allocated by law regarding housing. For instance, the Committee notes the Housing Development Programme in Slovakia (ESC, 2013), which adapts older persons' housing to their needs. This includes assistance with renting apartments or with purchasing necessary technical equipment.

The Committee notes that in Sweden in 2008, around 75 000 cases of housing adaptation were granted at a total cost of €108 million (ESC, 2013, Sweden). In addition, Sweden established a special organization in 2007 called the National Board of Housing, whose role is to build special housing for older persons. Up to the delivery date of the conclusions, 5714 such apartments had been built in Sweden, and another 2203 were being constructed.

In its conclusions on housing, the Committee also criticizes the States. For instance, it states that Turkey had no government programme for older persons' housing, and the Committee demands to know whether older persons' needs were taken into consideration in building plans

(ESC, 2013, Turkey). In its conclusions regarding Italy (ESC, 2013), the Committee asks whether financial aid is provided to older persons for home refurbishment or adaptation. Overall then, the Committee requests details and data about budgeting and current programmes for adapting older persons' housing to their needs. The Committee sees budgeting and accessibility to these programmes as part of the State's obligation as it emerges from the Charter (ESC, 2013, Turkey).

2.3.6 Health care

The Committee examines whether health programmes for the older population exist in the States in question as part of the overall State health programme. The Committee's expectations of the States can be learned from its comments to the conclusions regarding Andorra (ESC, 2013, p. 3):

> The Committee previously asked for information on specific health care services aimed at the elderly, mental health programmes, palliative care services and special training for individuals caring for elderly persons. The Committee also asked to be kept informed of any measures aimed at improving the accessibility and quality of geriatric and long-term care, and the coordination of social and health care services in respect of the elderly. Since the report does not address these issues, the Committee reiterates its questions.

Further to these comments, in the case of Montenegro (ESC, 2013), the Committee emphasizes the need to create health programmes designed to care for the older population. Clearly, the question of funding medical services for older persons is examined by the Committee. In its conclusions regarding the Netherlands (ESC, 2013), the Committee provides details of the sources of funding and of which medical services for older persons are funded.

The Committee also examines the study and treatment of illnesses characteristic of the older population, such as dementia. For example, in its conclusions regarding the Netherlands (ESC, 2013), the Committee describes an integrative programme for treating patients with dementia. In the conclusions pertaining to Malta (ESC, 2013), the Committee mentions special clinics that have been opened to treat medical problems unique to the older population such as those related to memory and stability, prevention of falling and so on.

It can be said that on the issue of health, the Committee urges the greatest possible expansion of the medical network for older persons. It wishes to see resources allocated to this area and to ensure that the medical system indeed covers all the different fields. It seems that in its conclusions the Committee is not in a hurry to declare that States are not in conformity with the demands of Article 23 of the Charter and mainly refers to a broad topic that cannot be clearly marked as "pass" or "fail".

2.3.7   Institutional care

The emphasis in the Charter on the topic of nursing care is placed on providing appropriate care while maintaining older persons' privacy, control over their own care, and the ability to make their own lifestyle decisions.

In its conclusions, the Committee examines an array of issues. A central topic is the degree of availability of nursing institutions. For example, in its conclusions regarding Norway (ESC, 2013), the Committee provides a report about the number of beds in the nursing institutions and the percentage of octogenarians hospitalized in them in 2011.[9] Regarding the Netherlands (ESC, 2013), it reports that a certain waiting time is considered reasonable (but this is not actually specified in the report) and that the State's target is that 90 per cent of people over 65 will receive a place within a given time. In its conclusions regarding Turkey (ESC, 2013), the Committee notes that the number of beds in private and public nursing homes amounts to 23 529, divided between 289 institutions, and that 862 persons were waiting for a bed in such an institution.

In its conclusions, the Committee also examines the quality, professionalism, and extent of supervizion of the nursing institutions. Regarding the Netherlands (ESC, 2013), it mentions efforts to reduce the number of shared rooms. It states that in Slovakia (ESC, 2013) the local authorities bear responsibility for the quality of care and emphasizes the importance of inspection, which should be settled more appropriately through State legislation than via the local authorities. The Committee also names States that have a special training system for carers in nursing institutions for older persons (for example, Slovakia, ESC, 2013).

As part of the trend to allow ageing within the community, the Committee examines the extent to which institutional nursing care is being replaced by care at home. For example, in its conclusions regarding Norway (ESC, 2013), it reported an increasing number of older persons moving out of institutions to home care. The Committee's conclusions regarding Sweden (ESC, 2013) state that patients suffering from dementia should be cared for, as far as possible, in specialized institutions allowing treatment of all aspects of the illness and not as patients requiring nursing 24/7.

2.4   Findings: the Committee's policy on conformity to norms

After describing the seven categories that are subject to the Committee's scrutiny in the various States, and after clarifying the norms demanded by the Committee, we now return to the overall picture. As presented in Figure 7.3, in 2013, the Committee delivered its conclusions to all 21 signatory States regarding Article 23. However, whereas 15 States were found to be not in conformity with the Article's requirements, the Committee deferred its conclusions regarding five of the States because of a lack of information. Only one State (France) was found to be in conformity with the requirements. It is asked for what reasons all States (20) except one did not conform to the Article's requirements in relation to older persons. Figure 7.4 depicts the distribution of reasons.

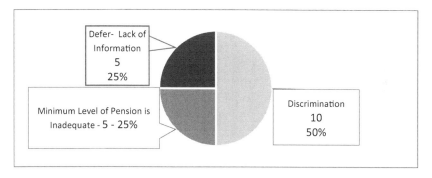

Figure 7.4   Reasons for being not in conformity with the requirements of Article 23 (2013)

If this is the case, as can be seen, the main reason for non-conformity with the requirements of Article 23 is the absence of legislation that will ensure no age discrimination in all areas of life. The Committee, in its review of Bosnia and Herzegovina (ESC, 2013), clarifies the importance of the subject as follows:

> As regards the protection of elderly persons from discrimination outside employment, the Committee recalls that Article 23 requires States Parties to combat age discrimination in a range of areas beyond employment, namely in access to goods, facilities and services. The European Older People's Platform and other sources point to the existence of pervasive age discrimination in many areas of society throughout Europe (health care, education, services such as insurance and banking products, participation in policy making/civil dialogue, allocation of resources and facilities) which leads the Committee to consider that an adequate legal framework is a fundamental measure to

combat age discrimination in these areas. It therefore asks whether such legislation exists. (p. 1).

The second most important reason is the absence of a minimal pension that is supposed to meet the needs of older persons. This reason already appears in the Committee's conclusions in 2009. In conclusions regarding the Czech Republic, the Committee has drafted policy on this issue: "The Committee notes that the minimum old-age pension is manifestly inadequate as it was considerably below the poverty threshold and therefore found that the situation was not in conformity with Article 4 of the Additional Protocol on this point" (p. 2).

In this sense, the test, as described above, regarding the Adequate Resources category, is relatively simple. A median income exists, which must be above the poverty line. Any State that does not adhere to this norm will be found to be not conforming with Article 23 of the Charter, as was the case with the Czech Republic, Montenegro, Serbia, Slovakia and Ukraine in 2013.

The third reason is the lack of information provided by the States themselves. The Committee spares no criticism on this issue and clarifies that the lack of information cannot provide an escape route for non-conformity with Article 23 of the Charter. The Committee refers to Andorra (ESC, 2013) as follows:

> Pending receipt of the information requested, the Committee defers its conclusion. The Committee considers that the absence of the information required amounts to a breach of the reporting obligation entered into by Andorra under the Charter. The Government consequently has an obligation to provide the requested information in the next report on this provision. (p. 4)

The States must know that they are obliged to deliver the information. This is a central point for the Committee because in the absence of information and the failure of the States to convey the facts, the Committee's work is inefficient. The Committee has the power of enforcement with the assistance of the Committee of Ministers of the Council of Europe, and this power is indeed enforced regarding Article 23 (as can be seen below in the complaint against Finland). However, as is apparent from other studies, the power of enforcement of the Committee of Ministers is very limited and is subject mainly to political needs and pressures (Churchill and Khaliq, 2004). The bottom line is that the States chose to join Article 23 of the Charter. The Committee can present the status quo, and the assumption is that, during the dialogue with the Committee, the States will improve their performance, including their level of reporting.

2.5 Qualitative Findings: The Collective Complaints System

As described in the sampling section, after the Committee database was reviewed, only three complaints under Article 23 were found to have been submitted. In this section, we will provide a very brief description of these three complaints.

2.5.1 Case 1: International Federation of Human Rights Leagues (IFHR) v. Ireland

The complaint was lodged by the International Federation of Human Rights Leagues (IFHR) and was registered on 26 February 2007. The IFHR alleged that Ireland discriminated against persons who were in receipt of Irish Contributory Old Age Pensions and who did not reside permanently in Ireland in that it refused to allow them access to a free travel scheme when they visited Ireland. The IFHR considered that this situation constituted a violation of Article 23 in conjunction with Article E (non-discrimination) and a violation of Article 12§4(a) of the Revised Charter (ensuring the effective exercize of the right to social security equality in case of treatment with their own nationals or the nationals of other Parties in respect of social security rights).

The free travel scheme, operated by the Department of Social and Family Affairs, allowed people aged 66 or over, and who permanently resided in Ireland, to travel free of charge on most public transport services, as well as on the public transport services of a large number of private operators in various parts of the country.

To avail oneself of free travel, one had first to apply for a free travel pass. The applicant qualified if he or she was living permanently in Ireland (that is, on a year round basis) and was aged 66 or over. The IFHR alleged that Ireland discriminated against persons in receipt of Irish Contributory Old Age Pensions who did not reside permanently in Ireland in that they were refused access to a free travel scheme for pensioners when returning to Ireland to visit relatives or friends. Moreover, the IFHR argued that the refusal by the Irish authorities to grant a free travel pass to these persons when visiting Ireland was in breach of Article 23 of the Charter. The provision of free travel for pensioners was clearly among the measures to be adopted by the States party within the meaning of Article 23 with a view to helping older persons remain full members of society, lead a decent life, and play an active part in public, social and cultural life.

In a majority vote, the Committee dismissed the case. In its decision, the majority asserted that, with regard to Irish nationals who were resident outside of Ireland, the Committee recognized the close links that led many to wish to maintain their public, social and cultural life in Ireland. However, the Committee considered that States might legitimately restrict the scope of application of measures adopted to give effect to Article 23. They could be restricted to residents, individuals regularly working in the State concerned, or to persons with an equivalent degree of integration into the society of that State if such a restriction was reasonable and did not constitute a denial of the core entitlement of older persons to essential social protection. Taking account of the nature of the benefits at issue in this complaint, the Committee considered that the inability of non-resident Irish nationals to avail themselves of the Free Travel Scheme did not, therefore, constitute an unreasonable restriction on the right to social protection recognized in Article 23.

Moreover, the Committee stressed the different treatment of residents and non-residents in respect of access to the free travel scheme at issue in this complaint. However, this difference in treatment could be justified as based upon a legitimate distinction between residents and non-residents. Therefore, this difference in treatment could not be deemed discrimination within the meaning of the Charter or its Article E. Finally, the Committee also discussed the alleged violation of Article 12(4), within the context of the right to social security, but, again, found that the free travel benefit could not be deemed to relate to any of the social security rights covered by this Article.

Interestingly, this case also included a minority opinion, which held that not only Article 23, but all the provisions of the Charter, are based on the principle of non-discrimination, which prohibits any differential treatment related to the criterion of permanent residence. Moreover, according to the minority opinion, Article 12(4) was also violated in the case, as social security rights are part of a "package" including the benefits or privileges granted by the State party concerned.

2.5.2   Case 2: The Central Association of Carers in Finland v. Finland (Complaint No. 70/2011)

The complaint presented by the Central Association of Carers in Finland was registered on 6 July 2011. The Association alleged that Finland had violated the right of older persons to social protection in breach of Article 23 of the revised ESC.

The complaint was about the funding and implementation of the Act of Informal Care Support (937/2005), as it applied to family members and other informal carers, who provided care for older persons in the community. The argument was that not only was the Act implemented very differently in the 336 municipalities in Finland, but there were no national standards for the amount and type of informal care provided under the minimum remuneration fixed by the law. For example, in some municipalities, a low level of care might have entitled a carer to the status of informal carer, whereas in some other municipalities even 24/7 care might not have been sufficient to achieve the status of informal carer. Moreover, the fact that the position of the informal carer was linked to the economic situation of the municipality not only created inequality between informal carers in the same situation, but also created situations in which the possibility to deliver informal services ended at the beginning of the year. Finally, as the state subsidy to the municipalities for informal care was not earmarked, municipal politicians could decide freely not to allocate it to support informal care for older persons (and indeed some localities in Finland cancelled all informal carer agreements).

The legal context was based on the Finnish legal framework: the Constitution of Finland bestows on public authorities the responsibility to guarantee adequate social welfare for everyone. Actual provision of social welfare is assigned to municipalities by the Social Welfare Act (710/1982). Section 17 of the Act stipulates that municipalities are responsible, *inter alia*, for "provision of support for informal care". However, municipalities have discretionary power to decide the ways and means of arranging social services, and on the type of service structure within which they respond to the needs of municipal residents. Moreover, Finland has separate legislation on informal care, namely the Act on Informal Care Support (937/2005). According to Section 3 of the Act, informal care support may be granted by a municipality in certain situations. This provision does not make payment an obligation but leaves it under the discretionary power of the municipality, although according to the Act on Planning and Government Grants for Social Welfare and Health Care (733/1992), municipalities receive financial support from the government in order to organize these services (on average, one-third of the costs).

After considering the case, the Committee, in its report of 4 December 2012, decided that:

> the lack of uniformity in the services provided for elderly persons throughout Finland resulting from the lack of uniformity in the funding of such services by municipalities does not as such violate Article 23 of the Charter. However, the fact that the legislation allows practices leading to a part of the elderly population being denied access to informal care allowances or other alternative support constitutes a violation of this Article. (p.14)

On 11 June 2013, the Committee of Ministers, after having considered the Committee's decision on the merits, and also after reviewing the

Government of Finland's reply to the decision, reaffirmed the Committee's decision.

Finally, on 4 November 2014, the Government of Finland provided the Committee with additional information about several steps that had been taken to remedy the situation. First, the Act on Supporting the Functional Capacity of the Older Population and on Social and Health Care Services for Older Persons entered into force on 1 July 2013. Second, the State budget for 2013, adopted by the Parliament, includes an increase in central government transfers to local governments with a view to developing support services for informal care in municipalities. Third, a working group appointed by the Ministry of Social Affairs and Health completed a proposal for a National Development Programme for the Support of Informal Care in March 2014. Fourth, the Act on the Arrangement of Social Welfare and Health Care Services and the new Social Welfare Act were to enter into force in 2015. Fifth, legislative reforms concerning informal care support and its administration and funding were to be assessed after 2015. Finally, in the framework of a structural policy programme, the Ministry of Social Affairs and Health prepared an action plan in February 2014 with a view to cutting back on institutional care for older persons and for extending services provided at home.

Despite these extensive steps, the assessment of the follow-up made by the Committee was that "the grounds that led to the finding of violation, namely that the legislation allows practices leading to a part of the elderly population being denied access to informal care allowances or other forms of support, have not yet been remedied" (ESC, 2011, p. 2). Hence, the Committee decided to assess the legislative and administrative measures, once adopted, when the information on the follow-up given to decisions was submitted in October 2017.

2.5.3 Case 3: The Central Association of Carers in Finland v. Finland (Complaint No. 71/2011)

As with the previous complaint, this complaint was also presented by "The Central Association of Carers in Finland". The Association alleged that Finland had violated the right of elderly persons to social and medical assistance, social services, and social, legal, and medical protection, in breach of Articles 13, 14, 16, and 23 of the revised ESC.

The complaint (71/2011) was about the reorganization of long-term care, whereby former institutional care facilities (elderly homes and long-term healthcare wards) that operated as residential homes and were part of the institutional care system, were changed into either service housing or service housing with 24-hour assistance, formally regarded as non-institutional (outpatient) care. However, the pricing systems of the two types of services were significantly different. As a result, persons in need of service housing and service housing with 24-hour assistance were charged higher fees than clients in institutional care because (1) there were no upper limits on fees for service housing and service housing with 24-hour assistance; (2) services, medicines and housing were charged separately.

The general legal context was similar to that described in the previous case, with regard to the large discretion that local municipalities in Finland hold concerning the provision of services under the Social Welfare Act. However, in particular, and compared to institutional care, service housing and service housing with 24-hour assistance were not subject to any specific legal regulation on determining the fees or on disposable incomes.

After considering this fact, the Committee concluded that inadequate regulation of fees for service housing and service housing with 24-hour assistance, combined with excessive demand for these services compared to supply, did not meet the requirements of Article 23 of the Charter insofar as these:

1. created legal uncertainties for older persons in need of care due to diverse and complex fee policies, since even if municipalities adjust the fees, no effective safeguards exist to assure that effective access to services is guaranteed to every older person whose condition necessitates services;
2. constituted an obstacle to the right to the provision of information about services and facilities available for older persons and their opportunities to make use of them as guaranteed by Article 23 of the Charter.

As to Article 14, Article 16 (the right of the family to social, legal, and economic protection), and Article 13 (the right to social and medical assistance), the Committee held that they were not applicable to the complaint.

On 11 June 2013, the Committee of Ministers, after having considered the Committee's decision on the merits and reviewing the Government of Finland's reply to the decision, reaffirmed the Committee's decision. Finally, as part of the assessment of the follow-up, the Finnish government indicated in the information registered on 4 November 2014, that the Ministry of Social Affairs and Health had set up a working group to prepare proposals for the legislation concerning user charges for service housing and service housing with 24-hour assistance. A draft of the proposed Act was circulated to municipalities for comments in July 2014. The bill was to be debated in Parliament in the autumn of 2014. Nevertheless, the Committee concluded that the situation had not been brought into conformity with the Charter and that it would assess the new legislation and its practical impact when the information on the follow-up given to decisions was submitted in October 2017.

3. DISCUSSION

The findings for screening all decisions of the Committee regarding Article 23 of the Charter reveal a rich and diverse picture. With such a broad scope of topics and issues, and such a diverse social policy landscape, it is difficult to draw unequivocal conclusions. Nevertheless, in our view, several key insights are revealed once one tries to analyze the above findings as they reflect the interconnections between law and ageism.

3.1 The "Invisibility" of Ageism and the Absence of Older Persons' NGOs

The first insight concerns the main topic of this book: ageism and the law. Reading all the decisions and proceedings of the Committee reveals an interesting picture. While there is a strong emphasis by the Committee on the social rights of older Europeans, and while acknowledging that many States do not meet the required standards under the Charter, the Committee makes no specific or direct reference to the concept of "ageism" (as such) or to the general negative social construction of old age.

One reason for this situation is that "ageism" as such does not appear in the Charter. Even in the formal digest to the ESC, there was no direct reference to ageism and very little reference to the social construction of old age. However, it should be noted that this finding is not unique to the Committee. A similar finding was made in empirical studies on the ECtHR and the CJEU. It seems then that "ageism" has not been adopted yet within the European jurisprudence and has not been adopted and promoted by organizations representing human and social rights in Europe.

To the invisibility of ageism should also be added the absence and lack of proactive behaviour by older persons' NGOs. NGOs can play a significant role in promoting human rights of older persons. Yet, as presented in our findings, they are almost "non-existent" in the legal and formal proceedings before the Committee. Once they understand the process and are aware of the material content, NGOs for older Europeans can easily facilitate the ESC mechanisms in order to promote the social rights of their constituents via the different legal mechanisms before the Committee.

3.2 The ESC and Committee as Instruments to Combat Ageism

On the one hand, the Committee's conclusions as described in the findings section above can be interpreted as evidence of a tendency toward the promotion of older persons' rights. Clear and stringent norms are becoming fixed. The signatory States to the Article are required to present data and demonstrate progress from one report to the next. If in the past it was considered that the rights of older persons, as belonging to socioeconomic rights were "weak", the Committee is proving otherwise. It shows that it is possible to enforce and promote such rights, in general, and the rights of older persons, in particular, while using existing formal, legal, social-rights instruments.

This optimistic perspective can also be supported from the historical perspective provided in our findings. What started as an almost "invisible" human right, which did not appear or receive special attention in the Committee's activities, transformed over the years into something that not only became "visible", but was gradually built up to a material and substantive social right unique to older Europeans. The dynamic seems to continue in a positive manner, promising that the social rights of older persons will continue to be developed in the future.

On the other hand, it should be noted that the decisions of the ESC – in general, and the Committee's decisions – are not automatically binding or legally enforceable. Unlike its "sister" convention, the ECHR, which has a unique court in which its decisions can be enforced under national law, or unlike the EU Charter and its Supreme Court of the EU, the decisions of which can be enforced under national law, the Committee lacks a court or national enforcement mechanism. It relies on political goodwill or political power relationships among European states, which often prefer not to adopt a non-consensual diplomacy.

3.3 The Importance of the "Empirical" Aspects of Ageism

One of the surprising findings of this study was the actual way in which the Committee reviewed the States' reports. The Committee was not satisfied by general descriptive arguments or normative articulations by the States. When it comes to social rights, the Committee is required to receive detailed empirical data about the numbers of older persons, the actual costs and budgets, and the real actual content of the services provided.

This finding relates to an important, and yet understudied, aspect of law and ageism. In many cases, arguments about the existence of ageism are asserted in a general manner, while anecdotal examples are provided. Case law regarding human rights of older persons often pictures a specific example or a specific older person. While some generalizations can be made, they should be made in this context with much caution. However, the reports and evaluations made by the Committee are based on data provided by governments on a large scale. If such data is not presented, the Committee insists that it be provided in order to make its legal assessment.

3.4 The Importance of "Measurability" of Social Rights of Older Persons

Drawing on the ESC, the Committee examined seven categories. The Committee defines, in certain areas that can be easily and clearly examined, a required standard norm, for example, the poverty line in the context of the required size of pensions or legislation regarding the prevention of discrimination. In areas less conducive to a clear assessment, the Committee sets suitable performance standards. However, above all, the Committee demands the provision of clear and current data, thereby creating a standard that is very important for everyone who wishes to learn about the status of older persons in the Council of Europe. This fits well with broader international trends of establishing comparative "measurement" tools (indexes) in various fields of life concerning older persons (for example, the Active Aging Index, and see also Spanier and Doron, 2016).

CONCLUSION

It is clear from the analysis and findings provided that the ESC and the ECSR can be important legal instruments in the development and promotion of social and human rights of older persons in Europe. More specifically, any attempt to understand the legal construction of old age and the socio-legal relationships between law and ageism cannot ignore the content, decisions and recommendations of the ECSR. On the one hand, the decision and proceedings of the ECSR seem to be still blind to the concept of ageism and to the importance of the understanding of the social construction of old age to the lives and human rights of older persons. On the other hand, the ECSR has given a strong and powerful interpretation to the material content of Article 23 of the ESC, while looking deeply and critically into all seven of its categories, which are central to the lives of older Europeans. Moreover, the Committee dives into the empirical data in the field and does not allow states to ignore or get around their legal commitments by general or empirically un-supported statements.

Overall then, it seems that the ECSR has a strong potential in developing a jurisprudence about the social rights of older persons. If the Committee adds to its existing work, the knowledge – theoretical and empirical – regarding ageism and the social construction of age in Europe, and "connects" it to its current decision-making foundations, the outcome in our view would be very promising in promoting the human rights of the older population in Europe and around the world.

Finally, it is clear that many more empirical studies are needed to better understand not only the activities of the Committee under the ESC, but also the actual experience of social rights of older Europeans. Future research can compare, for example, the differences in the social rights of older persons between different regions in Europe, between "older" and "younger" countries, or between different European social welfare regimes, while examining the extent to which such variables shape or influence the social rights of older persons in real life.

NOTES

1. While we believe that from an anti-ageist perspective, "elderly" is less appropriate terminology to use than "older persons" or "older adults", we use this term in the chapter to the extent that it is used within the ESC and its official documents.
2. See http://www.coe.int/en/web/turin-european-social-charter/national-reports (accessed February 2017), hereinafter "Reporting system of the European Social Charter".
3. See http://www.coe.int/en/web/turin-european-social-charter/national-reports (accessed February 2017), hereinafter, "National Reports".
4. See http://www.coe.int/en/web/turin-european-social-charter/signatures-ratifications (accessed February 2017).
5. See http://www.coe.int/en/web/turin-european-social-charter/provisions-of-the-charter (accessed February 2017).
6. See, for example, Reporting system of the European Social Charter – Sweden and Finland, 1995, 1997.
7. Up until 2009, the Committee did not examine the category of "Prevention of elder abuse".
8. See Article 23, which states, "Provision of housing suited to their needs and their state of health or of adequate support for adapting their housing."

BIBLIOGRAPHY

Churchill, Robin R. and Khaliq, Urfan (2004), The collective complaints system of the European Social Charter: An effective mechanism for ensuring compliance with economic and social rights?, *European Journal of International Law*, **15**(3), 417–56.

Churchill, Robin R. and Khaliq, Urfan (2007), Violation of economic, social, and cultural rights: The current use and future potential of the collective complaints mechanism of the European Social Charter, in Mashood A. Baderin and Robert McCorquodale (eds), *Economic, Social and Cultural Rights in Action*, Oxford: Oxford University Press, pp. 195–240.

Convention for the Protection of Human Rights and Fundamental Freedoms (As amended by the provisions of Protocol No. 14 (CETS no. 194) as from its entry into force on 1 June 2010).

Cullen, H. (2009), The collective complaints system of the European Social Charter: Interpretative methods of the European Committee of Social Rights, *Human Rights Law Review*, **9**(1), 61–93.

Dashwood, Hevina S. (2004), Corporate Social Responsibility and the evolution of international norms, in John J. Kirton and Michael J. Trebilcock (eds), *Hard Choices, Soft Law: Voluntary Standards in Global Trade, Environment and Social Governance*, Abingdon: Ashgate, pp. 189–202.

De Schutter, O. (2016), *The European Social Charter in the Context of Implementation of the EU Charter of Fundamental Rights*, Brussels: European Parliament.

Doron, I. (2013), Older Europeans and the European Court of Justice, *Age & Ageing*, **42**, 604–8.

ESC (2011), Complaint 70/2011. *The Central Association of Carers in Finland v. Finland*. Follow up of the complaint, accessed at https://www.coe.int/en/web/turin-european-social-charter/processed-complaints/-/asset_publisher/5GEFkJmH2bYG/content/no-70-2011-the-central-association-of-carers-in-finland-v-finland?inheritRedirect=false.

ESC (2013), Reporting system of the European Social Charter, accessed July 2018 at http://www.coe.int/en/web/turin-european-social-charter/national-reports.

ESC (2018), The Charter in Four Steps. The Council of Europe Portal, accessed 9 January 2018 at https://www.coe.int/en/web/turin-european-social-charter/about-the-charter.

ESC Reporting (2018), Reporting System of the European Social Charter. The Council of Europe Portal, accessed 9 January 2018 at https://www.coe.int/en/web/turin-european-social-charter/national-reports.

ESC Complaints (2018), Reporting System of the European Social Charter. The Council of Europe Portal, accessed 9 January 2018 at https://www.coe.int/en/web/turin-european-social-charter/collective-complaints-procedure.

European Social Charter (Revised) (1999), Entered into force 7 January 1999, European Treaty Series No. 163.

European Union – Consolidated versions of the Treaty on European Union and the Treaty on the Functioning of the European Union, 2008/C 115/01. Signed on 13 December 2007 in Lisbon, entered into force on 1 December 2009.

Gomien, Donna, Harris, David and Zwaak, Leo (1996), *Law and Practice of the European Convention on Human Rights and the European Social Charter*, Strasbourg: Council of Europe Publishing.

Koch, Ida Elisabeth (2002), Social rights as components in civil rights to personal liberty: Another possible step forward in the integrated human rights approach?, *Netherlands Quarterly of Human Rights*, **20**(1), 29–51.

Koch, Ida Elisabeth (2009), *Human Rights as Indivisible Rights: The Protection of Socio-Economic Demands Under the European Convention on Human Rights*, Leiden: Martinus Nijhoff Publishers.

Mikołajczyk, B. (2013), Is the ECHR ready for global ageing? *The International Journal of Human Rights*, **17**(4), 511–29.

Oliveira, A. (2016), A freedom under supervision: The EU Court and mandatory retirement age. In S. Manfredi and L. Vickers (eds), *Challenges of Active Ageing*. London: Palgrave Macmillan, pp. 29–45.

Rodriguez-Pinzon, Diego and Martin, Claudia (2003), The international human rights status of elderly persons, *American University International Law Review*, **18**(4), 915–1008.

Seatzu, F. (2015), Reshaping EU old age law in light of the normative standards in international human rights law in relation to older persons. In F. Ippolito and S.I. Sanchez (eds), *Protecting Vulnerable Groups: The European Human Rights Framework*. Oxford: Hart Publishing.

Spanier, B. and Doron, I. (2016), From wellbeing to rights: Creating an International Older Persons' Rights Index (IOPRI), *The Elder Law Journal*, **24**(2), 245.

Spanier, B., Doron, I. and Milman, F. (2013), Older persons and the European Court of Human Rights, *Journal of Cross-Cultural Gerontology*, **28**, 407–20.

8. Ageism and age discrimination in international human rights law

Marijke De Pauw, Bridget Sleap and Nena Georgantzi

1. INTRODUCTION

Older men and women have been listed as a group that faces many human rights violations.[1] However, they have remained almost invisible in the existing international human rights landscape. Few provisions take into account the particular situation of persons in old age, and those that do are scattered over a wide range of instruments as part of human rights treaties, declarations, principles, plans of action, and treaty body recommendations. Unlike other groups – such as women, children, migrants, and persons with disabilities – no comprehensive and unifying international treaty exists on the human rights of older persons. An increasing number of civil society organizations, human rights experts and States therefore see a solution for improving the situation of the older population in the drafting of a new UN convention. Although the debate has been ongoing for several years, no international consensus has been reached yet regarding the need for such a new binding human rights treaty.

In light of this continuous debate, this chapter aims to discuss how international human rights law currently addresses ageism, but also how it can be improved. First, the following paragraphs (Section 2) expose ageism from a human rights perspective, exploring key concepts that clarify the link between ageism, age discrimination and the rights of older persons, and guides the authors' analysis throughout this chapter. Section 3 subsequently identifies the position of older persons as human rights subjects within the existing international policy framework and international human rights framework, demonstrating the significant protection gap at the international level. In Section 4, the chapter discusses how the increased focus on the rights of older persons has led to calls for a new UN convention, and what (limited) role 'ageism' has played in these developments. It also looks into the discourse of the UN Open-Ended Working Group on Ageing (OEWG), the main forum in which the debate for a new international binding instrument on the rights of older persons is taking place. Here, we critically analyze the extent to which ageism has been addressed in this debate as a key barrier to the equal enjoyment of human rights by older persons, as well as whether it has been identified as an important substantive element of a new treaty. On the basis of our analysis we conclude that there remains insufficient attention in international human rights law for the widespread ageism that lies at the root of many human rights violations faced by older persons worldwide. And finally, in section 5 we formulate recommendations on how to ensure sufficient regard for ageism in future international law and practice.

2. AGEISM AND HUMAN RIGHTS

Ageism is a widespread form of prejudice against older persons. Palmore even diagnosed an 'epidemic of ageism' – a spreading negative attitude toward older persons, which basically consists in humiliating them.[2] Persistent negative perceptions and behaviour, or ageism, often lie at the very basis of the human rights violations older persons suffer worldwide.[3] More specifically, ageist bias results in older persons being treated less favourably and restricts their enjoyment of human rights on an equal basis with others. In the following paragraphs, we will discuss more in depth how ageism relates to and affects the human rights of older persons. It will be determined what constitutes 'ageism' (2.1), how old age is the result of social rather than just biological processes (2.2), and how this leads to discrimination against older persons in practice (2.3).

2.1 What is Ageism?

For the purposes of this chapter, we will start from the interpretation of Dr Robert N. Butler, who first coined the term 'ageism' in 1969. According to Butler, ageism 'reflects a deep-seated uneasiness on the part of the young and middle-aged – a personal revulsion to and distaste for growing old, disease, disability; and fear of powerlessness, 'uselessness,' and death.'[4] In his later work Butler further clarified the term 'ageism' as comprising three distinguishable, yet interconnected aspects:

1. *prejudicial attitudes* towards older people, old age and the ageing process, which includes attitudes held by older adults themselves;

2.   *discriminatory practices* against older people; and
3.   *institutional practices and policies* that perpetuate stereotypes about older adults, reduce their opportunity for life satisfaction and undermine their personal dignity.[5]

In other words, it is important to note that ageism is not limited to how we perceive older persons or how we 'feel' about them, but also includes how we act towards older persons, individually or as a society. Consequently, both ageist perceptions as well as actual discriminatory actions (see *infra*) fall under the broader concept of 'ageism'. Butler also refers to ageism as 'another form of bigotry', in addition to sexism and racism.[6] A specific characteristic of ageism, however, is that it is to a great extent still accepted in society and social sanctions against it are close to non-existent.[7] In addition, prejudice against older persons is not necessarily something that we identify within our own thoughts and behaviour. Research has shown that ageism can occur 'without conscious awareness, control or intention to harm',[8] otherwise referred to as 'unintentional ageism'.[9]

2.2   Age as a Social Construct and the Persistence of Age Barriers

Since the 1970s there has been a growing consensus among gerontologists that the experience of old age is socially constructed.[10] As described by Estes, the 'experience of old age is dependent in large part upon how others react to the aged; that is, social context and cultural meanings are important. Meanings are crucial in influencing how growing old is experienced by the ageing in any given society: these meanings are shaped through interaction of the aged with the individuals, organizations and institutions that comprise the social context.'[11] Age has indeed become an important factor in organizing certain areas of society, such as education and work.[12] By categorizing persons in such age groups, age also becomes 'naturalized',[13] leading to certain characteristics being attributed to people based solely on the fact that they belong to a specific age group.[14] Another way of describing this process is the emergence of 'age norms', referring to what society expects from people based on their age.[15] The emergence of such age norms can therefore become a source of personal constriction and social oppression.[16] As will be discussed further below, from a human rights perspective it is important to note that such age norms can lead to discriminatory behaviour and treatment towards older persons in a wide range of areas and can restrict their human right to equality and non-discrimination in general, and to the right to education, the right to work, and the right to health more specifically, to name just a few. For instance, as we tend to assume that pursuing an education takes place in our younger years, older persons can be discriminated against when scholarships and other financial aid measures are limited to a certain age.

Finally, it should be noted that the impact of social processes in shaping how old age is experienced also has important consequences for understanding the intersection with other potential disadvantages. Changing pension systems, for example, will especially affect older persons in a weaker socio-economic position.[17] The negative effects of such reforms are not caused by chronological age as such, but rather by the existing inequality of economic resources in all societies. Other factors contributing to inequality in old age include gender discrimination, racial discrimination and negative cultural images of ageing (also see, *infra*, 2.3).[18] It is therefore crucial to take into account and stress the importance of existing social inequalities in order to understand the problems faced by older persons. As a result, when addressing or implementing the human rights of older persons, adequate attention should be given to existing inequalities that intersect with ageing.

2.3 Age Discrimination

As noted above, age discrimination is one of the ways in which ageism manifests itself, namely its behavioural component. It is well rooted in society and especially difficult to overcome. In fact, age discrimination in itself is both one of the most common human rights violations faced by older persons,[19] as well as one of the root causes of other human rights infringements affecting the older population.[20] Many of the obstacles faced in old age, such as limited access to social security, employment and healthcare, are thus intrinsically linked with and caused by stereotyping and prejudice, leading to direct or indirect age discrimination.[21] Direct discrimination takes place when a person is treated less favourably than another is, has been or would be treated in a comparable situation.[22] It includes, for example, refusing work based on a person's age, but can also take on very extreme forms such as witch-hunting.[23] Indirect discrimination, on the other hand, takes place when an apparently neutral provision puts a (group of) person(s) at a particular disadvantage compared with other persons.[24] For instance, indirect discrimination can be caused by the lack of data collection on HIV infection among older persons, resulting in their exclusion from HIV and AIDS prevention programmes.[25]

The most well known and documented form of age discrimination relates to employment. However, discrimination on the basis of age takes place in many other areas of older persons' lives, including education and training; healthcare services; social security; insurance; financial services; housing; the media; access to public spaces, transport and modern technologies; measurement in statistics and monitoring information; participation in political life; and taxation.[26] For example, older persons are often denied insurance after they have reached a certain age limit or are subjected to paying higher contributions than younger persons.[27] Such age barriers have been identified in, *inter alia*, health insurance, travel insurance, car insurance for rental cars, and motor insurance. In addition, age limits apply to financial services, such as credit offers, credit cards, investment plans and mortgages.[28] With regard to housing, older persons are particularly affected by the practice of forced evictions.[29] Although these are only a few examples, the large number of areas in which age discrimination is identified shows how it permeates many different spheres of older persons' lives. This multitude of age barriers therefore has the potential of negatively affecting older persons' ability to participate in society fully and actively.

As inequality in old age is to a great extent influenced by other social inequalities, the cumulative impact of a lifetime of discrimination can also be devastating in old age.[30] In many cases age intersects with other discrimination grounds, especially gender, disability and racial or ethnic origin. Multiple discrimination particularly affects older women worldwide. This is exacerbated by deep-rooted cultural bias, higher rates of illiteracy and women's reliance on family for financial and other support.[31] This financial dependence in itself is caused by, *inter alia*, a significant employment and pension gap among older women. Women, especially widows who live alone, are considered to be particularly at risk of economic destitution, social isolation, poor health and death. A specific problem for older women in certain countries consists of the patriarchal customary systems and discriminatory inheritance laws, denying women the right to inherit property after their husbands die.[32] A large part of the older population is also faced with disabilities; approximately 46 per cent of people aged 60 years and over worldwide have disabilities.[33] Rates of disability are also much higher among those aged 80 to 89 years, projected to account for 20 per cent of the global population 60 years or older by 2050.[34] As populations age, an increasing number of persons with intellectual disabilities will also live longer lives.[35] Many older persons will thus not only face ageist prejudice and behaviour, but will simultaneously be affected by discrimination on the basis of their disabilities. Older migrants, refugees and ethnic minorities also face particular obstacles, caused by racist bias and ageism, discriminatory laws and practices regarding education, employment and social security, as well as language barriers. Likewise, a person's sexual orientation in combination with their old age may create additional barriers in the enjoyment of their right to private and family life in a residential setting[36]

We therefore witness a widespread discrimination impact on many areas of older persons' lives. The following section sets out to discuss to what extent these issues have been addressed by the international human rights and policy framework.

3. AGEING, AGEISM AND AGE DISCRIMINATION IN INTERNATIONAL POLICY AND HUMAN RIGHTS INSTRUMENTS

Although older persons are faced with various forms of discrimination on one or more grounds (*supra*, 2.3), this group has overall remained almost invisible within the international human rights system. Age discrimination is often not considered together with other discrimination grounds, such as sex, race and disability, and ageism receives even less attention. Over time, however, an increasing number of international policy documents on older persons' rights have been adopted and today discussions are taking place within the OEWG on a potential new UN human rights treaty for this particular group. The following paragraphs will first provide a more detailed assessment of this international policy development (3.1), followed by a reflection on the position of older persons in international human rights law (3.2) and regional human rights instruments (3.3).

3.1 International Policy Framework on Ageing

Despite the universality of human rights, a human rights perspective has generally been missing in the evolution of global ageing policies. In fact, most ageing instruments address older people from a population and development perspective rather than as human rights holders. Particularly noteworthy in this regard is the Vienna Plan of Action on Ageing (VIPAA). In 1982, UN Member States gathered for the World Assembly on Ageing, the world's first meeting that served as a forum to launch an international action programme aimed at guaranteeing economic and social security to older persons, and opportunities to contribute to national development. At the Assembly, the VIPAA was adopted unanimously, confirming the full and undiminished application of the rights enshrined in the Universal Declaration of Human Rights to older persons.[37] This document, however, has a residual concern about age discrimination, including very few references and focusing merely on employment and education. In 1991, in preparation of the VIPAA's tenth anniversary, the UN General Assembly (GA) also adopted the United Nations Principles for Older Persons.[38] These were based on the Vienna International Plan of Action on Ageing and related to five main topics; independence, participation, care, self-fulfilment and dignity. The 1991 Principles do not refer to ageism or discrimination but they advance that 'older persons should be treated fairly regardless of age, gender, racial or ethnic background, disability or other status'. Whether fair treatment (*'with justice'* in the French version of the text) entails the same level of protection as the principle of equal treatment and non-discrimination is a matter subject to interpretation. The lack of clarity of this provision is noteworthy and probably reveals the discomfort of the drafters to adopt a strong language prohibiting age discrimination in the same way human rights law does for other grounds.

Two decades after the adoption of the VIPAA, the instrument was followed-up by the Madrid International Plan of Action on Ageing (MIPAA), an international response to opportunities and challenges of population ageing in the twenty-first century.[39] The MIPAA was a turning point as it was the first time that States came to a consensus on linking the population ageing debate to existing human rights frameworks.[40] The growing attention for equality was notable and was followed by a consideration of a wider range of areas where equal treatment is at stake than what was included in the VIPAA, extending to equal access to healthcare, social services, economic resources, credits, markets and assets, as well as emergencies and political participation. In practice, however, the document fails to reflect a true human rights approach to ageing. Whilst including multiple references to discrimination,[41] the MIPAA does not enshrine a *right* to equality and non-discrimination. This means that the MIPAA also does not include a duty of States to prevent discrimination from happening and to promote equal treatment, but only an objective towards equality. Moreover, this approach considerably limits accountability in case of failure to comply and leaves the application of this human right (including exceptions to the rule of equal treatment) open to political interpretation. Regardless of the MIPAA's aspiration to create a society for all ages, the outcome of the 2012 Review process also showed significant gaps in the implementation of the MIPAA and concluded that even after ten years, it had only had limited impact at the national and international level.[42] Age discrimination counted among the persisting challenges across the world, while instances of unequal access to employment and healthcare as well as discriminatory treatment against older persons in emergency situations were particularly noted.[43] Similar considerations also led the UN Independent Expert on the Enjoyment of All Human Rights by Older Persons to recommend that legislation should contain 'an explicit prohibition of direct and indirect discrimination on the basis of age'.[44]

The assessment of the MIPAA implementation brings evidence of the pervasive nature of discrimination that has not been adequately tackled to date. This is due to flawed or limited non-discrimination recommendations in the MIPAA that address a narrow range of issues but also to the lack of monitoring and accountability mechanisms. Moreover, the failure to recognize ageism as a social norm across many areas of older people's lives is noteworthy. The Plan of Action of Madrid makes a single reference to ageism, which is limited to the labour market. Additionally, none of the political commitments in the MIPAA include a positive duty to eradicate ageist prejudices and structural discrimination that create barriers to the equal participation of older people in society. This gap considerably limits the scope of political action and its potential to create truly inclusive societies for all ages, through prevention, institutional changes and mainstreaming. In contrast, countries bound by the Convention on the Elimination of all forms of Discrimination Against Women have a duty to eliminate prejudices against women, and several governments also have a duty to take due regard of the impact of policies on women. Consequently, the commitments made in MIPAA are not only weak in nature due to the lack of binding force, but they are also limited in scope.

3.2 Age Discrimination in International Human Rights Law

Essentially, international human rights treaties of a general scope – such as the two 1966 Covenants[45] – apply to *all* persons, including older persons. For those groups found to face particular obstacles, however, specific human rights provisions are often included, mainly regarding women and children. Over time, treaties entirely dedicated to the specific needs of those groups were also adopted, such as the 1965 Convention against All Forms of Racial Discrimination; the 1979 Convention against All Forms of Discrimination against Women; the 1989 Convention on the Rights of the Child; the 1990 Convention on the Rights of all Migrant Workers; and the 2006 Convention on the Rights of Persons with Disabilities. So far there has been little regard, however, for the particular experience of human rights in older age. Since dedicated conventions have been recognized as valuable tools for addressing particular barriers to the enjoyment of rights for certain groups and circumstances, a reflection on the particular challenges of older persons might be able to build the case for a new convention as an appropriate response. To date, a specific treaty on this group does not exist and human rights provisions focusing on older persons remain rare.

Especially problematic is the lack of international human rights provisions explicitly prohibiting discrimination on the basis of age. Apart from the Convention on the Rights of Migrant Workers (ICMW),[46] age is not mentioned in the discrimination clauses of any of the core UN human rights treaties.[47] It is noteworthy that despite the relatively more frequent references to age discrimination and ageism in employment (see for instance the MIPAA discussed above), no provisions are to be found in the core human rights treaties with regard to age discrimination or the particular needs of older persons in employment either. Although the list of discrimination clauses is often a non-exhaustive one – referring to discrimination on the basis of 'any other status' – the lack of an *explicit* reference to age tends to render older persons invisible within the normative framework. For example, all UN Member States have to report periodically to the UN's Human Rights Council on how they are protecting and promoting human rights. Only 177 (0.3 per cent) of the 57 686 recommendations made within the Human Rights Council's Universal Periodic Review process to October 2017 address the rights of older people.[48]

Moreover, the UN Office of the High Commissioner for Human Rights has highlighted that:

> the practice of considering age as 'other status' is far from consistent among human rights bodies, allows for a significantly broad margin of discretion, lacks the benefit of legal clarity and requires the argument to be specifically made on a case by case basis. Moreover, the consideration of age as 'other status' for the purpose of anti-discrimination protection still raises the question of the standard of scrutiny employed to decide the claim: even if age might be considered an 'other status' in order to trigger anti-discrimination analysis, if the standard of scrutiny utilised is too deferent, distinctions on the basis of age might be easily justified. Furthermore, as age is in general not explicitly identified as a forbidden ground of discrimination, the need for positive measures to eradicate age-based discrimination might also be challenged.[49]

In other words, the use of age limits to organize society, including employment and retirement, in itself still promotes the view that treating older persons differently is not that problematic.[50] Age-based discrimination is just as serious as any other form of discrimination, yet age-based *differentiations* are not considered as grave as those based on other grounds, and therefore are not as easily considered as discrimination in the first place.[51] It can thus be concluded that considering the pervasiveness of ageism and age discrimination in societies today, the lack of an international prohibition of all forms of discrimination on the basis of age constitutes a serious protection gap.

Finally, it should be noted that the adoption of the most recent category-specific treaty – the UN Convention on the Rights of Persons with Disabilities (CRPD) – has been an important development in determining the rights of persons who are faced with declining physical and/or mental health in old age.[52] Several provisions of the CRPD also explicitly require age-sensitive measures.[53] However, in principle the consideration of age in the CRPD targets the needs of children and not those of older persons. Unlike women and children for whom the Convention includes specific provisions, the CRPD does not have an article dedicated to the rights of those individuals who may face challenges at the intersection of ageing and disability. Despite its potential to address disability issues that arise in old age, as it was drafted with the aim of addressing the particular needs of persons with disabilities, the CRPD is not well equipped to ensure the effective enjoyment of the rights of older persons that have nothing to do with disability, nor does it preclude age discrimination.[54]

An explicit unambiguous prohibition of age discrimination should thus be in place at the global level and should, *inter alia*, cover every aspect of life and forms of discrimination, including the obligation to take positive measures to address disadvantage; to tackle ageist stereotypes as well as harmful social, institutional and cultural practices; and 'not be subject to a wider range of exceptions to the principle of equal treatment than is permitted for any other prohibited ground'.[55] Any exceptions should require specific justification and review under a duty to ensure that they do not undermine human rights principles including those of non-discrimination, equality and dignity.[56]

3.3   Age Discrimination in Regional Human Rights Instruments

At the regional level, age is not explicitly listed as a prohibited ground in the American Convention on Human Rights (1969, Article 1), but discrimination based on the age of older persons is prohibited under the Inter-American Convention on Protecting the Human Rights of Older Persons, which was adopted in 2015 (Article 5).

Similarly, the Protocol to the African Charter on Human and Peoples' Rights on the Rights of Older Persons in Africa (2016) prohibits all forms of discrimination against older persons (Article 3), although the African Charter itself does not explicitly list age as a prohibited ground

(1981, Article 2). However, the African Charter does create a positive action duty to take special measures in Article 18(4): The aged and the disabled shall also have the right to special measures of protection in keeping with their physical or moral needs.

Age is not explicitly listed as a ground for discrimination in the European Convention on Human Rights and Fundamental Freedoms (1950, Article 14), nor in the non-discrimination clause in the Revised European Social Charter (1996, Article E). Age is, however, listed as a prohibited ground in the Charter of Fundamental Rights of the European Union (2007, Article 21), which applies only to Member States when they apply Union law and does not create a general obligation for states to take action to eliminate age discrimination. This is why across the EU 'the scope of legal protection on grounds of age hardly goes beyond the employment sector'.[57] The Council of Europe's Recommendation CM/Rec(2014)2 of the Committee of Ministers to member states on the promotion of the human rights of older persons (2014, paragraphs 6–8) has recognized the gap in the protection of age discrimination and urged member states to make explicit reference to 'age' in their national anti-discrimination legislation. However, this is merely a recommendation and not a binding obligation.

There is no binding regional Asian human rights treaty that addresses age discrimination, although the non-binding sub-regional ASEAN Declaration on Human Rights (2012) guarantees that everyone is entitled to the rights set out in that instrument 'without distinction of any kind, such as […] age'.

In sum, at the regional level binding human rights provisions that explicitly prohibit age discrimination are also missing. It is thanks to dedicated treaties that were recently adopted by the Organisation of American States and the African Union that the normative gap has been addressed for the respective jurisdictions. In the meantime Asia and Europe are lagging behind, because regional standards (binding and non-binding) have not managed to offer to age discrimination the same level of protection available for other grounds.

4. TACKLING AGEISM AND AGE DISCRIMINATION THROUGH A NEW UN CONVENTION ON THE RIGHTS OF OLDER PERSONS

Considering these protection gaps and the deficits of implementation of the MIPAA, it is not surprising that support has grown among various actors for the adoption of a new UN convention on the rights of older persons. This section takes stock of the political developments that led to increasing state support for a new international treaty (4.1) and further discusses how far ageism has played a role in discussions around a new convention (4.2).

4.1 Increasing Support for a New Binding Instrument on the Rights of Older Persons

In 2007, the Second Regional Intergovernmental Conference on Ageing in Latin America and the Caribbean resulted in the adoption of the Brasilia Declaration, in which participating States pledged to promote the drafting of a UN convention on the rights of older persons.[58] This commitment was an important step in the promotion of a new convention as, unlike previous proposals, there was sufficient State follow-up. Additional regional meetings were held in 2008 and 2009 to discuss ways to achieve an International Convention to Promote the Human Rights of Older Persons[59] and Latin American States have since been an essential driving force in the negotiations at UN level. The Latin American support for a convention was also quickly picked up on by civil society,[60] as they themselves continued and increased calls for a specialized binding instrument.[61]

Gradually, the debate on the need for a new convention also emerged within the UN bodies and a first Expert Group Meeting was organized in 2009 to provide the General Assembly with the necessary information on the human rights situation of the older population.[62] The Expert Group concluded that a normative gap existed within the international human rights law framework, resulting in the 'invisibility' of older persons. Concerns were raised about the fragmentation of existing norms as well, which jeopardize legal clarity.[63] In addition to abuse, ageism and age discrimination were identified as the root causes of human rights violations suffered by older persons.[64] Specific recommendations were therefore also made to combat ageism and stereotyping of older people, and to enhance awareness and data collection regarding discrimination.[65]

With regard to the need for a new international binding instrument, the report of the Expert Group Meeting emphasized that a new convention would create obligatory and binding international law and bring about a paradigm shift in the way older persons are viewed as a social group.[66] These outcomes were confirmed in the UN Secretary General's report on the follow-up to the Second World Assembly on Ageing, which reiterated that the inadequate protection of older persons' rights (in part) stems from the lack of an older person's perspective on human rights.[67]

Finally, an additional study was undertaken by Ms Chinsung Chung at the request of the Human Rights Council Advisory Committee.[68] With regard to age discrimination, it was stressed that most legislation is too limited in scope to tackle age discrimination effectively in practice.[69] Again, weak implementation of existing norms was attributed to their non-binding nature and concerns were raised regarding the lack of explicit references to age in international non-discrimination clauses and the lack of a comprehensive mechanism to protect the rights of older persons. Overall, the report called for a human rights-based approach to the older population and the recognition that older persons 'have particular needs and care, and require special protection'.[70] At the same time, it emphasized the need to identify older persons as rights holders, potentially through the drafting of an international convention on the human rights of older persons.[71]

The development of an international human rights approach to ageing and the calls for a binding instrument finally culminated in the establishment of the Open-Ended Working Group on Ageing (OEWG) in 2010. The OEWG was created with the aim of 'considering the existing international framework on the human rights of older persons and to identifying possible gaps and how best to address them, including by considering the feasibility of new instruments and measures'.[72] Although it proved especially difficult to find agreement on *how* to improve the human rights situation of the older population, States did agree that additional steps must be taken to achieve that goal. In addition, States found consensus on the added value of creating a new human rights mandate on the rights of older persons. The Human Rights Council thus appointed Ms Rosa Kornfeld-Matte in May 2014 as the first UN Independent Expert on the enjoyment of all human rights by older persons.[73] Her mandate, which was recently extended, consists of assessing the implementation of existing international instruments; identifying best practices; awareness raising regarding the challenges older persons face in the enjoyment of their rights; and working with States to foster implementation of measures that contribute to the promotion and protection of older persons' rights.[74]

These developments mark the increased global recognition to move forward to enhance the protection of older people's rights, although a consensus on the need for a new convention has not yet been reached. In the final part of this chapter we look into how far ageism has played an important role in the debate around a new treaty in the frame of the OEWG.

4.2   Ageism at the Open-Ended Working Group on Ageing

Based on the wide acknowledgement of the need to eliminate age discrimination it would be surprising if the OEWG only had a residual concern of unequal treatment of older persons. Indeed, in our analysis, which spans from the establishment of the OEWG until 2016, all but one of the UN General Assembly Resolutions addressing the mandate of the Working Group recognize the need to address discrimination on the basis of age. Multiple discrimination on the basis of age and gender is recognized in five of the six Resolutions, yet ageism as a social norm that drives this discrimination is not included in any.[75]

Likewise, discrimination on the basis of age, but not ageism specifically, has been the topic of panel discussions at four of the six Working Group sessions.[76] A review of the summaries produced by the Chair of the Working Group of these panel discussions shows that age discrimination and its effects on older people and society were raised as a concern by some Member States.[77] Ageism as a social norm was raised in some civil society organizations' interventions in the discussions in 2012[78] but was only addressed in any depth by one panellist, Professor Israel Doron, in 2013, linking ageism to social injustice and arguing that ageism is as prevalent as racism and sexism and it is this social injustice that older people are subjected to in their daily lives which governments need to address.[79] Other panellists in different sessions referred to stigma, prejudice and negative stereotypes and perceptions of older people and older age, including in the workplace, within healthcare systems, in the family and society more widely; the historical and cultural traditions that constrain the role of older people; and that ageism is a driver of elder abuse.

Member States, however, have not given the elimination of ageism as a justification for a new convention on the rights of older persons. Rather, a review of available Member State interventions shows that population ageing and the growing numbers of older people is referred to as a common reason why ageing and the rights of older people must be addressed.[80] A number of Member States have also referred to the challenges of the rising numbers of older people reinforcing, possibly inadvertently, negative ageist attitudes towards older people and ageing.[81]

Civil society organizations, on the other hand, have paid greater attention to ageism as a driver of human rights violations. For example, ageism has been cited as a cause of different forms of violence and abuse;[82] as overruling fundamental rights in Europe;[83] as being one of the reasons we need a new convention;[84] and as being a universal concern that requires a universal response.[85] The impact of an inadequate existing international human rights system on ageism was also raised in terms of how this system allows ageism to continue in law and practice,[86] and that expecting older persons to be satisfied with a limited list of non-binding principles perpetuates ageism.[87] It was also recognized that few examples of how to eliminate ageism had been presented by Member States in the exchange of best practices.[88] Civil society interventions have also referred to the role a new convention could play in ending ageism and transforming negative ageist social norms.[89]

Overall, ageism as a driver of discrimination and denial of rights in older age has not featured as prominently as might be expected in the deliberations of the Open-Ended Working Group on Ageing in its seven sessions between 2011 and 2016. References have been inconsistent and sporadic. What can be drawn from this analysis is that the interplay between ageism and human rights violations remains underexplored. In addition, the duty to eliminate ageism as part of States' existing human rights obligations has not been articulated. Likewise, a narrative about how ageist norms have compromised the universal application of human rights is missing from the debate. In addition, the contradiction of committing to equality while continuing to treat older people with less dignity or maintaining age barriers has not emerged as an important topic. Finally, limited attention has been drawn to the issue of multiple discrimination, primarily focusing on the intersection of age and gender. Some consideration of age and disability has also taken place, albeit without questioning the legitimacy of age barriers in national disability provisions. Other groups at risk of discrimination, however, and the impact of ageism in the enjoyment of their rights have barely been addressed by the OEWG.[90] More generally, our analysis reveals the need for more consistency and refocusing on ageism as a harmful social norm and driver of discrimination and violation of rights in the debate around a new UN treaty.

5. CONCLUSION

The adoption of international policy instruments on ageing and older persons, such as the UN Principles on Older Persons and the MIPAA, certainly constitute important developments in the promotion of the well-being of the older population. Nevertheless, it must be concluded that a comprehensive international human rights framework for older persons is still missing today. Ageism has only been marginally addressed by human rights law, policy and discourse around a new treaty. As the process moves towards the drafting of a new convention, a more substantive discussion is necessary on the implications of ageism on the contents of a new convention in that regard. A mere prohibition of age discrimination alongside an affirmation that generic human rights standards apply in older age will not be sufficient to transform ageist social norms or tackle systemic and structural ageism. Rather, to be effective, a new instrument must directly address and provide for the reality and lived experience of ageism in all its forms.

First of all, this should include an obligation for States parties to take positive action to eliminate all forms of discrimination against older persons. In other words, States obligations are not limited to recognizing older persons' right to equality and prohibiting discrimination, they are to *guarantee* that older persons receive equal and effective legal protection against discrimination on all grounds.[91] Second, a new convention should include a specific obligation for States parties to raise awareness in society on ageist stereotypes, to tackle ageist bias in all areas of life, and to promote awareness of the contributions of older persons.[92] Third, a new treaty should address multiple discrimination on the basis of all grounds. Human rights supervisory bodies undoubtedly play an important role in monitoring compliance with such provisions and should therefore actively identify and address all forms of age-based discrimination and multiple discrimination. More so, in reviewing State reports and individual complaints, there should be sufficient regard for ageist stereotypes and age norms that may lie at the basis of human rights infringements.

Considering the current protection gap and invisibility of ageism within the international human rights framework, the adoption of a new binding instrument including such a comprehensive non-discrimination and anti-stereotyping approach could prove to be an important tool in tackling ageism worldwide.

NOTES

1. Report of the United Nations High Commissioner for Human Rights, UN Doc. E/2012/51, 20 April 2012, § 2–4.
2. E. Palmore (2001), 'The Ageism Survey: First Findings', *The Gerontologist*, **41**(5), p. 574.
3. UNDESA, Division for Social Policy and Division, Report of the Expert Group Meeting 'Rights of Older Persons', 5–7 May 2009, Bonn, Germany, p. 5.
4. R.N. Butler (1980), 'Ageism: A foreword', *Journal of Social Issues*, **36**(2), 8–11.
5. Butler (1980).
6. R.N. Butler (1969), 'Age-ism: Another form of bigotry', *The Gerontologist*, **9**(4), 243–6.
7. B.R. Levy and M.R. Banaji (2004), 'Implicit ageism', in T.D. Nelson (ed.), *Ageism: Stereotyping and Prejudice against Older Persons*, Cambridge, MA: MIT Press, p. 50.
8. Levy and Banaji (2004).
9. International Longevity Centre (2006), *Ageism in America*, International Longevity Centre, p. 21; E. Palmore, *Ageism: Negative and Positive* (1999), Springer Publishing, p. 44.

10. C.L. Estes, S. Biggs and C. Phillipson (2003), *Social Theory, Social Policy and Ageing: A Critical Introduction*, Maidenhead: Open University Press, p. 17.
11. C.L. Estes (1981), 'The social construction of reality: A framework for inquiry', in P.R. Lee, N.B. Ramsay and I. Red (eds), *The Aging Enterprise*, San Francisco, CA: Jossey-Bass Publishers, p. 400.
12. D. Dannefer and R.A. Settersten Jr (2010), 'The study of the life course: Implications for social gerontology' in D. Dannefer and C. Phillipson (eds), *The SAGE Handbook of Social Gerontology*, London: SAGE Publications, p. 4.
13. Dannefer and Settersten Jr (2010), p. 4.
14. H.P. Chudacoff (1989), *How Old Are You? Age Consciousness in American Culture*, Princeton, NJ: Princeton University Press, p. 4.
15. Dannefer and Settersten Jr (2010), p. 9.
16. Dannefer and Settersten Jr (2010), p. 10.
17. Dannefer and Settersten Jr (2010).
18. Dannefer and Settersten Jr (2010).
19. See UNDESA (2009), Report of the Expert Group Meeting 'Rights of Older Persons', 4–5; HRC Advisory Committee (2010), 'The necessity of a human rights approach and effective United Nations Mechanism for the human rights of the older person', Working paper prepared by Ms Chinsung Chung, *UN Doc.* A/HRC/AC/4/CRP.1, 4-5; UNGA (2011), Follow-up to the Second World Assembly on Ageing: Report of the Secretary-General, *UN Doc.* A/66/173, 5; HelpAge (2012), 'International human rights law and older people: Gaps, fragments and loopholes', pp. 8–9.
20. UNDESA (2009), pp. 4–5.
21. HRC Advisory Committee (2010), p. 5.
22. Article 2(a) Council Directive 2000/78/EC of 27 November 2000 establishing a general framework for equal treatment in employment and occupation, *OJ.L.* 303, 22 December 2000, 16–22 ('EU Employment Equality Directive').
23. HelpAge International (2009), 'Why it's time for a convention on the rights of older people', p. 2.
24. Article 2(b) EU Employment Equality Directive.
25. HelpAge International (2009), p. 2.
26. The European Older People's Platform (2004), 'Age barriers: Older people's experience of discrimination in access to goods, facilities and services'.
27. AGE Platform Europe (2012), 'Background document for Hearing 'Unblocking the Anti-Discrimination Directive' on age discrimination in access to financial services', accessed 12 February 2018 at http://www.age-platform.eu/images/stories/Background_document_anti-discrimination_directive_AGE.pdf.
28. AGE Platform Europe (2012), pp. 11–12; T.M. Nhongo (2006), 'Age discrimination in Africa', paper presented at the International Federation on Ageing Conference Copenhagen, 31 May, p. 8.
29. UN ECOSOC (2012), Report of the United Nations High Commissioner for Human Rights *UN Doc.* E/2012/51, paras 45–7; CESCR Committee (1997), General comment No. 7: The right to adequate housing: Forced evictions, para. 10.
30. HelpAge International (2011), 'Discrimination in old age: Multiple, cumulative and on the increase'.
31. Report of the Chairperson of the Working Group on Older Persons and People with Disabilities in Africa, presented during the 52nd ordinary session of the African Commission on Human and People's Rights, Yamoussoukro, Cote d'Ivoire, 9–22 October 2012; F.A. Begum (2011), 'Ageing, discrimination and older women's human rights from the perspectives of the CEDAW Convention' available at: http://www.ngocoa-ny.org/perspective_human_rights.pdf, p. 5; European Commission (2017), '2017 Report on equality between men and women in the EU'.
32. Nhongo (2006), p. 8; F.A. Asiimwe (2009), 'Statutory law, patriarchy and inheritance: Home ownership among widows in Uganda', *African Sociological Review*, **13**(1), p. 139; E. Scalise (2009), 'Women's inheritance rights to land and property in South Asia: A study

of Afghanistan, Bangladesh, India, Nepal, Pakistan and Sri Lanka, Rural Development Institute Report on Foreign Aid and Development (Rural Development Institute, p. 21).

33. WHO (2008), The Global Burden of Disease: 2004 Update, p. 34.
34. WHO (2011), World Report on Disability, p. 35.
35. WHO (2002), Active Ageing: a Policy Framework, p. 34.
36. AGE Platform Europe, ILGA Europe (2012), 'Equality for older lesbian, gay, bisexual, trans and intersex people in Europe' accessed 12 February 2018 at https://www.ilga-europe.org/sites/default/files/Attachments/combating_discrimination_on_the_grounds_of_age_and_sogi_final_vs_19-11-12.pdf.
37. Preamble to the Vienna International Plan of Action on Ageing, adopted by the World Assembly on Aging held in Vienna, Austria from 26 July to 6 August 1982; Report of the World Assembly on Ageing, Vienna, 26 July–6 August 1982, U.N. Sales No. E.82.1.16 (1982).
38. United Nations Principles on Older Persons, UNGA Resolution 46/91, "Implementation of the International Plan of Action and Related Activities", 16 December 1991, *UN Doc.* A/RES/46/91.
39. United Nations, Political Declaration of the Second World Assembly on Ageing, Madrid, Spain, 8–12 April 2002, Article 1.
40. United Nations, Political Declaration and Madrid International Plan of Action on Ageing, Second World Assembly on Ageing, Madrid, Spain, 8–12 April 2002, Foreword by Kofi A. Annan.
41. A commitment to eliminate age-based discrimination and the vision of equality of all ages was included in the political declaration of governments.
42. UN Economic and Social Council (2002), Second review and appraisal of the Madrid International Plan of Action on Ageing, 2002, Report of the Secretary-General, UN Doc. E/CN.5/2013/6, paras 81–4.
43. UN Economic and Social Council (2002), para. 80.
44. UN General Assembly (2016), Report of the Independent Expert on the Enjoyment of all Human Rights by Older Persons, A/HRC/33/44.
45. The 1966 International Covenant on Civil and Political Rights (ICCPR) and the 1966 International Covenant on Economic, Social and Cultural Rights (ICESCR).
46. See Article 7 of ICMW.
47. See Article 2(1) ICCPR; Article 2(2) CESCR.
48. Search by HelpAge International of UPR database for key words: older people, older persons, elderly, age discrimination, 2 November 2017, https://www.upr-info.org/database/ Visited 02/11/17.
49. Office of the High Commissioner for Human Rights, Normative standards in international human rights law in relation to older persons – Analytical Outcome Paper, August 2012, pp. 8–9. Accessed 12 February 2018 at http://social.un.org/ageing-working-group/documents/ohchr-outcome-paper-olderpersons12.pdf.
50. A. Gosseries (2014), 'What makes age discrimination special? A philosophical look at the ECJ Case Law', *Netherlands Journal of Legal Philosophy*, **43**(1), p. 70.
51. A. Gosseries (2009), 'La singularité de l'âge: Reflexions sur la jurisprudence commun-autaire', *Mouvements*, **3**(59), 48–9.
52. Article 1 CRPD provides that 'Persons with disabilities include those who have long-term physical, mental, intellectual or sensory impairments which in interaction with various barriers may hinder their full and effective participation in society on an equal basis with others.'
53. See Articles 8 (1)(b) (Awareness-raising); Article 13(1) (Access to justice); Article 16 (2) and (4) (Freedom from exploitation, violence and abuse); Article (23) (b) Respect for home and the family.
54. Most importantly, the Convention does not address the issue of age discrimination. Also see HelpAge International (2012), p. 5.
55. AGE Platform Europe (2017), HelpAge International, The Law in the Service of the Elderly, and National Association of Community Legal Centres Australia, *Equality and*

Non-discrimination, p. 11. Accessed 12 February 2018 at https://social.un.org/ageing-working-group/documents/eighth/Inputs%20NGOs/Joint_Paper_Equality.pdf.

56. AGE Platform Europe (2017).
57. Lassen, Eva Maria et al. (2014), *Factors which Enable or Hinder the Protection of Human Rights*, FRAME, p. 106.
58. ECLAC (2007), *Brasilia Declaration*, adopted at the Second Regional Intergovernmental Conference on Ageing in Latin America and the Caribbean: towards a society for all ages and rights-based social protection, 6 December, paras 25–6, accessed 26 February 2018 at http://www.cepal.org/cgi-bin/getProd.asp?xml=/prensa/noticias/comunicados/5/31945/P319 45.xml&xsl=/prensa/tpl-i/p6f.xsl&base=/prensa/tpl/top-bottom.xslt.
59. ECLAC (2008), Follow-up Meeting on the December 2007 Brasilia Declaration, 16–17 September, Rio de Janeiro, Brazil; ECLAC (2009), Second Follow-Up Meeting of the Brasilia Declaration Towards a Convention on the Rights of Older Persons, 21–22 May, Buenos Aires, Argentina; ECLAC (2009), Third Follow-Up to the Brasilia Declaration of 2007 calling for a UN Convention or a Special Rapporteur on the Rights of Older Persons, 5–6 October Santiago, Chile.
60. At the 18th annual celebration of the International Day of Older Persons in October 2010, the NGO Committee on Ageing launched its call for a Convention on the Rights of Older Persons, arguing that it would assure the effective implementation of the recommendations made in the MIPAA. See NGO Committee on Ageing (2008), 'Proceedings of the Eighteenth Annual Celebration of the International Day of Older Persons: A Call for a Convention on the Rights of Older Persons', 2 October, p. 2. The same year, a group of NGOs working on the rights of older persons – including the International Network for the Prevention of Elder Abuse (INPEA), International Federation on Ageing (IFA), Age UK and HelpAge – also published their call for a new binding instrument. International Network for the Prevention of Elder Abuse et al. (2010), 'Strengthening older people's rights: Towards a UN Convention'. Also see HelpAge International (2012), 'International human rights law and older people: Gaps, fragments and loopholes'; HelpAge International (2012), What are the options? Potential human rights instruments on the rights of older people.
61. In most instances, the call for the appointment for a UN Special Rapporteur on the rights of older persons was made as well, yet was not the primary goal.
62. See UNGA (2008), Resolution 63/151, Follow-up to the Second World Assembly on Ageing, 18 December *UN Doc.* A/RES/63/151; UNDESA (2009), Division for Social Policy and Division, Report of the Expert Group Meeting 'Rights of Older Persons', 5–7 May Bonn, Germany.
63. Report of the 2009 Expert Group Meeting, pp. 14–16.
64. Report of the 2009 Expert Group Meeting, p. 5.
65. Report of the 2009 Expert Group Meeting, p. 8.
66. Report of the 2009 Expert Group Meeting, pp. 18–19.
67. Member States were recommended to consider how best to improve international norms and standards pertaining to older persons, and to consider the recommendations formulated by the experts in Bonn. UNGA (2009), Follow-up to the Second World Assembly on Ageing: Report of the Secretary-General, sixty-fourth session, 6 July, *UN Doc.* A/64/127, paras 19, 66–7.
68. Human Rights Council Advisory Committee (2010), The necessity of a human rights approach and effective United Nations Mechanism for the human rights of the older person, Working paper prepared by Ms Chinsung Chung, *UN Doc.* A/HRC/AC/4/CRP.1, para. 1.
69. Human Rights Council Advisory Committee (2010), para. 7.
70. Human Rights Council Advisory Committee (2010), para. 56.
71. Human Rights Council Advisory Committee (2010), paras 28, 44–53.
72. UNGA (2010), Resolution 65/182, Follow-up to the Second World Assembly on Ageing, 21 December, UN Doc. A/RES/65/182, para. 28.

73. Human Rights Council (2013), Resolution 24/20, The human rights of older persons, 27 September, *UN Doc.* A/HRC/RES/24/20; OHCHR, "The Independent Expert on the enjoyment of all human rights by older persons", accessed 25 February 2018 at http://www.ohchr.org/EN/Issues/OlderPersons/IE/Pages/IEOlderPersons.aspx.

74. OHCHR, "The Independent Expert on the enjoyment of all human rights by older persons", accessed 25 February 2018 at http://www.ohchr.org/EN/Issues/OlderPersons/IE/Pages/IEOlderPersons.aspx.

75. A/RES/65/182, accessed 12 February 2018 at http://www.un.org/en/ga/search/view_doc.asp?symbol=A/RES/65/182; A/RES/66/127, accessed 12 February 2018 at http://www.un.org/en/ga/search/view_doc.asp?symbol=%20A/RES/66/127; A/RES/66/127 accessed 24 February 2018 at http://undocs.org/A/RES/67/139; A/RES/68/134 accessed 24 February 2018 at http://www.un.org/en/ga/search/view_doc.asp?symbol=A/RES/68/134; A/RES/69/146 accessed 24 February 2018 at https://undocs.org/en/A/RES/69/146; A/RES/70/164 accessed 24 February 2018 at http://undocs.org/A/RES/70/164.

76. See agendas of 2nd session, 3rd session, 4th session and 6th session, accessed 12 February 2018 at https://social.un.org/ageing-working-group/.

77. See Chair's Summary of the 1st and 2nd sessions of the Working Group in 2011, accessed 27 October 2016 at http://social.un.org/ageing-working-group/documents/chairmans%20-%205%205%20May.pdf and http://social.un.org/ageing-working-group/documents/Chair_summary_2nd_session_OEWG_final.pdf.

78. See Chair's Summary of the 3rd session of the OEWG in 2012, accessed 27 October 2016 at http://social.un.org/ageing-working-group/thirdsession.shtml.

79. Chair's Summary of the 4th session of the OEWG in 2013, accessed 27 October 2016 at http://social.un.org/ageing-working-group/documents/Chair'sSummary4thOEWGA.pdf.

80. For example, see statements by Bangladesh 4th Session accessed 24 February 2018 at https://social.un.org/ageing-working-group/documents/fourth/statements/Bangladesh.pdf; India, 3rd Session accessed 24 February 2018 at https://social.un.org/ageing-working-group/documents/India.pdf; Japan, 3rd session accessed 24 February 2018 at https://social.un.org/ageing-working-group/documents/Japan.pdf; Pakistan, 1st Session accessed 24 February 2018 at https://social.un.org/ageing-working-group/documents/Pakistan%20opening%20statement%20on%2018%20april%202011.pdf; Turkey 3rd session accessed 27 October 2016 at http://social.un.org/ageing-working-group/index.shtml.

81. For example, see statements by Brazil, 5th session accessed 24 February 2018 at https://social.un.org/ageing-working-group/documents/fifth/Brazil.pdf; Denmark, 1st Session accessed 24 February 2018 at https://social.un.org/ageing-working-group/documents/Statement%20by%20Denmark%20-%20EOWG%20Ageing.pdf; the European Union, 5th Session accessed 24 February 2018 at https://social.un.org/ageing-working-group/documents/fifth/European%20Union_Opening%20Statement.pdf; China, 1st session accessed 24 February 2018 at https://social.un.org/ageing-working-group/documents/Statements%20China.pdf.

82. See statements by International Network for the Prevention of Elder Abuse and International Longevity Centre, 4th Session; HelpAge International 5th Session; accessed 27 October 2016 at http://social.un.org/ageing-working-group/index.shtml.

83. See statements by AGE Platform Europe, 4th Session; Age Action Ireland, 5th Session; accessed 27 October 2016 at http://social.un.org/ageing-working-group/index.shtml.

84. See statement by Global Alliance for the Rights of Older People, 3rd Session; accessed 27 October 2016 at http://social.un.org/ageing-working-group/index.shtml.

85. See statement by HelpAge International, 2nd Session, accessed 27 October 2016 at http://social.un.org/ageing-working-group/index.shtml.

86. See statement by HelpAge International, 3rd Session accessed 27 October 2016 at http://social.un.org/ageing-working-group/index.shtml.

87. See statement by National Association of Community Legal Centers, Australia, 4th session; accessed 27 October 2016 at http://social.un.org/ageing-working-group/index.shtml.

88. See statement by HelpAge International, 6th and 7th Sessions accessed 27 October 2016 at http://social.un.org/ageing-working-group/index.shtml.
89. See statement by AARP, 1st Session accessed 27 October 2016 at http://social.un.org/ageing-working-group/index.shtml.
90. Herro, Annie (2017), The human rights of older persons: The politics and substance of the UN Open-Ended Working Group on Ageing. *Australian Journal of Human Rights*, **23**(1), 90–108.
91. Cf. Article 5(2) CRPD.
92. Cf. Article 8(1)(a)(b) and (c) CRPD.

Index